DO NOT BE DECEIVED IN THESE LAST DAYS

"WHICH CHURCH DID

JESUS CHRIST SAY

HE IS RETURNING FOR?"

Are you a part of it
or something else?

Written by: Rick Evans

Trafford PUBLISHING   www.trafford.com
North America & international
toll-free: 1 888 232 4444 (USA & Canada)
fax: 812 355 4082

Contents

Prologue

Please pray before you read this book for insight from the Holy Spirit and pay special attention to the scriptures.

I did not want the task of writing this book. I was asked to write it in 1999 and eventually God had to give me a Jonah type experience to wake me up to the fact that if I was going to be his servant I would have to do as I was told.

It suffices to say that this book contains a very clear message to each and every single Church member, Pastor, Minister and every single person who professes to be a Christian. Even those who do not profess to be Christians should take note. No one is exempt from this message, not even the Pope, Arch Bishop or Dalai Lama. It does not matter what their business or personal status is either. Presidents, Kings and Queens had better take note. This message will reach all. Because this message is from The Judge of All who dwell on Earth, and who will shortly translate those who truly love Him off the Earth and many will ask why God did not "rapture" them, and now they have been left behind. Rather read this and mend your ways than be left behind, for the Word of God is very clear about which church Jesus Christ is returning for.

I have added the actual Scripture References to each point that I make. But I urge you to read the whole Old King James Bible 1611 - for that is a translation from God's original Word.

Proof that the translators of The Old King James Bible knew God can be found by Jesus own words about the lives they lead, how they were persecuted, tortured and killed getting God's original Word translated for the world to read. The writers of the newer translations have been welcomed by the world. Read what Jesus says about this test to know what is and is not Real Truth – As for me, I only want Real Truth. For when I stand before God I will stand before Real Truth. Nothing will be hidden and I want no more surprises that I got it wrong on that day.

Jesus speaks in John 15: 13 - 26

Greater love hath no man than this, that a man lay down his life for his friends.

Ye are my friends, if ye do whatsoever I command you.

Henceforth I call you not servants; for the servant knoweth not what his lord doeth: but I have called you friends; for all things that I have heard of my Father I have made known unto you.

Ye have not chosen me, but I have chosen you, and ordained you, that ye should go and bring forth fruit, and *that* your fruit should remain: that whatsoever ye shall ask of the Father in my name, he may give it you.

These things I command you, that ye love one another.

If the world hate you, ye know that it hated me before *it hated* you.

If ye were of the world, the world would love his own: but because ye are not of the world, but I have chosen you out of the world, therefore the world hateth you.

Remember the word that I said unto you, The servant is not greater than his lord. **If they have persecuted me, they will also persecute you; if they have kept my saying, they will keep yours also.**

But all these things will they do unto you for my name's sake, because they know not him that sent me.

If I had not come and spoken unto them, they had not had sin: but now they have no cloke for their sin.

He that hateth me hateth my Father also.

If I had not done among them the works which none other man did, they had not had sin: but now have they both seen and hated both me and my Father.

But *this cometh to pass,* that the word might be fulfilled that is written in their law, They hated me without a cause.

Joh 15:26 But when the Comforter is come, whom I will send unto you from the Father, *even* the Spirit of truth, which proceedeth from the Father, he shall testify of me:

Also please bear in mind that you are responsible for your own relationship with God, and that includes ensuring that scripture references quoted actually prove the point that is made in any book you read. This book is no exception to this rule either. This book is a revision of the first book which I published in around 2000.

The reason for this revision of the original book is that I, like so many other Christians, have discovered that the most recent Bibles have been translated off the corrupted Greek Alexandrian Codices. I have now corrected this. Please read the chapter on "The Real Truth" to find out more.

Jesus Himself warns all of us, and me included, to be on the lookout for corruption, and to correct our ways when we see we are in error. We are to watch for false teachers and prophets, and <u>when someone is translating the Word of God, they are to be very carefully scrutinised</u>.

Matthew 7:13 - 29

> Enter ye in at the strait gate: for wide *is* the gate, and broad *is* the way, that leadeth to destruction, and many there be which go in thereat:
>
> Because strait *is* the gate, and narrow *is* the way, which leadeth unto life, and few there be that find it.
>
> Beware of false prophets, which come to you in sheep's clothing, but inwardly they are ravening wolves.
>
> Ye shall know them by their fruits. Do men gather grapes of thorns, or figs of thistles?
>
> Even so every good tree bringeth forth good fruit; but a corrupt tree bringeth forth evil fruit.
>
> A good tree cannot bring forth evil fruit, neither *can* a corrupt tree bring forth good fruit.
>
> Every tree that bringeth not forth good fruit is hewn down, and cast into the fire.
>
> **Wherefore by their fruits ye shall know them.**
>
> Not every one that saith unto me, Lord, Lord, shall enter into the kingdom of heaven; but he that doeth the will of my Father which is in heaven.
>
> Many will say to me in that day, Lord, Lord, have we not prophesied in thy name? and in thy name have cast out devils? and in thy name done many wonderful works?
>
> And then will I profess unto them, I never knew you: depart from me, ye that work iniquity.
>
> Therefore whosoever heareth these sayings of mine, and doeth them, I will liken him unto a wise man, which built his house upon a rock:

And the rain descended, and the floods came, and
the winds blew, and beat upon that house; and
it fell not: for it was founded upon a rock.

And every one that heareth these sayings of mine,
and doeth them not, shall be likened unto a
foolish man, which built his house upon the
sand:

And the rain descended, and the floods came, and
the winds blew, and beat upon that house; and
it fell: and great was the fall of it.

And it came to pass, when Jesus had ended these
sayings, the people were astonished at his
doctrine:

For he taught them as *one* having authority, and
not as the scribes.

The Problem a Non-Believer faces

There is an urban legend that very clearly explains the problem Non-Christians have with Christians.

During the Second World War a group of people escaped into hiding so as not to be found by the enemy. They found their way into a protected cave, which was well hidden and inaccessible to the enemy.

They learnt to survive off the bats, moss and insects within the cave. As there was water within the cave they did not need to leave. They became accustomed to this life and preferred it to the threat of what war would do to them and their families. They developed a defence system, demarcated safe and unsafe areas and warned everyone that the lines painted near the entrance to the cave were not to be crossed under any circumstances.

Their concern was that if any one of them were detected at the entrance then all of them would be at risk. A hierarchical structure of people in various degrees of authority developed over time, with the leader becoming more and more autocratic and dictatorial. He became so consumed with power (as is the temptation with so many leaders) that he introduced harsh and uncalled for laws.

He led primarily through the use of fear and made examples of those who broke his laws and persecuted any who opposed him or introduced any opposing thoughts. The greatest law was that if anyone tried to leave the cave they were to be killed. To ensure that this law was enforced guards were placed near the line at the cave entrance.

The leader, in his desire to maintain control, had slowly indoctrinated the children and adults. The leader twisted the stories of the enemy so much in order to make the outside "people" appear to be monstrous beings, out to kill and destroy them. With this dread instilled within his subjects he ensured that even those who did not like him would side with him simply because there is safety in numbers. The leader had also ensured that this, and other, indoctrination filtered through his colony of hideaways.

Not long after they had entered the cave the leader sealed off the cave entrance saying to the people that it was for their own good that they removed all possibility of an outside surprise attack. Through many years of indoctrination this leader ensured that eventually the members of the colony believed, that the stories told by the older generations of an outside world was a myth.

Children were born and raised under this philosophy. All to the fulfilment of the leaders own desire to maintain control and power.

As time went by however, the war going on outside the cave came to an end, but no one in the cave could hear about this, as they were completely cut off from all outside communication.

Late in the 1990's a mining company began excavating near this cave and during their working the cave entrance was uncovered. Inquisitive a few miners entered the cave and were captured and brought before the leader. The leader now had a problem.

He could not simply throw them out or have them executed, as they did not fit the description of the monstrous beings he had portrayed the outside world beings to be like. The miners looked just like they did, with the exception that their clothes were different.

After allowing them to speak to the people about what the outside world was like he then gave the people the choice. If they chose to leave and never return, they could. They would have to leave all that they knew behind them, their way of life, traditions, and their sense of security, of knowing the rules and understanding the system, language and culture. They would also have to leave all their family members and friends who chose to stay.

A few did leave, however most of them stayed. Those that left returned later to inform the cave dwellers that the leader was in fact misleading them about the Truth of the real world (the one that they could not see, because they would not go outside for one fear or another had gripped them and they were not going to fight their fears.)

Unfortunately they were too late. All they found were the charred remains of the cave dwellers. It appeared as though the leader had chosen to destroy all his subjects and himself rather than to lose his power, (unfounded) respect and the control he had over them.

The analogy of this story is as follows:
The leader is the devil (satan)
The cave dwellers are Human beings who have not found Jesus Christ yet
The miners are the evangelists.

The non-Christians of this world have been kept in an indoctrinated state for thousands of years, with new religions springing up to distract them from finding the original single Truth. This has been going on so long that people on Earth no longer believe in a Heaven, a Hell and many do not believe in God Almighty.

Then there are so-called christians who think everyone gets to go to Heaven, No one actually needs to accept Jesus Christ as personal Lord and Saviour, neither do they need to turn from doing and saying things that are wrong. There are also those of the "New Age" who believe people should speak with the angels and seek them out because they believe God is just a force we cannot actually reach. God is just there and impersonal.

There are hundreds of lying and distracting beliefs and customs and many idols are worshipped. All this to get the Earth-dwellers to remain in a state of confusion (each believing they are right of course) so that they do not turn to the original One who created them, sustains them, and will have to judge the evil they do which sticks to them like urine and faeces.

God does not send people to Hell. He sends sin to Hell. God must flush all sin down into Hell, but has prepared the sacrificial blood of God Himself (brought to earth through Jesus) and shed on a cross at Calvary to wash the sin off you and me.

God is a gentleman, He will not force us. It is our choice.

If we get clean (and stay clean) we get to go to Heaven.

If we choose to keep the sin on us and keep playing in it and with it, then when this sin is judged and flushed down into Hell, then that sin will pull us down with it, where we will wish forever we had accepted the priceless gift God had offered. satan tries to mislead us (through our own stubbornness, desires and lusts of this physical body and mind) into rejecting this gift that God has offered by bringing doubt.

But what Non-Christians struggle with too is that they cannot comprehend the things that the Christians speak about. They cannot identify with a lot of the Christian words used such as "Joy", "Peace that passes all Understanding", being "saved" or "delivered". They do not recognise their own sinfulness.

The Christians appear to be the same as they are on the outside. As this is the only part of a person the Non-Christian can identify with, they do not believe that what they are hearing is True. Or if they do believe, they might misinterpret the Christian terms in a rather frightening light and lump Christianity together with many other cults this world has experienced.

Satan is however is a lot more cunning than the leader in the "cave" story, spoken of earlier, as he realised that he needs to keep his lies so close to the real world as to make differences unnoticeable. Why would satan want to do this? Well just like in the story, satan has taken the people of this world and hidden them away from the Truth. Away from what God is offering. You see, long ago, satan was in charge of all of Heaven. God had given him this position (Ezekiel 28:11-18). But then satan become proud and arrogant and he challenged God by changing the laws of "loving and giving, not worrying about what you will receive for God knows what you need and will provide it." Into the law of Trading (that is to "only give if someone could give something of equal value in return".)

Jesus Himself repeated God's law when He was on Earth in His physical body. Here are just a few pointers, and the one in Acts showed how the Christians obeyed the Laws of God

Luke 6:17-38

Bless them that curse you, and pray for them which despitefully use you.
Give to every man that asketh of thee
lend, hoping for nothing again

Luke 12:22 – 34

If then God so clothe the grass, which is to day in the field, and tomorrow is cast into the oven; how much more will he clothe you, O ye of little faith?

But rather seek ye the kingdom of God; and all these things shall be added unto you.

Acts 4:32 – 35

And the multitude of them that believed were of one heart and of one soul: neither said any of them that ought of the things which he possessed was his own; but they had all things common.

But here on earth he has found subjects that are easily led by the majority. He has found subjects that in most cases accept without question most things (given the right information Methods).

Satan has chosen to do to humans what the leader in the story did to his subjects and will continue to do to them until the time when God Almighty judges the earth and everyone on it and in it. Then too satan will be judged and will for eternity be damned to Hell. As in the story, he will take as many of the people on this earth with him as possible.

If a Christian is zealous in telling a Non-Christian about Jesus' saving power, it is because they love that person enough to risk their relationship to be able to lead them out into the light of the Truth.

But what exactly has satan done through the centuries since Jesus Christ broke through the cave wall and exposed satan's lies.

If satan wants to control all of the Non-Christians on the earth, he needs to be everywhere all at once. satan cannot do this. Only God can be everywhere all at once. So satan had to find a way to overcome his limitations. His only means of doing this was to apply a hierarchical structure within his demonic forces. His demonic forces in turn rely on the hierarchical structures that man himself imposes on his own sphere of influence.

For example a well-respected person has a number of people who would look up to him/her and follow his/her view of the world (in most cases unquestioningly). Another example would be where a person is placed in a position of authority over others, and is given the power to force certain procedures and policies to be adopted. If they are not followed then he/she has the authority to remove the offender from his/her sphere of authority. Naturally this is so open to abuse that an entire sector of industry has sprung up to be the watchdog to make sure that people do not abuse their authority. Now we see that there are cases where even amongst this watchdog body, bribery and corruption defeat the ends of justice. So satan is winning on all fronts in the physical world with his control through hierarchy. However, satan's desire is to win on all spiritual fronts too.

I must make it clear at this point that this world is not at the point where the principal of hierarchy is no longer required. There is one ingredient however, that if added, removes the need for hierarchy. However this ingredient needs to be the ONLY control each individual within the world chooses to follow for this to work.

This of course is how God has designed Heaven.

In the Church, there is no place for such a hierarchy (Matthew 23:8-10) in Jesus' own words:

> "But be not ye called Rabbi: for one is your Master, *even* Christ; and all ye are brethren.
> And call no *man* your father upon the earth: for one is your Father, which is in heaven.
> Neither be ye called masters: for one is your Master, *even* Christ."

Before we go any further, I need to warn you now not to say anything negative about The Holy Spirit. You will be tempted to if you are not a Christian, consider this temptation proof that satan Is real, hates you, and wants to destroy you.

I am telling you this to keep my conscience clear that I am not endangering your future.

Jesus specifically warns that anyone who says anything against The Holy Spirit will not be forgiven that sin and they would be punished for it.

Consider yourself warned. (Matthew 12:31-32), (Mark 3:28-29)

You have probably guessed it by now, The Holy Spirit is the missing ingredient.

The world has left the Holy Spirit out of the equation. In some church organisations He has also been left out of the equation in terms of church management. (I stressed church <u>organizations</u> in this sentence because these are not churches. According to the word of God (<u>Romans 12:5</u>) there is only one Church, the body of Christ, which consists of all Christians - past, present and future - who truly believe (i.e. they act on the True, original Word of God).

The Holy Spirit is ordained to be the teacher and guide to each one of God's Children (<u>1 John 2:27</u>). In the Christian faith, to impose a hierarchy is to clearly state that The Holy Spirit is incapable of teaching and guiding and using each of Gods Children in the best way. In fact it is so blasphemous a statement that it really means that those that require a Hierarchical Structure of authority really believe that they can do a better job than God can/do of doing God's work.

God Is not confined to simply saving souls. The Holy Spirit is the best at running church affairs too. The church governing body is in no way separate from the church nor should it see itself as divorced from the real work that God is about. Do not think that God needs you, because you are the greatest. God wants humble obedient servants in tune with The Holy Spirit. Any one not fitting this description, He could replace with a donkey tomorrow just as he did with Balaam's Donkey and gave it the power of speech to speak to him and save him from the angel that was about to kill him. (<u>Numbers 22: 28</u>).

Those who think they are high and mighty in the church or are really important in the governing body are hereby warned that their days are numbered. Disaster will strike them and their families from a direction they do not expect. They will be reduced to bumbling idiots until they should humble themselves and come on servant's knees with a servant's heart and beg The God of Heaven and Earth to forgive them for their arrogance. God Almighty did this to King Nebuchadnezzar (Daniel 4:33). To do it to these people is no great effort for Him who holds the very air they breathe in the palm of His hand and can remove it or refrain from filtering it at His will.

Your church shouldn't have a hierarchy.

OK so now I have said it some of you may be nodding your heads but there will be many, many more who are probably flaming mad at me.

Well, let us take this statement and let us see what Jesus Christ teaches about it.

1. Jesus was in charge of the 12 Disciples.

   This Is True. But Jesus is still in Charge of the Church who is His Bride. (Ephesians 5:23)

2. Jesus appointed 12 Disciples & 70 Apostles to go out and spread the word. (Luke 9:1-6 & 10:1-4)

   This is also true. Jesus has also appointed each and every single Christian to do the same as these Apostles. (Matthew 28:18-20)

OK, so maybe you now agree that Jesus (The Head) cannot be used as a measure for how the Church (His Body) should work, because He is the head of it and has left clear instructions on how the church, His body, should work. The church leaders should be wary to take headship of the body of Christ for our God is a jealous God and will not tolerate any rivals. How many great Christian leaders have been cut down in their ministries because they allowed the people to praise them and they assumed the headship of their church organization or church community. You my dear brother/sister, remain our brother/sister and if you take headship, your days are numbered. So then what does God's Word teach us about how the church should be run and managed?

Well, let us look at how the Apostles worked.

Jesus sent them out with the power to use His Name to the various cities to spread the Gospel. They were to go without any belongings or means of taking care of themselves. (Luke 9:1-6 & 10:1-4)

Why that is so stupid!' Why send people out with nothing....

Is it so stupid?....

Of course, if you leave out the missing ingredient I would agree with you wholeheartedly. But the Holy Spirit made sure that all their needs were met.

Jesus also made it very clear that the Disciples were not to leave Jerusalem until The Holy Spirit had come upon them. Jesus was no longer going to be there (He was soon to be crucified to pay the death penalty for those who chose to accept His free gift) so they needed God's Guidance from within them.

Those who run church organisations or denominations often claim to be so guided by the spirit that those who attend their church think that they do not have the Spirit within them. They listen attentively to the Minister, Pastor, Priest, Evangelist, Prophet, Bishop, Arch Bishop, Pope, or other church leader as though he/she were the only divine link to God Almighty.

The Holy Spirit did NOT anoint the disciple Peter and tell the rest of the Believers to submit to Peter's authority. No! - Again Each and every single one of these Believers was anointed. (Acts 2:1-4)

The Holy Spirit can be within you too. You just have to accept Jesus, reject living contrary to God's original Word and ask God to give you His Holy Spirit to live within you. God promises He will and that same Spirit is limited only by your free will. The Holy Spirit will only work through you what you believe He can do through you.

The Minister, Pastor, Priest, Evangelist, Prophet, Bishop, Arch Bishop, Pope, or any other leader of a church congregation or denomination, who does not promote the movement of the Holy Spirit in and amongst those attending the congregation, or denomination they lead or serve, is answerable directly to God Almighty for treason and usurping His Authority, and God punishes such leaders very severely.

They have committed the same sin that satan committed, which got him thrown out of Heaven. These people have gone one step further though. They have claimed to have God's Blessing on their behaviour. Something they are lying about to themselves, and to others.

John the Baptist called the Pharisees snakes (Matthew 3:7).

He was so accurate and yet, I think today there are many who stand up in the church who are modern day Pharisees. Do not think that The Almighty Father will one day say to these "Well done My good and faithful servant"

If this is you then be warned your time is not far off. Turn and repent, take up the servant heart you had when you first came to know Jesus Christ, before it is too late.

Let us return to the question of how the church should work, by looking at the church in the 1st century. How did it work?

The Church members asked God who He had appointed as judges to rule on issues. (1 Corinthians 6:1-10) The Holy Spirit anointed each of these.

The Apostles asked God who He had appointed as helpers in the church. (Acts 6:1-4) The Holy Spirit anointed each of these.

The Church members asked God who He had appointed as leaders in the church. (1 Timothy 3:1-7) The Holy Spirit anointed each of these.

Paul appointed Elders in the Church. Each was anointed by the Holy Spirit and was there to be used by The Holy Spirit in the Guidance of the church and the healing of its members

"AHA'!! So you see the Church Hierarchy was established."

Did you perhaps think that?

Well actually no, there was no hierarchy.

Each merely had a different function.

None of these people or functions had any authority over anyone else including the members of the church. (1 Corinthians 14:26-33)

Jesus, whose words gives context to Paul's words (Paul can never contradict or override Jesus' words, for Jesus is God) made it very clear that there was not to be a hierarchy within the Church. (Matthew 23:8-12) reads as follows:

"But be not ye called Rabbi: for one is your Master, *even* Christ; and all ye are brethren.

Mat 23:9 And call no *man* your father upon the earth: for one is your Father, which is in heaven.

Neither be ye called masters: for one is your Master, *even* Christ.

But he that is greatest among you shall be your servant.

And whosoever shall exalt himself shall be abased; and he that shall humble himself shall be exalted"

The Most powerful example of this is when Jesus, who is The Word of Almighty God, represented to us as The Son of Almighty God, within whom is the power to create and destroy the entire Universe, knelt before the Disciples and washed their feet. (John 13:12-17)

If there is a Hierarchy in the church then it is not a top down dissemination of authority, but rather a bottom up dissemination of service to God Almighty where each and every single Christian is responsible to God Almighty, and to Him ALONE.

Another example of this would be, that should a member of the Church sin, this should be brought to his/her attention by one person. If they did not listen to this person speaking in private, then they must be told by this person and another from the Church.

(I imagine these were probably people close to the offender. People who had a relationship with him/her and were able to rebuke them, in love, and it would be received that way.)

Should the offender not listen to this rebuke and continue to sin, then It should be brought before all the members of the church. (<u>Matthew 18:15-17</u>)

You see, The Holy Spirit has tried to reach the sinner directly. They did not listen. The Holy Spirit has tried to reach them through one caring person. The Holy Spirit has tried to reach them through a few church members (There Is no authority here). They still did not listen. The Holy Spirit tried to reach them through all the members standing together on God's already laid down principles. Each member on the same level as every other member including the Judges, Elders, Helpers, Leaders. Once again no hierarchy exists. If he/she still did not listen then what?

<u>ALL</u> THE MEMBERS OF THE CHURCH had to treat him/her as one who does not know Christ. It was not just the elders. He was not simply struck from membership. He was completely ostracised from the Christian Community by each and every single member. (<u>Matthew 18:15-17</u>), (<u>1 Corinthians 5:1-13</u>) & (<u>1 Timothy 5:20</u>)

Please note that this is the only way to keep The Church from impurity. Love the person, hate the deed, and be open about hating the deed. If that person chooses to cling to the deed above clinging to Jesus, do not mislead them into believing they are Christians. You who do this will be held responsible for their destinies. Be warned.

Some churches discipline by, lying to people, because they still want their money, fame, respect, etc.... This is because they do not trust God Almighty to provide for them, even though He owns all the resources on earth. If this is you, you had better consider a different career because you have lost the faith and are flavourless salt and will soon be thrown out and trodden under foot.

It is the practice of not ostracising wilful sinners from the church that has lead the world to scoffing at Christianity.

The church is full of people who think they have bought a seat in Heaven because of their weekly visits to church and sometimes more often. They sit in the church, but when they leave they return to their previous ways and do not change and shun the wilful sins.

Consider this:

Why did Paul need to write letters to the various churches to rectify their behaviour?

If each individual had The Holy Spirit working within them, surely this would not have been necessary.

Here comes the Reality Check

Answer this question honestly before continuing:

If you were the Devil, would you want to control these churches?

Absolutely!

The church members are a threat to your Authority over the people you control. What is worse is that these Church Members do not shut up. They talk to others who are under your control. You will most definitely want to control them. In fact, if you do not control them they are going to destroy your ability to control the world because they who are not governed by a hierarchy are going to make those who are under your control question the need for hierarchy. That hierarchy is your only means to control all of mankind.

Now the truth begins to show its light on the lies you have been told all your life. The lie is "You have to have a hierarchy to control the church."

Well If you were satan how would you accomplish this?

1. Set up a hierarchy of key people within The Church.
2. Assist them in introducing a top down structure of Authority.
3. Introduce the element of fear of reprisal from these key elements.
4. Twist slowly, over many, many years and centuries The Truth. (Do not twist it completely out of shape. This would be detected. Just sufficient to shut them up and if possible trick them into believing that they are saved from going to Hell, when in actual fact they still are going there.)

How then do we define what a believer is? A Believer is a God-Appointed Christian i.e. A Child of Almighty God.

A BELIEVER is someone who ACTS ON WHAT GOD SAYS.

(As an Analogy you could tell me that you believe that a chair will hold you up. BUT UNTIL YOU PROVE THAT YOU BELIEVE IT by sitting in it, YOU ARE NOT A BELIEVER. It does not matter what you call yourself or for that matter what the Church says you are. When you stand before God and face Heaven or Hell;

it will be what God says you are, and nothing can influence that. What He says you are is clearly defined within the Bible, and is outlined in this book.) James 2:14-26). Of course you can change and become a believer, but God does not change for you.

What then is a Non-Believer (A self-appointed, Church-Appointed or Other-Appointed Christian; It also Includes all those who do not believe what Believers believe.)

I apologise if you are angry with me, but I am only the messenger. The Bible, written by God through 40 authors over thousands of years, is His message.

If you are angry, you have good reason to be.

How could I write things like this? In your mind it is totally outrageous, and a direct attack on everything you believe in. Just like the cave dwellers in the story in chapter one I am asking you to leave behind all that you know and trust.

I am NOT asking you to listen to what I am telling you. I am asking you to listen to what God Almighty has clearly and specifically spelt out in His original Word, The Bibles translated prior to 1881 (See the chapter titled "The Real Truth" for more insight on the differences between the original and current Bibles.)

So you see, you cannot get angry with me. If you want to be angry with God for what He has spelt out then do it. I do not suggest this though. He Is going to out-live you and out-love you anyway. You would simply waste what is left of your life away.

If you are angry, perhaps the right person to be angry with is yourself.

Why?

You did not take personal responsibility for ensuring that the people you are following are following what the original Bible teaches. (<u>Matthew 16:1-11</u>). If you have The Holy Spirit living within you and you are angry with me, I suggest you go into a quiet room and find out if you have been listening to what The Holy Spirit has been telling you.

(Just to ensure there is no confusion about God's Message. There is a book called "The Message" which is supposed to be an explanation of the Bible. Some have however used this instead of the Bible, which is an error.

Please note that the book "The Message" is not a Bible, but a commentary. It is one man's view of the interpretation, and it is flavoured with his view. For pure scripture, go back to the original Bibles translated prior to 1881.)

God Almighty's Standard

The Ten Commandments are summed up by Jesus in the following conversation:

"Master, which *is* the great commandment in the law?
Jesus said unto him,
Thou shalt love the Lord thy God with all thy heart, and with all thy soul, and with all thy mind. This is the first and great commandment.
And the second *is* like unto it, Thou shalt love thy neighbour as thyself.
On these two commandments hang all the law and the prophets. " (Matthew 22:36-40)

Let us look at The Ten Commandments to get to understand how to apply these commandments.

(Deuteronomy 5:6-21)

Commandment 1

I *am* the LORD thy God, which brought thee out of the land of Egypt, from the house of bondage.
Thou shalt have none other gods before me.
Thou shalt not make thee *any* graven image, *or* any likeness *of any thing* that *is* in heaven above, or that *is* in the earth beneath, or that *is* in the waters beneath the earth:

(Anything that is more important to you than serving or being with God is an idol. Search out too all things that have their origin in idolatry which includes any object or ritual used in other religions and get rid of it, even if it is on you such as a tattoo or piercing – remove it. God made your physical body to be a shell within which you, who are a spirit, will develop to become all you are supposed to be. Physical deformities require greater spiritual growth on the inside to overcome the physical challenges of the earthly shell we live in. The same is true of mental and emotional handicaps. The spirits of these people have to develop more strongly in other areas. God knows the incredible spiritual journey you have ahead of you once you "hatch" out of this earthly shell. Do not try to hatch early, you need to develop fully to God's satisfaction, before He "hatches" you out.

But when we make a choice to change that which God made, then we are allowing the spirits that God said are on this planet, to brand us like cattle, with marks printed on our bodies, or objects piercing our bodies like rings in the nose of pigs or bulls to lead them where we want them to go, and make them become what we want them to become. These marks and piercings give spirits ownership rights over our bodies because we have stepped out of God's divine protection by disobeying God's Word.

Take back your life. Remove the marks, and give yourself back to God as whole. Restore your body, remove your piercings and adornments, and modifications and go back to what He intended you to be. Eat correctly, exercise and take care of the shell God gave you to grow in. Clear out your home and house of all that detracts from God, or is of another religion, or is of magic, or things which are not true or are misguiding. (Acts 19:19) Then God will return to you the correct beautiful perception of yourself that sets you free.

Anything that you will one day have to admit to your child is not true, should not be told to them, for this is how satan destroys a child's trust in their parents, leaving them vulnerable to satan bringing the wrong people into their lives. Let children be excited about Jesus and not about lies such as santa clause (father christmas), fairies, or even that angels want us to talk to them. All this leads to distrust and disbelief in God, and from then onwards, this child will struggle to keep this first commandment. Do you see why satan pushes christmas so hard? Nowhere in the Bible are we commanded to keep a feast to the birth of Jesus Christ. This is satan's doing.)

Commandment 2

Thou shalt not bow down thyself unto them, nor serve them: for I the LORD thy God *am* a jealous God, visiting the iniquity of the fathers upon the children unto the third and fourth *generation* of them that hate me,
And shewing mercy unto thousands of them that love me and keep my commandments.

(Bowing down is an expression of your wish to have it at the expense of God or His commands)

Commandment 3

Thou shalt not take the name of the LORD thy God in vain: for the LORD will not hold *him* guiltless that taketh his name in vain.

(The Name of "Jesus", "YHWH", "Yahweh", "Yashua" is to be used only when you are addressing Him or when using His authority to change the world we live in. Never use the word "Holy" before any word, excepting when that person or object has been completely dedicated and set apart for the use of God Almighty Alone.

Exclamations of "Holy ...!" as are found among non-believers, and more and more frequently among believers (as society twists them away from loving God) are an insult to God, and especially to The Holy Spirit. Don't do it.

Any religion not proclaiming that Jesus came in the flesh, died physically, and that His blood can be received by faith to cleanse the receiver from all unrighteousness, and set them in the right relationship with the One and Only True God (Father, His Word (who He transformed into the physical Jesus, His Son, equal to and part of Himself), and The Holy Spirit (who, if invited, lives within those who have accepted Jesus' sacrifice as paying for their sins and that they can now be called "Holy", for God has made them Holy. The Holy Spirit comforts, leads, guides and helps us to understand His Word, as spelt out in the Old King James Bible, and all Bibles translated prior to 1881. (Read the chapter titled "The Real Truth" further in this book to understand this statement better.)

Commandment 4

Keep the sabbath day to sanctify it, as the LORD thy God hath commanded thee.
Six days thou shalt labour, and do all thy work:
But the seventh day *is* the sabbath of the LORD thy God: *in it* thou shalt not do any work, thou, nor thy son, nor thy daughter, nor thy manservant, nor thy maidservant, nor thine ox, nor thine ass, nor any of thy cattle, nor thy stranger that *is* within thy gates; that thy manservant and thy maidservant may rest as well as thou. And remember that thou wast a servant in the land of Egypt, and that the LORD thy God brought thee out thence through a mighty hand and by a stretched out arm: therefore the LORD thy God commanded thee to keep the sabbath day.

(God has ensured that the Jews have kept His Sabbath day cycle going continuously, and without missing a beat of God's supernatural rhythm. The Sabbath is from sunset to sunset in Israel, running from Friday evening to Saturday evening. On this day you must rest and relax. Have good clean fun with those you love and care for (If you do not have anyone, pray, and ask God for a friend, and then go and be a friend to everyone).

On this day do not do work that earns an income. And do not ask anyone to work for you or your family or your company. Feel free to happily serve and help others (people and animals) during this time, but rest from your work. God has a double blessing of restoration flowing, enough to sustain you for the next 6 days, however, He only pours this blessing out on those who are resting on His Sabbath day. If you keep His day like this, you confirm that He created The Sabbath on the 7th day. You are therefore confirming, not only that He is God, but also that He owns this planet, and is The One and Only Creator of everything, both seen and unseen.

My personal testimony on keeping the Sabbath:

I have discovered, that just as when God lead the Israelites through the desert in the book of Exodus, on the day before the Sabbath, if I have purposed in my heart to keep the Sabbath the next day, (evening to evening), the work I do on the 6th day (Friday) is supercharged, and time and success are doubled to me. I achieve so much if I work hard on this last day, knowing that at the end of it is a day of rest and recovery with my Lord and Saviour, who still rests with us on this day. In the Millennium Kingdom, we will observe the Sabbath in this way too. I am convinced that we will do so in Heaven as well, for it is the only thing which God both sanctified and blessed at Creation. I still go to a church service on Sunday for convenience sake. Paul said, some esteem one day more important than another, I spend my whole week with God. As I am a part of His Church so when and where I worship

Him is actually irrelevant. People esteeming one day different from another does not mean that God has done away with the Sabbath. So rest and relax and recover Friday evening and Saturday.

A final warning. I have also found, and scripture bears witness to this, that if I do work on the Sabbath, the spirit of confusion causes me to mess up the work, and many things go wrong, not the least of which is that the quality of my relationships with my loved ones are poorer, due to my absence from them during this day of blessing. Do not curse your relationships or work by working on the Sabbath. I keep Sabbath from Friday evening (sunset in Jerusalem) to Saturday evening (sunset in Jerusalem). I use Jerusalem as God's perfect Time Zone, because it was God Himself who chose His Name to be put there. Using this time zone is not a law, I just love to do things that line up with what God loves and does.

Commandment 5

Honour thy father and thy mother, as the LORD thy God hath commanded thee; that thy days may be prolonged, and that it may go well with thee, in the land which the LORD thy God giveth thee.

(Solomon wrote that if you do not chasten your child they could go to Hell. As a parent this would make you partly responsible for his/her eternal destiny.

What does the word "Chasten" mean
(רסי " " Hebrew word for "Chasten" written "ya'sar" pronounced "yaw-sar'")
A primitive root;
to chastise,
literally (with blows)
or figuratively (with words);
hence to instruct:

- 43 -

- Proverbs 13:24
  He that spareth his rod hateth his son: but he that loveth him chasteneth him betimes.

- Proverbs 22:15
  Foolishness is bound in the heart of a child; but the rod of correction shall drive it far from him.

- Proverbs 19:18
  Chasten thy son while there is hope, and let not thy soul spare for his crying.

- Proverbs 23:13
  Withhold not correction from the child: for if thou beatest him with the rod, he shall not die.

- Proverbs 23:14 - 15
  Thou shalt beat him with the rod, and shalt deliver his soul from hell. The rod and reproof give wisdom: but a child left to himself bringeth his mother to shame.

- Deuteronomy 8:5
  Thou shalt also consider in thine heart, that, as a man chasteneth his son, so the LORD thy God chasteneth thee.

- Hebrews 12:6
  For whom the Lord loveth he chasteneth, and scourgeth every son whom he receiveth.

- Hebrews 12:7
  If ye endure chastening, God dealeth with you as with sons; for what son is he whom the father chasteneth not?

Synonyms: - bind, chasten, chastise, correct, instruct, punish, reform, reprove, sore, teach.]

Also note that this is the only commandment that has a promise to the one who keeps it. Bless yourself by keeping it. And always chastise in love and always use a rod and not your hand. Hands are for love and sacrificing yourself for others. Whether your parents are alive or dead, or you yourself are a parent or grandparent this commandment to honour your parent's holds.

Please also note that your parents never need to earn your honour, nor do they need to deserve your honour. For God's own reasons they are your parents and so it is their God given right for you to honour them. To go against this is to go directly against God therefore speak only the good you can find to speak about them and/or to them.

If you cannot learn to discipline with a rod in love you will not be able to rule in the millennium kingdom. Please note the "**he**" referred to below speaks to the Christians that overcome. This does not refer to Jesus, because Jesus is speaking, and He is speaking to us. This rod of iron is our standing fast in what is right and correcting those around us whom we have authority over.

- Rev 2:26 - 29
  And **he** that overcometh, and keepeth my works unto the end, to **him** will I give power over the nations: And **he** shall rule them with a rod of iron; as the vessels of a potter shall they be broken to shivers: even as I received of my Father. And I will give **him** the morning star. **He** that hath an ear, let him hear what the Spirit saith unto the churches.]

Take this seriously.

Commandment 6
Thou shalt not kill.

(Jesus extended this to anger. Do not watch movies or read books that have violence in them or play electronic games with hurting and killing in them. Do not tell or laugh at jokes that have violence and/or anger and/or revenge and and/or bitterness and and/or unforgiveness in them.)

Commandment 7
Neither shalt thou commit adultery.

(Jesus extended this to merely lustful thinking - Pornography is clearly of the Devil. Do not watch movies or read books that have sex and/or nudity in them, neither laugh at jokes about sex and nudity. Sex and nudity are God's gift to a marriage partners of opposite sexes. And then only for when such marriage partners both mutually respect and treat one another with love and care. Keep lust and other people, animals and ideas and fantasies out of sexual acts between a husband and a wife. Get married first, do not live together. Never tempt or seduce someone away from someone else. Ask God to give you his choice and be patient. Get on with doing something that you love doing. Run away from prostitution, go where God leads you. He will provide for you.)

Commandment 8
Neither shalt thou steal.

(Including stationary from work or Overcharging or under servicing your clients. Do not watch movies or read books where stealing is done, nor laugh at jokes about stealing. As far as electronic equipment is concerned, do not download, nor pass through your electronic systems any pirated movies, songs or other stuff that has been stolen. Find, apologise to, and repay (with interest) adding an extra fifth of the value to those you have stolen from. Make a list, and start to restore.)

Commandment 9
Neither shalt thou bear false witness against thy neighbour.

(It is better not to Gossip than to be guilty of accusing falsely. Do not lie, but tell the whole truth. Do not watch movies or read books where there is lying in them, nor play games where you have to lie in the game, nor laugh at jokes where lying is part of the joke. God is clear that no liar gets into Heaven. So ask God to forgive you, and tell the truth from now on. Make a list of lies to correct and start correcting them. Recompense all who have been hurt by your lies.)

Commandment 10
Neither shalt thou desire thy neighbour's wife, [or woman's husband] neither shalt thou covet thy neighbour's house, his field, or his manservant, or his maidservant, his ox, or his ass, or any *thing* that *is* thy neighbour's.

(Trust that God knows what you need and will supply it. If you do not have it yet, God is trying to give you something better, or you do not need it yet. Keep your eyes open for what God wants to show you.)

Does your church in any way Condone or treat as normal, accept or tolerate, the practices mentioned in these ten commandments. Are members of your Church practicing such things and getting away with it? If so, you are in danger and should leave this church and serve where the church organization does as God Almighty instructs.

Jesus gave a final commandment at his ascension into Heaven. We are to go into the entire world and make disciples of the nations. (<u>Mat 28:18-20</u>)

Is your Church actively evangelising the local community as well as internationally?

There are 7 things mentioned in the Old Testament that God HATES AND CANNOT TOLERATE. (<u>Proverbs 6:16-19</u>)

As God does not change He still hates these things. They are:

1. A proud look (Pride),

2. a lying tongue,
   (Including so called "little white lies", which also includes keeping back a part of the truth. Before you speak, make sure what you will say is real truth, and not someone else's version of the truth. If you did not see it or hear it personally, or if you might have misunderstood, do not repeat it, for this is gossip, and gossiping is lying too.)

3. and hands that shed innocent blood,
   (Including those that support such killers, with their money, time etc... - watch out for brand purchases – symbols tell you so much about who you are supporting with your money. Do not buy from those who pay other religions to certify their goods or foods as acceptable to that religion, you are "tithing to their god/ gods.)"

4. An heart that deviseth wicked imaginations,
   (The word "wicked" means anything God does NOT permit. Take captive every thought that is

- 48 -

not in line with God's Word. Satan has tried to change the meanings of words to twist society away from knowing they are disobeying God. Do not follow the world. Any thing "Wicked", or any "Wicked" action is hated by God it is evil. Do not do anything wicked, or call something wicked that is good, and do not call something good when it is wicked. Watch out for the labels and words and pictures on the clothes you wear and things you own. These also change you. They are not called "Brands" for nothing. "Branding is what we do to cows to say we own them. Stay away from everything wicked and keep to that which is of God. Plain clothes are the safest –no branding – you are good enough, just as you are. Others will also see what you wear, your brands and will draw you into what they are doing that is in line with that which they see you are branded as. No branding – no problem, and wickedness is then easy to stay away from.

5. feet that be swift in running to mischief,
   (Jesus extended this to merely entertaining the thoughts of doing evil. This includes games and stories and joking about them.)

6. A false witness *that* speaketh lies,
   (This includes those who spread gossip.)

7. and he that soweth discord among brethren,
   (Interesting that this one should be part of this list. This verse should not be used to silence those who speak accurate scriptural rebuke against another person or the church's leadership. In such cases, the discord between God and the person or persons or leadership is a greater issue to God than discord experienced

by the brethren. This is because the person or leadership has distanced themselves from scripture and prophets have been sent to bring scriptural correction. But were rejected.)

Does your Church in any way Condone or treat as normal, accept or tolerate the practices mentioned in these seven abominations. Are members of your Church practicing such things and getting away with it?

Does your Church campaign against abortion (The Right to Kill a Life that God has created)

Is the Family Unit of extreme importance to your Church?

God's design for a family is a Man and a Woman joined in Holy Matrimony that God joins together in some unknown and supernatural way. (Matthew 19:3-6) Following from this matrimony alone may sex be engaged in and may children be brought into the world. (1 Corinthians 7:2-5), (Colossians 3:18-21)

Does your Church Condone or treat as normal, accept or tolerate, Same Sex Marriages, or Sex before Marriage, or Divorce? (1 Corinthians 7:2-5), (1 Corinthians 6:12-20), (Romans 7:2-3), (Matthew 5:31-32) & (Matthew 19:1-9)

Are 'Sex before Marriage' and 'Same Sex Sexual Relationships' actively abhorred?

(John 8:1-11 forgiveness from adultery applies only if there is repentance - Note verse 11)

Is it made clear to members that those who do not forgive others ARE going to go to Hell? (Matthew 18: 21-35) because our forgiveness by Jesus Christ is directly related to our total forgiveness of others — be warned!

Anyone who prays The Lord's Prayer is actually making it very clear that God should ONLY forgive them if they have already forgiven everyone else (Matthew 6:12). In fact, whether we pray this prayer or not, this is how forgiveness works. Forgive everyone else first, then God's forgiveness can be received. He gives it, but we cannot receive it until we forgive everyone we have a problem with. Ask the Holy Spirit to reveal who you have buried unforgiveness with. You may have forgotten it, but God can see it, and it is like a spreading virus that must be removed.

Does The Holy Spirit have the freedom to use whomever he wishes during the service to bless and teach the Church Members? (1 Corinthians 14: 26-33)

If you are guilty of any of the above then do not despair. God promised to forgive you provided you repent (Stop doing it and try your best, in His strength, to resist all future temptations to start doing it again.)

This forgiveness is for all Church Members including those currently in hierarchical positions within a Church.

The Holy Spirit will let you know what you need to do about your situation. Simply ask Him and wait on His answer. You will know when His answer comes.

You see, that is an example of allowing the Holy Spirit to move. I have not told you what action you are to take.

Why?

I do not know Gods Strategic Plan. I do not even know God's Action Plan. All I know is the little bit The

Holy Spirit chooses to tell me. I am the servant and He is the Master.

I am content with not understanding what Gods Plan is.

I am quite happy just to do as I am told. (That which I am told to do which is not in line with God's Character and his Word, I do not accept as coming from The Holy Spirit.)

The bottom Line is that I openly accept that I have no control over what God has planned for me and I also accept whatever He chooses to send my way.

Jesus said that if we love Him we will obey His commands. Which commands was He talking about. None of Paul's letters had been written yet. Jesus, being The Word of God was speaking about the books of The Law and The Prophets. He continued to say that not one tiny letter or emphasis of the Law would be done away with until everything was fulfilled. So the following is not to be disputed. Just obeyed.

John 14:21 - 24
> He that hath my commandments, and keepeth them, he it is that loveth me: and he that loveth me shall be loved of my Father, and I will love him, and will manifest myself to him.
> Judas saith unto him, not Iscariot, Lord, how is it that thou wilt manifest thyself unto us, and not unto the world?
> Jesus answered and said unto him, If a man love me, he will keep my words: and my Father will love him, and we will come unto him, and make our abode with him.
> He that loveth me not keepeth not my sayings: and the word which ye hear is not mine, but the Father's which sent me.

John 15:10

If ye keep my commandments, ye shall abide in my love; even as I have kept my Father's commandments, and abide in his love.

There are three chapters in the book of Leviticus that apply to all human beings:

Chapter 17 speaks to how you will treat life on God's Earth, and how you will respect it and honour God in the sacrifices we make each day. Every animal we eat has been killed (or sacrificed) that our physical bodies might be sustained. We must respect that God created each animal, and that as this is His creation, we must respect His commands about how we eat of it, and what we eat from it.

Chapter 18 speaks of how our bodies (or "earth-suits") are designed and that they leak different substances, and how we should treat such leakages and how we should respect the "earth-suits" of others, and the genetic lines that God has created.

Chapter 19 speaks of how our bodies (or "earth-suits") belong to God. They are our spiritual egg shells housing our highly complex spiritual nature and allowing us, the spirit, to develop within it. Satan knows that if he can get us to believe we are the "earth-suit", that we will not realise we are in fact spiritual beings within it, and so we will follow physical temptations, never stand against him and ultimately die and be dragged into places where we will be misled and destroyed. God gives no reasons for these laws, just as He gave none to Adam and Eve, when He told them not to eat of the fruit of the tree of knowledge of good and evil. We are to simply obey Him because He is God and His thinking is vastly beyond our capabilities. If we love him we will simply obey Him.

Leviticus 17 6:16

And the LORD spake unto Moses, saying,

Speak unto Aaron, and unto his sons, and unto all the children of Israel, and say unto them; This *is* the thing which the LORD hath commanded, saying,

And thou shalt say unto them, Whatsoever man *there be* of the house of Israel, or of the strangers which sojourn among you, that offereth a burnt offering or sacrifice,

And bringeth it not unto the door of the tabernacle of the congregation, to offer it unto the LORD; even that man shall be cut off from among his people.

And whatsoever man *there be* of the house of Israel, or of the strangers that sojourn among you, that eateth any manner of blood; I will even set my face against that soul that eateth blood, and will cut him off from among his people.

For the life of the flesh *is* in the blood: and I have given it to you upon the altar to make an atonement for your souls: for it *is* the blood *that* maketh an atonement for the soul.

Therefore I said unto the children of Israel, No soul of you shall eat blood, neither shall any stranger that sojourneth among you eat blood.

And whatsoever man *there be* of the children of Israel, or of the strangers that sojourn among you, which hunteth and catcheth any beast or fowl that may be eaten; he shall even pour out the blood thereof, and cover it with dust.

For *it is* the life of all flesh; the blood of it *is* for the life thereof: therefore I said unto the children of Israel, Ye shall eat the blood of no manner of flesh: for the life of all flesh *is* the blood thereof: whosoever eateth it shall be cut off.

And every soul that eateth that which died *of itself,* or that which was torn *with beasts,* *whether it be* one of your own country, or a stranger, he shall both wash his clothes, and bathe *himself* in water, and be unclean until the even: then shall he be clean.

But if he wash *them* not, nor bathe his flesh; then he shall bear his iniquity.

Leviticus 18 1:30

And the LORD spake unto Moses, saying,

Speak unto the children of Israel, and say unto them, I am the LORD your God.

After the doings of the land of Egypt, wherein ye dwelt, shall ye not do: and after the doings of the land of Canaan, whither I bring you, shall ye not do: neither shall ye walk in their ordinances.

Ye shall do my judgments, and keep mine ordinances, to walk therein: I *am* the LORD your God.

Ye shall therefore keep my statutes, and my judgments: which if a man do, he shall live in them: I *am* the LORD.

None of you shall approach to any that is near of kin to him, to uncover *their* nakedness: I *am* the LORD.

The nakedness of thy father, or the nakedness of thy mother, shalt thou not uncover: she *is* thy mother; thou shalt not uncover her nakedness.

The nakedness of thy father's wife shalt thou not uncover: it *is* thy father's nakedness.

The nakedness of thy sister, the daughter of thy father, or daughter of thy mother, *whether she be* born at home, or born abroad, *even* their nakedness thou shalt not uncover.

The nakedness of thy son's daughter, or of thy daughter's daughter, *even* their nakedness thou shalt not uncover: for theirs *is* thine own nakedness.

The nakedness of thy father's wife's daughter, begotten of thy father, she *is* thy sister, thou shalt not uncover her nakedness.

Thou shalt not uncover the nakedness of thy father's sister: she *is* thy father's near kinswoman.

Thou shalt not uncover the nakedness of thy mother's sister: for she *is* thy mother's near kinswoman.

Thou shalt not uncover the nakedness of thy father's brother, thou shalt not approach to his wife: she *is* thine aunt.

Thou shalt not uncover the nakedness of thy daughter in law: she *is* thy son's wife; thou shalt not uncover her nakedness.

Thou shalt not uncover the nakedness of thy brother's wife: it *is* thy brother's nakedness.

Thou shalt not uncover the nakedness of a woman and her daughter, neither shalt thou take her son's daughter, or her daughter's daughter, to uncover her nakedness; *for* they *are* her near kinswomen: it *is* wickedness.

Neither shalt thou take a wife to her sister, to vex *her,* to uncover her nakedness, beside the other in her life *time.*

Also thou shalt not approach unto a woman to uncover her nakedness, as long as she is put apart for her uncleanness.

Moreover thou shalt not lie carnally with thy neighbour's wife, to defile thyself with her.

And thou shalt not let any of thy seed pass through *the fire* to Molech, neither shalt thou profane the name of thy God: I *am* the LORD.

Thou shalt not lie with mankind, as with womankind: it *is* abomination.

Neither shalt thou lie with any beast to defile thyself therewith: neither shall any woman stand before a beast to lie down thereto: it *is* confusion.

Defile not ye yourselves in any of these things: for in all these the nations are defiled which I cast out before you:

And the land is defiled: therefore I do visit the iniquity thereof upon it, and the land itself vomiteth out her inhabitants.

Ye shall therefore keep my statutes and my judgments, and shall not commit *any* of these abominations; *neither* any of your own nation, nor any stranger that sojourneth among you:

(For all these abominations have the men of the land done, which *were* before you, and the land is defiled;)

That the land spue not you out also, when ye defile it, as it spued out the nations that *were* before you.

For whosoever shall commit any of these abominations, even the souls that commit *them* shall be cut off from among their people.

Therefore shall ye keep mine ordinance, that *ye* commit not *any one* of these abominable customs, which were committed before you, and that ye defile not yourselves therein: I *am* the LORD your God.

Leviticus 19 1:37

And the LORD spake unto Moses, saying,

Speak unto all the congregation of the children of Israel, and say unto them, Ye shall be holy: for I the LORD your God *am* holy.

Ye shall fear every man his mother, and his father, and keep my sabbaths: I *am* the LORD your God.

Turn ye not unto idols, nor make to yourselves molten gods: I *am* the LORD your God.

And if ye offer a sacrifice of peace offerings unto the LORD, ye shall offer it at your own will.

It shall be eaten the same day ye offer it, and on the morrow: and if ought remain until the third day, it shall be burnt in the fire.

And if it be eaten at all on the third day, it *is* abominable; it shall not be accepted.

Therefore *every one* that eateth it shall bear his iniquity, because he hath profaned the hallowed thing of the LORD: and that soul shall be cut off from among his people.

And when ye reap the harvest of your land, thou shalt not wholly reap the corners of thy field, neither shalt thou gather the gleanings of thy harvest.

And thou shalt not glean thy vineyard, neither shalt thou gather *every* grape of thy vineyard; thou shalt leave them for the poor and stranger: I *am* the LORD your God.

Ye shall not steal, neither deal falsely, neither lie one to another.

And ye shall not swear by my name falsely, neither shalt thou profane the name of thy God: I *am* the LORD.

Thou shalt not defraud thy neighbour, neither rob *him:* the wages of him that is hired shall not abide with thee all night until the morning.

Thou shalt not curse the deaf, nor put a stumblingblock before the blind, but shalt fear thy God: I *am* the LORD.

Ye shall do no unrighteousness in judgment: thou shalt not respect the person of the poor, nor honour the person of the mighty: *but* in righteousness shalt thou judge thy neighbour.

Thou shalt not go up and down *as* a talebearer among thy people: neither shalt thou stand against the blood of thy neighbour: I *am* the LORD.

Thou shalt not hate thy brother in thine heart: thou shalt in any wise rebuke thy neighbour, and not suffer sin upon him.

Thou shalt not avenge, nor bear any grudge against the children of thy people, but thou shalt love thy neighbour as thyself: I *am* the LORD.

Ye shall keep my statutes. Thou shalt not let thy cattle gender with a diverse kind: thou shalt not sow thy field with mingled seed: neither shall a garment mingled of linen and woollen come upon thee.

And whosoever lieth carnally with a woman, that *is* a bondmaid, betrothed to an husband, and not at all redeemed, nor freedom given her; she shall be scourged; they shall not be put to death, because she was not free.

And he shall bring his trespass offering unto the LORD, unto the door of the tabernacle of the congregation, *even* a ram for a trespass offering.

And the priest shall make an atonement for him with the ram of the trespass offering before the LORD for his sin which he hath done: and the sin which he hath done shall be forgiven him.

And when ye shall come into the land, and shall have planted all manner of trees for food, then ye shall count the fruit thereof as uncircumcised: three years shall it be as uncircumcised unto you: it shall not be eaten of.

But in the fourth year all the fruit thereof shall be holy to praise the LORD *withal*.

And in the fifth year shall ye eat of the fruit thereof, that it may yield unto you the increase thereof: I *am* the LORD your God.

Ye shall not eat *any thing* with the blood: neither shall ye use enchantment, nor observe times.

Ye shall not round the corners of your heads, neither shalt thou mar the corners of thy beard.

Ye shall not make any cuttings in your flesh for the dead, nor print any marks upon you: I *am* the LORD.

Do not prostitute thy daughter, to cause her to be a whore; lest the land fall to whoredom, and the land become full of wickedness.

Ye shall keep my sabbaths, and reverence my sanctuary: I *am* the LORD.

Regard not them that have familiar spirits, neither seek after wizards, to be defiled by them: I *am* the LORD your God.

Thou shalt rise up before the hoary head, and honour the face of the old man, and fear thy God: I *am* the LORD.

And if a stranger sojourn with thee in your land, ye shall not vex him.

L*But* the stranger that dwelleth with you shall be unto you as one born among you, and thou shalt love him as thyself; for ye were strangers in the land of Egypt: I *am* the LORD your God.

Ye shall do no unrighteousness in judgment, in meteyard, in weight, or in measure.

Just balances, just weights, a just ephah, and a just hin, shall ye have: I *am* the LORD your God, which brought you out of the land of Egypt.

Therefore shall ye observe all my statutes, and all my judgments, and do them: I *am* the LORD.

White Fire from within

So then.

Has the devil (satan) succeeded in ruling the churches of today? Does he control them? How would you measure the church you attend or its Priest, Minister, Pastor, Evangelist, Prophet, Eldership, governing body or leadership? How do you ascertain if your church is one of those under satan's Control?

The Measurement is God Almighty's required behaviour pattern for Human Beings on this Planet.

This standard has never changed.

But the standard that churches apply is being watered down, and the words are given meanings that they do not have to justify the behaviour of the members of the church, or to bring in new converts on the basis of accepting their behaviour just to get them in. Sometimes it is simply because the church wants their money.

If a church needs to change God's Standard (Which cannot change) to accommodate new converts then those new converts should not be welcome. These new converts have to accept God's standard as unchanging and should repent and continuously strive to attain it.

There is no space in Heaven for those who condone or preach a standard other than that set by God Almighty. (James 4:1-10)

Satan has realised that to twist the church he first has to twist society. A twisted society will demand a church that allows a set of standards that suits the members.

Christians living in a twisted society find it harder and harder to live according to the standards God Almighty has laid down. Indeed it is impossible to meet God's standard without using The Power of God, through His Holy Spirit.

In fact had Jesus Christ not died to give each and every single human being the opportunity to be forgiven then it would be completely unattainable.

This is the difference between Christianity and every single other religion. While every religion says there are laws which if you obey them perfectly you will get into Heaven.

Christianity says you will never get in to Heaven, no matter how hard you try. The One True God tells us that, ONLY IF HE swaps His perfect Son's perfect blood for your/my sinful blood, can we get into Heaven, because His son's death penalty price, gives us the chance to swap sinfulness for perfection. God does this supernaturally, if we ask Him to. We do not have to do anything else, except mean it, and when He does it, it doesn't hurt either, because it is our spiritual blood which He purifies, so that our spirit becomes perfect.

God does this because He loves us so much.

And because Jesus is God, He can die and rise again and smash Hell's gates open and take the power satan used to have, and take the keys of Hell away from satan, and defeat satan and all his demons, and leave him desolate and still return back to Heaven. Very soon satan will be bound for the 1000 year millennium reign of Jesus on Earth.

God tells us that He loves us, and then He also tells each of us "If you love Me, you will accept My sacrifice to bring you back to Me. Accept Jesus' payment for your sins, become Mine, and My Holy Spirit will help you to learn, understand and change your ways to be right."

God in His wisdom also realised that without The Holy Spirit within His children. His child that has not asked for The Holy Spirit to live within them would not withstand the extreme pressures satan is placing on our society. It is up to those Christians who have received The Holy Spirit to give the opportunity of receiving The Precious, Gentle and Mighty Holy Spirit to those who have not so He can live within them.

The Holy Spirit is the source of all a Christian's supernatural strength, peace, love, forgiveness, patience, kindness, goodness, faithfulness, humility, self-control and joy. (Galatians 5:16-26)

The Holy Spirit is also a WHITE HOT FIRE that burns a Christian deep inside when they see or sense evil. But how many "Christians" bow to society and its rules and norms and do not allow that Fire within them to make known God's True Standards. (John 16: 7-14)

Satan has succeeded in twisting society.

If your church has accepted society's standards then get out of there. (2 Timothy 3:1-5)

It is too late to try and save the whole ship. Those who are in such a church, who decide to follow the churches standards, which no longer follow God's Standard, will follow them no matter what you do or say.

Those who choose to follow Gods Standards must allow The Holy Spirit to lead them and enable them to find fellow believers, who truly believe.

The Religious leaders of today have fallen into the same trap as the Pharisees. There are among them genuine God Fearing Children of God and I pray that these will be useful tools in the Hands of God in bringing this truth out into the open. For the rest, unless they turn from their views and hypotheses and return to the original (pre-1881) scripture, as the base for all they do, they are damned.

Satan has attacked every church on this planet and he started in the early Christian church. Why did Paul need to send those letters to the churches? Various reasons are evident.

On the surface there are many individual issues dealt with. The underlying cause of each and every single one of them is the way that The Holy Spirit had been removed from being the key element within each and every individual of the Church.

To remove The Holy Spirit from the church, satan had to create a Hierarchy within the Church. Satan had to place such society pressures on the leaders within these Hierarchies that they had to bend. They were now in a hierarchy and those beneath them gave them tremendous status. They did not want to risk losing this status. (James 4:1-10) So they chose status or job security above God.

But they did not have to bend. Every one of them that did bend, bent because they had forgotten the most essential Ingredient.

The Holy Spirit and his Awesome Power.

They fell into the trap and will be the Last for all eternity because they made themselves the first on earth. (Luke 13:22-31) & (Matthew 7:21-23)

Galatians Chapter 1: 6- 10 All over again. You have
been warned. Do something about it.

> Gal 1:6 I marvel that ye are so soon removed from
> him that called you into the grace of Christ
> unto another gospel:
> Gal 1:7 Which is not another; but there be some
> that trouble you, and would pervert the gospel
> of Christ.
> Gal 1:8 But though we, or an angel from heaven,
> preach any other gospel unto you than that
> which we have preached unto you, let him be
> accursed.
> Gal 1:9 As we said before, so say I now again,
> If any *man* preach any other gospel unto
> you than that ye have received, let him be
> accursed.
> Gal 1:10 For do I now persuade men, or God? or
> do I seek to please men? for if I yet pleased
> men, I should not be the servant of Christ.

Do not take this lightly. You no longer have any
excuse (Hebrews 10:26-31), (Hebrews 12:25-29) & (2
John 1:9-11)

Who then is Jesus Coming back for?

There are no church organisations in Heaven, Jesus is not coming back for one or other denomination, but for children of God who truly love Him and truly serve Him from their heart in whatever they do and wherever they go. No matter what church organisation these people are found, they will be saved, while the rest in that church are left behind to face God's Wrath.

How then should each of us, as individuals, live to do all that God requires of us as shown in the preceding chapters of this book.

1. Accept that God is Perfect and Holy, and that we cannot save ourselves from eternal separation from Him, which is Hell.

2. Submit ourselves to God, and accept that He is God, and that what He says we must do is what we must do.

3. Understand how much He loves us and wants to save us.

4. Accept that Jesus Christ died to pay for our sins, and that there is no other way to have our sins paid for.

5. Ask Jesus to come into your life, take over controlling it, and teach you to be the best person you can be.

6. Ask the Holy Spirit to enter you and help you to change.

7. Read God's Word at least once a day, (Read the chapter "The greatest sign and wonder" before you buy a Bible, and throw away those Bibles that are contaminated.)

8. Spend time with your eyes closed, talking to the Father, Jesus and the Holy Spirit.

9. Get rid of the things in your life which cause you to stumble in habitual sin.

10. Make new friends at church, but choose your church and friends carefully, based on what you have read so far, and also what you will read in the next chapters.

How does the true Church that Jesus Christ is coming back for work?

The death of Jesus Christ, The perfect Son of God is the only Sacrifice acceptable to God to pay for our sins. In fact Jesus went further and asked Peter a question "But whom say ye that I am?" (Matthew 16:15 – 19) to which Peter replied, "Thou art the Christ, the Son of the living God". Then Jesus said to Peter "Blessed art thou, Simon Barjona: for flesh and blood hath not revealed it unto thee, but my Father which is in heaven. And I say also unto thee, That thou art Peter, and upon this rock I will build my church; and the gates of hell shall not prevail against it."

On what did Jesus build His Church?
On this principle:

God, in Heaven, would communicate through His Spirit with mankind

This is why those who try to use their carnal thinking, cannot accept, or understand Christianity. God reveals it, when, and only when, man first puts his faith in God and accepts Jesus Christ as his Lord and Saviour. Only then does Jesus enter the person and "switch on the ability to understand" from within the person. It seems as though the switches are all on the inside of you. Jesus is a gentleman and will never barge in and take over. He will only come in if you ask and He will only switch the switches you allow Him to.

So what is the purpose of this Church that Jesus came to build?

Question:
What is Christianity?

Answer:
God is Holy, Pure and Abides by his own Laws at All Times.

One of his Laws is that any Sin is punishable by Death. (Romans 6:23) We on the other hand have committed so many Sins:

- Heart Sins (e.g. Lust, Jealousy, Greed, Idolatry, Anger, etc);
- Verbal Sins (e.g. Using the Name of Jesus inappropriately, Swearing, Maligning, Gossiping, Lying (including "little white lies"), etc);
- Physical Sins (e.g. Theft, Assault, Fighting, Sexual immorality, inappropriate use of our resources, etc).

In fact if you have just once done any of the above things only once, from the day you could understand right from wrong, God's Law states that you must die. (Romans 6:23)

Well you might say that that is a bit harsh. Well yes. You see in the entire universe it is only man who was created in the image of God. And in the entire universe it is only man that would dare to disobey God. Not one creature, planet, solar system or spec of space dust would dare to move out of alignment with what God ordains, none but man. So then, is it God who is overly harsh, or is it man who is arrogant and contemptuous of The Almighty God. If it is the latter, then it is no real surprise that this is the only planet satan has been banished to, and these characteristics, are not ours but that of satan and his fallen angels.

Before the Holy Spirit was available to us, mankind allowed satan to control them because they were and still are week helpless and puny beings by comparison. Nevertheless, Death is the punishment for disobedience to God.

But because God Almighty Loves you so much and wants you to be with Him in Heaven for eternity He has provided a way for you to escape this death judgement hanging over your head. But someone will still have to die to pay for your sins, if not you ... then someone who has never sinned. If someone has sinned, he must die for his own sins, he cannot again die for someone else's sins. So none of us mortals could ever do it. We humans would only be able to pay the penalty for the sins we have committed, not anyone else's.

Scripture tells us that all have sinned and fallen short of reaching God (Romans 3:23 - 26)

Sure, We have been tempted, by a being far more slimy and devious than we can imagine, with greater power than we ourselves have. But that is no excuse. God's laws are God's laws and dare not be broken.

God cannot change His Law. Because God cannot change, He is the same, yesterday, today and forever

(Malachi 3:6). - You Sin, Your spirit dies. It is that simple.

As we know, it is God who created satan. He created him as the most powerful being in the universe second only to himself (Ezekiel 28:11–18). Naturally satan was created as a finite being, with limitations, unlike God who is infinite and has no limitations. (excepting those He chooses to place on Himself.)

So then, to provide a person who could withstand all satan's temptations, who, could live a perfect life and then die for the sins of others. He would have to take on satan himself... but as a human. Naturally he did not stand even a breath of a chance against The Almighty who cast him out of Heaven and down to earth to live among us humans (Ezekiel 28:11–18).

So in the form of a person, Jesus Christ, he exposed the character and nature of God, His Love for people, compassion for their situations, power over all of creation, and ability to resist all temptations, He was born of a virgin by the name of Mary.

Mary was a highly favoured woman to have had this opportunity to be used by God. To place an emphasis on Mary, Jesus' earthly mother, who was human and not to place that emphasis on Jesus Christ, the Mighty Son of God, as the means to receiving favour with God, is obviously a means to distract you, ever so slightly, but sufficiently, to ensure that you miss receiving what God provided for you...

Escape from eternal Death.
Jesus Christ fulfilled every single prophecy regarding the Jewish Messiah, which, according to chance, is impossible for one person to achieve in a lifetime. He fought the Devil on his own turf and resisted every

temptation satan could throw at Him. Eventually He was crucified on a cross and the final prophecies were fulfilled at His resurrection.

Why did God raise Jesus from the dead?

Jesus Christ had carried with Him to Hell, all the sins that were to be forgiven, past, present and future until the end of time, but He Himself had committed no Sin and therefore satan was not entitled to keep Him.

Jesus is now seated on a throne in Heaven at the Right Hand of God. He is waiting for the appointed time, the end of the countdown, and very soon, when we will all have to appear before Him and be judged by Him, whether we die our earthly death before then or are still alive when the time of the end comes.

The penalty for sin had now been paid. God is now able to forgive those who ask Him to forgive them. I am still studying the subject of those born prior to Jesus death on the cross, but so far I am convinced that for us who live after the penalty for sin was paid by Jesus Christ, there remains only one path open to Heaven.

God cannot save those who hear and understand the message and yet still choose to throw away God's gift of a means of escape from eternal death. Not because He does not want to, but simply because He will never interfere in your free will. He gave you your free will and for some reason he chooses to respect your choice to exercise it in whatever manner you choose. There is no doubt that He is distressed when a person chooses to reject the escape route, He has provided at so great a price, to so undeserving a species.

Scripture tells us that God does not want any of us to be lost (2 Peter 3:9). And in fact we know that when just one person accepts the escape route and is saved then there is great joy in Heaven (Luke 15:7).

But at the end of the day there will be those who choose to go to their own destruction through obstinacy, despite all that God does to try and save them, and these, even God cannot save.

If you are one of those who has heard this message of Jesus Christ, which by reading this you have, and for any reason still choose to ignore His call (God appointed this day and time for you to receive His call for you to escape) then you have judged yourself, and chosen Hell as your eternal destination. God sends no one to Hell. People choose to go there by default of not choosing the one and only path God has provided to get to Heaven.

You might just have said that you doubt that this is the one and only path?

Well let me ask you this then. If there were any other ways to get to God, then why would He suffer the pain of watching His only Son murdered to pay the price of sin, which is death (Romans 08:01-17).

So now we have seen the escape route God has created, how then do we escape through it? Jesus said that He is the door, and that no one comes to The Father but through Him. (John 14:5 - 7; John 10:9). John 3:1-36 tells us how to escape through this door. Read it for yourself at least 5 times. Study it until you understand it clearly. Then act on it. By confessing with your mouth that Jesus Christ is your Lord (Reason for your existence, your Master, and that you wish that He use you for the rest of your days on this earth) and by being Baptised (Submersed in water) where the old you is destroyed and God places a spirit which can enter Heaven within you, you will be able to enter into heaven when you die. However you have now become an enemy of satan and your life is going to be very difficult from this day on unless you ask The Holy Spirit to enter into you (Luke 11:13).

(The Holy Spirit will never force himself on you, as he will never encroach on your free will. You have to ask Him to enter you.)

You will find it an absolute necessity to have the Power of God operating from within you in the form of The Holy Spirit.

If you have done all this then you are guaranteed his presence, peace, security, and so much more He will never leave you nor forsake you.
(Hebrews 13:5 & 6; Deuteronomy 31:6, 8; Joshua 1:5)

What Church did God raise up in the beginning of the Last Days?

(... for this is the Church you want to belong to.)

Firstly it should be noted that brothers and sisters of Christ are physically sexual beings being male and female. Spiritually however we are asexual and therefore there is no spiritual difference between the spirits of males and females.

Sex is required only to keep the earth populated with vessels within which God can place His Spirit and so gain children for his eternal Kingdom. Marriage only lasts as long as people are alive. Jesus taught that there is no marriage after death (Matthew 22: 23 - 30) and in fact there is separation of marriages on the death of a spouse.

Secondly Brothers and Sisters of Christ should note that it is Servant hood to God and to others, which is the key requirement of any believer (Matthew 23: 8 – 12). No emphasis should be placed on any believer in terms of Authority.

All believers are equal in authority and none are subject to another (Matthew 23: 8 – 12). All are subject to the Holy Spirit of God and are accountable to Him and to Him alone.

So then the Church is not a building, organisation, or any top- down hierarchical structure.

The Church is in fact each believer interacting with other believers where they are a servant to other believers, supplying them with whatever goods, skills, knowledge, encouragement and spiritual gifts they have wherever and whenever possible. Moreover, Believers must supply these when prompted by the Spirit of God even when it is not in line with the worldly way of doing things.

So what happened to the Church?
satan, being a finite creature, can only be in one place at one time. He relies on demons in a hierarchical reporting structure to provide him with the information he requires to cause the maximum damage to God's Church of believers.

During the first century, he attempted to wipe out all Christians. This did not work, so he infiltrated them. Not with satanists, but with people who would call themselves Christians, Ambitious people, who <u>wanted Power and not Servant hood</u>. These satan knew had not received the Holy Spirit within them and so were powerless to detect his presence and prompting. Demons were assigned to these "more powerful Christians" and with their influence churches were established which had a Hierarchy. Those of greater influence, who chose to be "in charge of", as opposed to "subordinate to" others, were ever so slowly and without their being aware of it, moulded to carry out satan's Plan B.

Plan B was to get all the real Christians together into a club, make everyone pleased to be there but hinder them from speaking to anyone outside of the church. To place them under such a list of rules they must obey and Things they must not do that they would spend all their time trying to be "Holy in God's sight", when in fact they were already perfectly Holy to God the moment Jesus took all their sins away.

No amount of doing good was going to make the Christians any more acceptable to God anyway, but satan kept this fact from them.

satan's plan did not completely succeed for there were still Christians who continued to talk to others about Jesus.

satan had to then come up with Plan C.

Plan C is a mixture of 3 different methods.

- Firstly kill as many of those who open their mouths, if you cannot kill them make them too busy, tired, sick, or distract them in any other way so that they will not talk.
- Secondly increase and strengthen the hold on the church hierarchies by getting people thrown out of the various churches. Using the spirits of judgement and gossip, get everyone belonging to churches to isolate these people from the church organisations.
- Thirdly turn the church into a club consisting of many who profess to be Christians but are not. People who aspire to the title of being a "good person" but never get to be children of the Most High God? - Using these people as examples get the people who are not in church to see what they do and so paint an incorrect picture of God because of what these supposed Christians are doing.

This has been his major approach since the first century AD but he has added a number of other little plans to trap and control believers. The latest is to enforce tolerance of one another and accepting of sinful practices within other believers lives and even more recently forcing the churches through

Government Legislation to endorse sinful practices such as Same-Sex Marriages.

How should the church operate?
In its current form the Church cannot function according to the actual definition of what it means to be a Christian.

A Christian is a true believer. He is a person who acts on what he sees Christ expects of him. A Christian is one who accepts the Grace Jesus bought for us by taking our sin upon the cross. We do this when we choose to accept Him as Lord and Master of every aspect of our lives. When He is our Lord, then we are to love one another ... First Jesus is our Lord, and then we love one another). (1 John 03 : 23)

The Church of The Last Days

Well let us look at what the Church looked like in the first century, when satan could not control it.

To put this in its proper context we must first look at the relationship between the believers and Jesus Christ.

When we accept Jesus into our hearts, we are in fact marrying Him. We do not take marriage to another human being lightly and we should not take marrying Jesus lightly either. We are the Bride of Christ, Jesus is the Bride Groom (Ephesians 5:21-27)

3. We must respect and honour him.
4. We must submit to His will for our lives.

There are various marriage vows used when I married my wife. This one was common at that time: (I have edited it a little for a better understanding of the analogy):

I (Your Name),
Take you Jesus Christ (My Bride Groom),
To be my eternal Lord and friend,
To have and to hold (in my being)
from this day forth (No turning back and no Divorce).
Whether my life gets better or worse,
Whether I get richer or poorer,
Whether I am sick or healthy,
I choose to love and to cherish You,
Forsaking all other gods and idols,
Making You my most important priority,
And this I pledge for eternity.
I give you my will as a sign that I belong to You,
With my Heart, Mind, Body and Soul I honour You,
All that I am I give to You,
      and

All that I have is Yours already,
Within the love of God, Father, Son/You and Holy Spirit,
And this is my solemn vow.

This really separates the Christ-followers from those who call themselves Christians. Read this carefully and understand all that you are giving up your right to.

There are always two sides to a marriage and in marrying Jesus it is no different. He has the following to say to you (remember, spirits are asexual, so do not think that this is about that sort of a relationship.)

I Jesus Christ,
Take you (Your Name),
To be my eternal subject and friend,

from this day forth (No turning back and no Divorce).
Whether you get better or worse,
Whether you get richer or poorer,
Whether you are sick or healthy,
I choose to love and to cherish you,
I will never leave you nor forsake you,
And this I pledge for eternity.
I give you my perfection and take all your sin away,
With my death I pay your death penalty,
All that I am I give to you,
         and
All that I have I share with you,
Within the love of God, Father, Son/Me and Holy Spirit,
And this is my solemn vow.

Now if this does not blow your mind then you still have not realised how much God has that He can share with you. How much He understands and knows that you will mess up in the future. How He will never leave you nor forsake you because He has accepted you by forgiving you, and how much, by dying for you He has made it possible to make this amazing promise to you.

I suggest you really study what these vows mean and how precious you are to God that He would offer such a promise to you. And He does because you are special. He created you because He loves you and wants you to be with Him forever (John 14:2 & 3).

Do not let satan say to you that this is not meant for you. The Bible says it is meant for you because God Almighty desires this relationship with you. You are special to Him. Even if no one else in the world thinks you are worth anything. Jesus proved you are worth His suffering and dying in your place. You are worth His Blood to Him (John 14: 1-31).

You might mess up, He never will, because He is perfect and keeps all His promises.

I have to stop here a while because this revelation has blown me away.

Excuse me while I take it in. Then we will look at how this relationship with Jesus affects our relationship with our Christian brothers and sisters.

Our relationship with our Christian brothers and sisters.

Well now that we have our relationship with The Son of God correctly aligned in our minds, now we can look at our relationship with our Christian brothers and sisters.

The first point to note is that you never know whether someone is your brother or sister. I am always excited to find out that someone is or has become my brother or sister. I just love knowing my family is getting bigger and there is someone else that Loves me and whom I can also Love. It is "really cool" as my children would say. I Love it.

Another thing you do not know is, what spiritual age your brother or sister, are at the moment. For example, you would never malign a baby and gossip behind their backs if they could not walk and talk at the age of 6 months would you? But Christians do that to each other all the time!

For the sake of Jesus, get your thinking straightened out.

Furthermore do not consider that because a person has been a Christian for many years that they are more spiritually mature or immature than you are.

In a race, if one person starts walking and another waits a while and then starts running you cannot say which will win or who should be at which stage when. The intensity of your devotion to Jesus Christ and the Study of His Word and His Will and the speed with which you conquer temptations and evil strong holds in your life will determine the speed with which you mature spiritually. (Take the plank out of your own eye (Matthew 7:1-5))

And lastly but most importantly you must understand that if someone claims to be a Christian and can say that Jesus is Lord he or she is your brother or sister (1 John 4:2). This means that no matter what they do, or say to hurt you, your loved ones, or anyone else, you have no right to hold it against them. They have been forgiven by Your Lord and Master to whom you Have to Submit your will, anger, frustration and every other negative feeling thought and emotion. Jesus chose to die for that sin they committed too. He paid a high price.

To be unforgiving when Jesus already paid the price to forgive that sin is to trample the blood of Jesus underfoot and Dishonour the very Jesus Christ you have pledged to honour. So you have to Love them and forgive them openly whether they deserve it or not, whether they continue to do it or not.

Gossipers, be warned!!! Jesus punishes those who cannot stop pouring forth filth from their mouths. Furthermore, if He has forgiven the sin that was committed which, you are gossiping about, then it has been thrown as far as the East is from the West and can be remembered no more. It never happened!!! This makes you a liar as well as a gossip. Do not be so quick to judge others, or God will judge you in the same light. (In this case on here-say, which is all that gossip is, and not on the real you) (<u>Matthew 7:1-5</u>), (<u>Mark 4:22-24</u>). If others begin to Gossip, politely ask to leave the conversation or remain silently praying for all those speaking and those spoken about. If asked, boldly explain this principle to those who ask after your silence. You may be ostracised, but it would be better not to be a part of a crowd who intends to make you feel uncomfortable by continuing in your presence.

This does not mean you should remain silent. But all that is good, encouraging, pleasing, kind, whatever is of a good report, think on these things (<u>Philippians 4:8-9</u>). Speak these things and build up your brothers and sisters.

Give to your brothers and sisters whatever they need if you have surplus of that item, skill, talent and time. Do this at no cost, asking nothing in return and accepting whatever they choose to offer. Do not offend them by making them feel like they are poorer or less than you are, by refusing to accept an offering from them. For you will be rewarded for what you give (<u>Luke 6:38</u>) and you should not deny them their reward for giving to you.

Exposing satan's biggest lie & destroying his grip on mankind

Now I want to destroy one of satan's Key Lies which rules human thinking, and most likely, yours too, by exposing His ultimate stronghold on, not just you, but also the church and in fact the whole world. Once you understand this properly you will be free from his control in most areas of your life, as were the early Christians. (Ezekiel 28 : 11 – 19)

Ezekiel is sent to give a message to the king of Tyre, which he delivers in Ezekiel 26:1 – 28:10. But then strangely, he suddenly receives another message for the King of Tyre, which he delivers in chapter 28: 11 – 19 (Ezekiel 28 : 11 – 19)

Now this blew my mind wide open. The second message was clearly not for any human being. Read it!! (Ezekiel 28 : 11 – 19). It is directed straight at satan himself who must have taken up temporary residence in the king of Tyre for Ezekiel to deliver the message to him.

The key sentence, tucked away in the Bible that explains what satan has always hidden from us is this: - satan was thrown out of heaven because of his Trade. So what was his Trade? God ascribes the creation of the principle of "Trade" to satan.

In heaven there is no Trade.

What????

Yes my friend in Heaven there is no Buying or Selling. No Barter.

The reason is that these remove the need for the giving out of Love for one another. You see both Trade and Barter have one prerequisite.

No one gets anything unless the values of the Trade or Barter Items are the same.

For example I cannot barter my old car for a new one and I cannot buy a new car for 5 cents. This is the System satan had introduced into Heaven. God however, knowing all things, seeing all things and knowing the future of all things, having wisdom beyond measure, could see that the minute you took Love out of giving and receiving you were heading for all kinds of evil consequences.

<u>Now Put down this book and think about this carefully, because satan will steal this revelation from you if you even give him the slightest chance.</u>

In fact, if you find yourself scoffing at this now, later, tomorrow, next week, next month or whenever, you can be sure he has succeeded in locking you up and stealing this one key.

I challenge you to find one evil thing that cannot be traced back to the principle of Trade.

Now that you've thought this through a bit let us continue.

So God never intended Trade or Barter to be on earth. What did he intend?

What did the early Christians discover that was so devastatingly dangerous to satan's Kingdom.

The lie

Well they discovered a simple truth: - Most people have more than they need of one thing and not enough of another. They also discovered that if they found out what their Christian brothers and sisters needed, they would all be able to meet one another's needs without actually running out themselves. (Acts 2 : 44 - 47), (Acts 4 : 34 & 35)

satan has the answer to your brother'/sister' needs locked away in your cupboard, store room, garage or somewhere else you tend to dump stuff. You may have a skill/talent that could solve a brother'/sister' need. So why do we not do anything about it?

Here is the crux!

Someone, somewhere, told someone a long time ago that to discuss your problems and needs with your brothers and sisters in Christ was to become a social outcast. It is to put yourself at the mercy of the Gossipers. "It is just not right to burden other people with my problems" some would say. Others would say, "It's just not done!"

Well I have news for you... I know who started this thing off. And I know the real reason some of you subscribe to this way of thinking.

satan started this off a long time ago and held it in motion by introducing social norms and rules commonly known that would ensure that those who did not subscribe to these rules would be ostracised. He introduced Gossipers to humiliate and keep the mouths of those who would confide in brothers and sisters shut. If no one knows your problems then no one can help you and that is exactly where he wants you. If a loving brother or sister starts to help you, satan loses control over you. Imagine if all the brothers and sisters shared their needs, belongings, talents, skills and time. Well, He would be back to the days of the early Church where he would have to persecute them in every possible way to stop them from destroying his control over the planet, which is centred on ..... Wait for it .... Trade... where Love is not required to transact.

If you cannot accept this and change, then you are too proud of yourself, your standing in society, and your situation. You think, "How can I stoop to that level?"

Well actually you are swimming upside down reaching for the bottom of hell. You need to turn yourself around. Start reaching for Heaven. Throw away all your pride, your concern about your social standing, and your need for power over other people. Throw it all away. It's all an illusion.

Jesus was never concerned about His social standing.
Why did he disrespect social standing so much? He knew the lie. And He knew the Liar. And He knew Heaven. And He knew how it really is. (Romans 12:2)

Until you get past this issue you will never operate according to the pattern of the Church as laid down by Jesus Christ. Do not play with this idea; do not con yourself that you are doing it.

DO IT!!! (Romans 12:1-21)

And then you will be free, to operate in the Love of God.

YOU WILL BE FREE - Because the Truth will set you free (<u>John 08: 31 - 34</u>).

There is a lot more to come on this subject but I need to recover. As much as this is new to you the way it has come out on paper, it is new to me too and I need to meditate on it a while and take stock of my own situation and where I stand on this issue.

So what could we do about this?
We could transform our churches to do what the 1st century churches did

Here follows a template that you can take to your church leaders to introduce a ministry which can assist in developing the re-institution of Love-based transactions instead of Trade-based transactions.

A 1st Century Church Ministry for our Church today

Primary Purpose:
To Care – Expose needs and hurts of those within our congregation, or those who visit our church, which brings compassion, a softened heart and a desire to resolve.

Secondary Purpose:
To Educate – Teach those attending our congregation, the same things Jesus taught, and experience how God taught and sustained the early church to meet the needs of those around them without having needs themselves.

To Demonstrate – Show how God can solve other people's problems by us passing on what belongs to Him, when we do not need it. God has already given us what we have needed and so we Demonstrate that Where the world and the devil say you can have if... God says you can have freely

To communicate – The good news to the poor, the widow, the fatherless and in so doing keep ourselves safe, by keeping our own hearts soft, and our own spirits humble, acknowledging we are just tenants on this planet and we are merely stewards of God's property.

Our Primary Target:

Committed Disciples of Jesus Christ

Secondary Target:

Those God brings to our congregation, small-group fellowship, and those outside of our fellowship too.

The Needs this ministry focuses on

The needs that this ministry focuses on is allowing the Holy Spirit to prompt those in the church congregation to meet one another's needs. And providing a way for those whom the Holy Spirit prompts, to be able to help their congregation brothers and sisters first, (Matthew 25:31-46) and thereafter to help the rest of the world

(Mark 9:41)
Mar 9:41 For whosoever shall give you a cup of water to drink in my name, because ye belong to Christ, verily I say unto you, he shall not lose his reward.

(Matthew 25:31 - 46)
Mat 25:40 And the King shall answer and say unto them, Verily I say unto you, Inasmuch as ye have done *it* unto one of the least of **these my brethren** [Referring to those who first gave themselves to God and were reborn as a living spirit and who also prove they are His by doing these things], ye have done *it* unto me.

The means to do this is so designed as to make known the needs of the individuals within the church congregation in such a way as to keep anonymous those who are in need. Only the need is made known to the Church congregation, so that the individual Christians can search their hearts and cupboards and stores for that which is being asked for, and which they no longer need, and respond and assist as they are lead by the Holy Spirit by bringing these to the

Church leadership to meet the need (without anyone but God knowing who gave and whom He will bless.)

The needs met may start off as physical needs, move to things like lift clubs, house sitting, Legal & Financial advice and eventually all the practitioners who normally charge for their services would assist church members in difficulty for nothing, simply because they recognise they are their brothers and sisters in Christ and that they love them as such.

One suggestion of how the ministry could work (Please note that the Holy Spirit will prompt you to use one or more methods in different situations so this is just an idea from which to start discussing what will work for you in your church

Description of Method?
Cards people can fill in with their needs that they can drop into the offering basket

1. Collect cards and place on the board (Wall). The card has two identical numbers. One can be torn off and kept by the member in need and the other remains on the card.
OR
2. Collect cards and enter them on a central database of needs. email or contact people that may provide for each particular need
OR
3. Website could have a needs page and anyone could add their need or answer to it

How to make this ministry reality?
We would need to test this on the small group initially

Board (Wall) design (Where cards will be put up on)

Card design (Cards/papers on which people can write their needs)

Printing Cards

If the Cards option is successful in the small groups then implement it in the church. Continuously pray so that the Holy Spirit can show you other ways to make this work in other parts of the church too.

The person(s) who should lead this ministry should be

Be Spirit Lead, Humble, Compassionate and desire mercy, They should not be one who gossips, But they should be empathetic, enthusiastic, patient, have leadership ability, be able to do administration (manage the needs and the meeting of these needs), Should be able to deal with people in a loving way (even when they are angry)

How do we expand this ministry?

Find people with compassion/mercy gifts (If anyone wants to serve in this ministry evaluate them according to the above criteria)

Give them an introductory training.

Give them hands on training.

The Primary type of work is

Administrative mostly....Some people skills required.

There is a completely flat structure of those who would operate in this ministry. The leader is only a coach and has no authority other than the Bible. If the leader cannot find scripture with which to guide a person to a different behaviour then the leader must re-evaluate his/her attitude on the subject. If a person does not wish to change their behaviour after the Word of God on the matter has been made known to them, then make this known to all of those who are working in this ministry that they should all try to dissuade the offender and assist them to change. If the offender still refuses then at a meeting the leader is to remain silent and all those in the ministry are to individually agree that the offender must leave the ministry until such time as he/she mends his/her ways. At no time is the leader to say a word about it, it is a matter of the Holy Spirit's Authority, and not the leader. The leader however remains accountable first to the Holy Spirit and then to the Church as a whole and finally to the Church Leadership.

Training Needed
Read this book

Understand the method your ministry has chosen to put in place and understand the part you are to play in it.

Regularly update their score cards for all to see

What will it cost to start this ministry?
It depends on the route....Cards...Website...phone calls ... It really should cost very little to start. A book would be used to record the needs, and when they were met.

What are the budget/financial needs to sustain our ministry?
It should not cost much at all. You will need some storage space and some volunteers. A book, pre-printed cards (or blank cards and a rubber stamp).

How can we (the Ministry team) find the money needed to support this ministry?

Pray for it and follow the prompting of the Holy Spirit. He will guide each of us in ways best for each of us.

Communication amongst one another could take place in some of these ways

- *With each other?*
  Cell Phone and Telephone and e-mail

- *With its leadership?*
  As above

- *With other ministries?*
  As above

- *With church staff?*
  As above

- *With the church at large?*
  Via weekly leaflet and from the Pulpit, quarterly magazine, email, sms, etc...

- *With whom ii is trying to serve?*
  Those whose needs are met will be contacted through a leaflet specifying which needs were met, unless contact details were left on the card (transcribed into the book but not publicised) in which case a message can be left for them.

Monitoring how well this ministry is doing?

Firstly bear in mind that there is often an adoption curve where slowly & cautiously those who have needs will use this ministry. So do not expect that suddenly everyone will respond. it will take time to grow.

Measure the ministry on whether people are getting there needs to us and are they being met, I.E. It is very measurable with stats.

Stats i.e. Mr. Bloggs needs a lift...Mr. Smith met the need. This will be documented but not publicised as to who needed the lift or who met the need. A certain amount of discretion is required for example it may not be prudent to simply say lift required. But the Holy Spirit will guide you as to what to write.

<u>The Ministry's success could be measured in some of the following ways</u>

The growing maturity in Jesus Christ of those who serve in this ministry

Are people making needs known and are they being met...Physical needs.

Anyone in the church leadership confirmed to have integrity within the church and who has not been found to be a gossip may check the books of requests made versus those met and those collected.

How do you measure someone who needed shoes for their child getting them and someone needing a lift and getting it? These must remain stories and not be reduced to 5 needs this month 6 the following. (We publicise stories not statistics. God is far more glorified in a story than he is in a set of numbers.)

The Ministry team's success would be enhanced by?
Prayer, Prayer and more Prayer. Pray for the Ministry team, and those in need and those who will give daily. An additional suggestion, that the group can meet periodically for Bible study is also a good one.

The Ministry team members would form a family unit?

We will all shepherd one another as brothers and sisters equal to each other before God as Jesus instructed.

The leader takes responsibility for his Ministry team and their growth

The Needs Board (Wall) will be available to the Ministry team members & church leadership too.

Negotiate the following between the leader and each individual Ministry team member.

One-on-one meetings to determine:

- *Time commitment*
- *Family matters*
- *Quiet Time*
- *Vocation vs. Ministry demands*
- *Small Groups/Accountability Relationships*

Support within the Ministry team:
- *Praying for each other*
- *Group devotionals*
- *Ministry team Fellowships*

The Vision for growth of this Ministry

One vision could be that God would grow this bigger than your church and use it as a means of outreach to your surrounding communities.

In all likelihood, God will put within the Ministry team and its leadership the passion for what he wants to achieve through them.

The purpose & dream (+ - 5 years from now)
The church of the days of Acts had 0 needs. We can achieve that. The needs board (Wall) disappearing and being replaced by people who can openly confess their needs and not feel that they are open to ridicule and at the mercy of the gossipers would be the ultimate goal

After about 3 years the ministry would ideally be
Needs board (Wall), fully functional and all needs within the membership being met.

Expanding this ministry is at the discretion of the Holy Spirit
The Holy Spirit will direct – We will not dictate His direction or limit his direction to the finite knowledge of our here and now.

Concerns some people have raised as to practicalities.

How do we minimise People abusing the system for their own gain?
(We needed to make it difficult enough so that those who are really in need will follow the process (at the same time making provision for problems like cultural differences, illiteracy, disability etc). The process must also be a bit of a pain so that those, not in real need will not bother to do it.)

The Church Leadership has certain Responsibilities
Proof of what we do with whose resources is an essential

(A record of needs publicized & Needs met must be kept by the Church)

Proof that negligence is at least mitigated is also essential

(A Needs Analysis on the situation & person should be done and some form of due diligence should be assured before needs are met.)

How will we ensure that mistakes made cause the least problems?

1. *This should be started on a small scale with dedicated Church Members (Preferably Cell Leaders).*
2. *Explain the entire concept (Best to let them read it for themselves and decide for themselves if they feel at peace starting this)*
3. *Select 5 of the cell leaders that volunteer.*
4. *Meet with the Cell Groups & explain the entire concept (Best to let the Cell Group work through the book.)*
5. *Ask that the cell group members submit one or more needs.)*
6. *The Cell Members can use the Needs Analysis Template below (Make Copies) to evaluate each other's real needs.*
7. *Draw up these needs and put them on the "Needs Wall". (NB No Names or identification of the person needing should be given on the need publicized on the Needs Wall)*
8. *The Needs Wall should be in a prominent place for the whole church to see.*

Is this God's work?

Proceed only when you have peace in your hearts that you have discovered God's Will in this matter.

A Needs Analysis Template

Below is a Needs Analysis Template that you could use (and adjust as the Holy Spirit dictates) which will assist you in finding and answering the real needs of people and not just their wants. Or what they think they need.

__Name of your Need__
Need Number
(Church to supply)

Original request - details of the need to be met.

All Information is treated as strictly confidential and all persons that will be handling your information are bound by Trust and Non-Disclosure Agreements.

__Please note that the process requires a fair amount of effort on the part of the Ministry Consultant (You who filled in this card) It is therefore essential that you provide valid contact details for day and night.__

Description of The Person in Need
(Names if possible)

Ministry Consultant:
Contact Details   (day)   :
Contact Details   (Night)   :
Contact Details   (Cell)   :

Description of the Need   :

Who (if any) amongst the Church Leaders &/or its members have you spoken to about this need?

NAME	FUNCTION	OUTCOME OF DISCUSSION	COMMENT

TAKE NOTE:

At no time will any consideration be given to even mentioning the person/business meeting the need.

All the Glory goes to God.

We do not Trade fame (advertising space) for that which should come naturally for God's Children.

Who is involved in this need?

Ministry Team Administrator to Complete:

Name	Function	Expected responsibility in the team	Contact no
	Ministry Consultant	Explain the Need and provide any proof of the Need if necessary.	
	Representative of the Church	To Counsel where necessary and to oversee the Church's Responsibilities	
	Ministry Team Administrator	To ensure that all Administration surrounding a Need is processed	
	Ministry Team – Leader	To ensure continuity throughout the process	
	Needs Analyst	To meet with the Needs Representative and to determine the exact nature of the need & to document it	
	Needs Supplier	The one who eventually Supplies the need	

What is the progress of this need being met?

Ministry Team - Leader to Complete:

STEP	RESPONSIBLE	START DATE	COMPLETION DATE
Need Fulfilment requested	Ministry Consultant		
Need Crystallised	Ministry Consultant		
Analyse the Need	Needs Analyst		
Request Supporting Information	Needs Analyst and Ministry Consultant		
Church Input	Representative of the Church		
Needs Request Draft	Needs Analyst		

What is the progress of this need being met? (Continued)

Ministry Team - Leader to Complete:

STEP	RESPONSIBLE	START DATE	COMPLETION DATE
QA of Needs Request Draft	Ministry Team – Leader		
Posting of Need on the Wall	Ministry Team Administrator		
Needs Provision received	Ministry Team Administrator		
Church Counsel for providers	Representative of the Church		
Permission to Witness	Ministry Team – Leader and Ministry Consultant		
Provide Need	Ministry Team – Leader and Ministry Consultant		
Witness Write up (if permitted by Needy)	Ministry Team – Leader and Ministry Consultant		
Witness Publication	Representative of the Church		
Needs Follow Up (1 Week after)	Ministry Team – Leader and Ministry Consultant		
Needs Follow Up (1 Month after)	Ministry Team – Leader and Ministry Consultant		
Needs Follow Up (3 Months after)	Ministry Team – Leader and Ministry Consultant		
Needs Follow Up (1 Year after)	Ministry Team – Leader and Ministry Consultant		

Why should you (Ministry Consultant) complete this?

Firstly

It is a need you are attempting to have satisfied that is being discussed. Only you really know the details of the real situation. The Church will bring your needs before the Body of Christ in such a way as to not mention your name or contact information publicly.

To do this without you personally standing up and telling the Church, the Body of Christ needs to know the details of what the real need is.

As an example:

If your real need is a lift to and from work, then you do not need a car. The car is one of many means to have your need met. Other ways would be a lift from a fellow Christian, or the ability to work from home, or a completely different way that the Holy Spirit wishes to meet your need.

If you need to have a safe place to stay then you do not need a house or money to rent a house. You need a safe place to stay. So remember to say it that way.

It is the purpose of this Guide to separate your real needs from how you think your needs should be met. God Almighty usually chooses ways that we do not see or expect to resolve our real needs. Our Church wants to free the Holy Spirit to deal with you and your need in the way that He chooses to, and not according to what you want done.

Secondly
The Church Leadership has a responsibility to God Almighty to act responsibly with the Resources God puts in their hands. There may be situations where the Church itself has a solution to the need. In such a case the Church Leadership must be a good steward of these.

Please note right up front that the Church will not be providing money to buy something to meet a need.

Thirdly
The Church is also a meeting place for the Body of Christ. Christians will be able to see these needs on the Needs Wall and they may be lead by the Holy Spirit to resolve the need.

Once again no money will be used to buy something to meet your need.

The Church is therefore responsible for making sure that there is no abuse of the Body of Christ that frequent this church community.

Fourthly
If you really need to have this need met, you will be prepared to make the effort to have your needs met.

May Almighty God lead you and guide you.

Church Leadership

Identifying the real need

Explain the current situation that is being faced

(Ministry Consultant to ask those in Need the questions & then fills in the boxes below)

What was the situation before this need arose?

```



```

What happened to cause this need?

```



```

What other problems are making this worse?

Unforgiveness, Bitterness, Physical or Mental Abuse, Divorce, Substance Abuse, Accident,

Sickness, Injury, Loss of Loved One(s), Death, Loss of Income, Ex Prisoner, Depression, Other

Circle those that are/have recently occurred.

(Please give details of each in the box below)

(You will not be disqualified based on the above – It is to ensure that we understand the nature of the Need in its context)

What is the exact nature of the needs you have?

(Ministry Consultant to discuss with those in Need & then Document)

What, besides money, do you think would meet your needs?

What do you expect of the church needs wall?

An example of Useful Questioning Techniques

The Person in Need	: "I need a car"
Ministry Consultant	: "Why do you need the car?"
The Person in Need	: "I need to take my children to School"
Ministry Consultant	: "Which School do you need to take them to?"
The Person in Need	: "I need to take my children to xxxxxx School"
Ministry Consultant	: "Is there someone you know who can take them to School for you?"
The Person in Need	: "No"
Ministry Consultant	: "So you need to get your children to School and Back?"
The Person in Need	: "Yes"
Ministry Consultant	: "Do you want us to find a way to get them to School for you?" (A)

Possible Responses:

One Response could be:
(A) Ministry Consultant: "Do you want us to find a way to get them to School for you?"

The Person in Need	: "Yes"
Ministry Consultant	: "So you want someone to help you get them to School?"
The Person in Need	: "Yes I do."
Ministry Consultant	: "Are there any special requests you have about this need?"
The Person in Need	: "Yes."
Ministry Consultant	: "What special requests do you have for this need?"
The Person in Need	: "I must be able to go with to drop off & pick up my children."
Ministry Consultant	: "Ok, Anything else?"
The Person in Need	: "No."

You have identified a Real Need and you know what the criteria for the need being met are.

Then Identify any other reasons for the person believing the car is the solution to the problem - Start from the beginning again

Ministry Consultant   : "What else do you need the car for?"

Another Response could be:
(A) Ministry Consultant: "Do you want us to find a way to get them to School for you?"
The Person in Need   : "No"
Ministry Consultant   : "So you do not need a car for this?"
The Person in Need   : "I need the car"
Ministry Consultant   : "If not for this then what?"
    This is Not the Real Need – Start from the beginning again.

Another Response could be:
(A) Ministry Consultant: "Do you want us to find a way to get them to School for you?"
The Person in Need   : "No"
Ministry Consultant   : "So you do not need a car for this?"
The Person in Need   : "I need the car"
Ministry Consultant   : "If not for this then what?"
The Person in Need   : "I need the car to go to coffee with my friends"

NB Do not write this off as not being a real need. Ask questions and let them decide if it is or is not a need. There may be other reasons why they go to the Coffee Shop that they do not want to disclose. Gently tell them that you can only give the needs you can explain in full to the Church.

Actual needs to be met:

(Ministry Consultant to discuss with those in Need & then Document)

Take a Specific Need and describe the real need not the solution (See Example discussion above)

Need # _____

Solution Detail:

Reason for this Solution:

Why would this solution solve the problem

Need Number _____

What is the real Need to be met

What will you <u>no longer</u> be able to do/have if this need is met by someone else? (Consider the effect of this solution).

The way you plan to do/get this – Are there possibly better ways of doing /getting this that will cause you less loss?

What problems could come from someone else meeting your need?

Special request when this need is met:
(This should also find a way around the problems)

Make extra copies of this page if necessary

Take another Specific Need and describe the real need not the solution

Actual needs to be met:
(Ministry Consultant to discuss with those in Need & then complete the form)

Take a Specific Need and describe the real need not the solution (See Example discussion above)

Need # _____

Solution Detail:

Reason for this Solution:

Why would this solution solve the problem

Need Number _____

What is the real Need to be met

What will you no longer be able to do/have if this need is met by someone else? (Consider the effect of this solution).

The way you plan to do/get this – Are there possibly better ways of doing /getting this that will cause you less loss?

What problems could come from someone else meeting your need?

Special request when this need is met:
(This should also find a way around the problems)

Make extra copies of this page if necessary

Take another Specific Need and describe the real need not the solution

Actual needs to be met:
(Ministry Consultant to discuss with those in Need & then complete the form)

Take a Specific Need and describe the real need not the solution (See Example discussion above)

Need # _____

Solution Detail:

Reason for this Solution:

Why would this solution solve the problem

Need Number _____

What is the real Need to be met

What will you <u>no longer</u> be able to do/have if this need is met by someone else? (Consider the effect of this solution).

The way you plan to do/get this – Are there possibly better ways of doing /getting this that will cause you less loss?

What problems could come from someone else meeting your need?

Special request when this need is met:
(This should also find a way around the problems)

Make extra copies of this page if necessary

Return this to the church and put it in the Offering for your Needs to be presented & prayed for.

The Ministry Consultant must get this completed document back to the Church and hand it in to the person who will get it to the right Person to review and pray through.

The person will then check if there is more information required and they will contact the Ministry Consultant for more information if necessary.

The Need will be posted on the Needs Wall. Only the Ministry Team will have your name and contact details. From then on you will need to pray that the Holy Spirit sends someone to meet your need. You have now done what is required of you, leave the rest to God.

God Almighty may choose to meet your need another way. If so, please let us know that your needs have been met so that we can take your need off the Wall.

Human Needs

Background
I would like to now explore the needs of all Humans first and how we are made up.

Think of yourself as a set of 3 spheres one inside the other.

1. The **Spiritual** area of your life is the centre sphere.
2. The **Emotional** is your middle sphere within which the spiritual sphere resides.
3. The **Physical** area of your life is the outer sphere or layer, which is that area of your life through which you experience this physical world.

Spiritual area (The real you is a spirit)

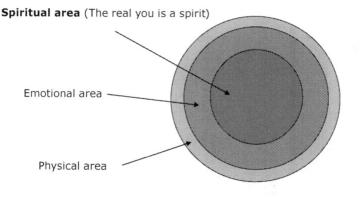

Emotional area

Physical area

A Table showing you and your needs.

Your Needs	Centre Spiritual	Middle Layer Emotional	Outer Layer Physical
Survival	- Eternal Salvation, - Prayer, - Quite Time with God, - Indwelling of the Holy Spirit, - Forgiving all others	- Ability to cry & laugh, - Ability to forgive yourself, - Someone to talk to, - Someone who loves you, - Someone to love.	- Air, - Food, - Water, - Sunlight, - Shelter.
Basic	- Encouragement, - Prayer Partners, - Group Bible Study, - Problems for spiritual exercise, - Understanding God's Will for you.	- A Clear Conscience, - Encouragement, - Someone who will listen without judging, - Someone who lovingly shows you your faults, - Someone who accepts you exactly as you are.	- Clothing, - Health, - Exercise, - Sound Mind, - Working Body.
General	- Friends, - Desires, - Understanding the spiritual world, - Being in constant dialogue with Jesus, - A Ministry	- A listening ear to which you can unload, - Peaceful environment to recharge, - Someone you can help, - Ability to control your emotions, - Ability to detect the spiritual atmosphere through your emotions.	- Friends, - Desires met, - Knowledge, - Intelligence, - Areas to still grow in.

These are just some of these needs, what is important to note is that you are a complex creation.

Why should we show your needs at 3 different layers

In answering this we must refer to the table above. (The block where "Survival" (heading on the left of the table above) and "Outer Layer Physical" (heading on the top of the table above) meet is the minimum requirement for existence). A balloon can be popped easily because it has a thin outer layer. So too your physical layer can easily be penetrated. If that person has nothing in any of their emotional and spiritual blocks they are just like this balloon, having nothing but hot air within it. They have nothing to fall back on when they receive a hard knock. The impact of such a hard knock is often extremely serious.

On the other hand you have people who have Solid Spiritual, Emotional, and Physical layers who can handle the most horrific of life's storms very easily. This is what we must strive to achieve.

DO NOT BE DECEIVED IN THESE LAST DAYS

Measure yourself and improve
In the last days, God will raise up His army

Will you be part of it?

Written by Rick Evans

The work is of my hands,
but not of my mind,
the work is of The Spirit,
and the work is for you.
The work is of Love,
a reminder to man,
that God is God forever,
before creation even began.

In all that Love can give,
and all that Love can do,
it is best expressed,
in Jesus' death for you.
Reject it or accept it,
That's for you to choose,
to test if this is God's work,
the Bible you must use.

Vain interpretations,
Scripture bent by man,
to suit man's own purpose,
to be their own 'I Am'.
"I sent you all my Prophets,
being different they were scorned,
I sent my Son to pay your price,
Him man also scorned."

"I cried out, called and knocked,
I have done all that I can,
this work will lead you to My Word,
The Word of The Almighty 'I AM'".

This book is not available in Printed form. It is an ebook see : http://www.freewebs.com/TheArmyofGod/index.htm

ISBN 0-620-36172-7

Please take special note of the warning on the next page

Author: Rick Evans
TheArmyofGod@SoftHome.net

This book must be given as a Love gift and received as one too. Nothing is to be exchanged for it either money or goods.

This work has taken over 3 years but it has been the work of the Holy Spirit and not mine.

I was commanded by Almighty God not to charge even a cost price for this book but to pass it on free of charge. This command is for everyone who has anything to do with this book. Once you have finished this book, this warning will make sense.

Some have prejudged this work because of this warning, creating within themselves an unteachable attitude and so they lost out on the blessings within it, I pray you can resist such a temptation. Take heed of the warning though - I need to have a clear conscience on this.

Warning:
The plagues that fell on the philistines when they stole the Ark of God (1 Samuel 5:6 – 12) are the plagues that will fall on the persons and their families should they charge even a cost price for this book or try to copyright, patent or own any aspect of it. God protects his own.

Contents

Prologue

When do the last days start?

Scripture tells us that in the last days you will see wars and rumours of wars. (Matthew 24: 6)

This has been going on almost since the great flood of Noah's time and in fact prior to this too.

This scripture, when quoted out of context of the Bible, has caused much confusion on the issue of the last days. I believe this Scripture has been given to us to encourage us by showing that God is always in control. Even through the hard times of War, Famine, Drought, etc., and even when there is a threat that War would start, He is still in control.

If this were the only scripture relating to the last days I might agree with the cynics that there does not appear to be a "Last Days". To their shame however there are many references to the last days and all of these need to be mapped together to get a correct picture of what God refers to as "The Last Days".

I believe that the "Last Days" started with the Death of Jesus Christ. My Reason for this is that scripture tells us that God said that in the last days He would pour out His Spirit on all flesh. (Joel 2 : 28 - 32)

Before this time only certain prophets received the Spirit of God and this came upon them (It did not dwell within them)

The outpouring of God's Spirit started at Pentecost when the Holy Spirit appeared as tongues of fire above the heads of the Disciples (Acts 2: 3& 4)

Since then, believers that ask God for the Holy Spirit, ask that He should come and live within them, receive the Holy Spirit. (Luke 11:13)

What is the Duration of the Last Days?
Nowhere in scripture do we find a time period for the last days. The book of Revelation and some of the prophetic books do indicate however that there will be an end to these last days. So there is definitely a countdown to this end and every second that goes by we are one second closer to that end.

Scripture also tells us that in the last days, people will increase their knowledge and rush to and fro.

(Daniel 12:4)
Daniel had received prophetic words for our time and was ordered to hide it until God revealed it to us. Who will be alive in a time where travel will increase (the picture of a rat trying to escape a maze comes to mind) and this will also be a time when men have ever increasing knowledge.

How true this is of the past 200 years.

God did raise up His Church though.

The death of Jesus Christ, The perfect Son of God is the only Sacrifice acceptable to God to pay for our sins. In fact Jesus went further and asked Peter a question "Who do you say that I am?" (Matthew 16:15 – 19) to which Peter replied, "You are the Messiah, the Son of the living God". Then Jesus said to Peter "Flesh and blood have not revealed this to you, but My Father, who is in Heaven ... and on this rock foundation I will build my church, and not even death will ever be able to overcome it."

On what did Jesus build His Church?

On the principle:

God, in Heaven, would communicate through His Spirit with mankind

This is why those who try to use their carnal thinking, cannot accept, or understand Christianity. God reveals it, when, and only when, man first puts his faith in God and accepts Jesus Christ as his Lord and Saviour. Only then does Jesus enter the person and "switch on the ability to understand" from within the person. It seems as though the switches are all on the inside of you. Jesus is a gentleman and will never barge in and take over. He will only come in if you ask and He will only switch the switches you allow Him to.

So what is the purpose of this Church that Jesus came to build?
Question:
What is Christianity?

Answer:
God is Holy, Pure and Abides by his own Laws at All Times.

One of his Laws is that any Sin is punishable by Death. (Romans 6:23) We on the other hand have committed so many Sins:

- Heart Sins (e.g. Lust, Jealousy, Greed, Idolatry, Anger, etc);
- Verbal Sins (e.g. Using the Name of Jesus inappropriately, Swearing, Maligning, Gossiping, Lying (including "little white lies"), etc);

- Physical Sins(e.g. Theft, Assault, Fighting, Sexual immorality, inappropriate use of our resources, etc).

In fact if you have just once done any of the above things only once, from the day you could understand right from wrong, God's Law states that you must die. (Romans 6:23)

Well you might say that that is a bit harsh. Well yes. You see in the entire universe it is only man who was created in the image of God. And in the entire universe it is only man that would dare to disobey God. Not one creature, planet, solar system or spec of space dust would dare to move out of alignment with what God ordains, none but man. So then, is it God who is overly harsh, or is it man who is arrogant and contemptuous of The Almighty God. If it is the latter, then it is no real surprise that this is the only planet satan has been banished to, and these characteristics, are not ours but that of satan and his fallen angels.

Before the Holy Spirit was available to us, mankind allowed satan to control them because they were and still are week helpless and puny beings by comparison. Nevertheless, Death is the punishment for disobedience to God.

But because God Almighty Loves you so much and wants you to be with Him in Heaven for eternity He has provided a way for you to escape this death judgement hanging over your head. But someone will still have to die to pay for your sins, if not you ... then someone who has never sinned. If someone has sinned, he must die for his own sins, he cannot again die for someone else's sins. So none of us mortals could ever do it. We humans would only be able to pay the penalty for the sins we have committed, not anyone else's.

Scripture tells us that all have sinned and fallen short of reaching God (Romans 3:23 - 26).

Sure, We have been tempted, by a being far more slimy and devious than we can imagine, with greater power than we ourselves have. But that is no excuse. God's laws are God's laws and dare not be broken.

God cannot change His Law. Because God cannot change, He is the same, yesterday, today and forever (Malachi 3:6). - You Sin, Your spirit dies. It is that simple.

As we know, it is God who created satan. He created him as the most powerful being in the universe second only to himself (Ezekiel 28:11 – 15). Naturally satan was created as a finite being, with limitations, unlike God who is infinite and has no limitations. (excepting those He chooses to place on Himself.)

So then, to provide a person who could withstand all satan's temptations, who, could live a perfect life and then die for the sins of others. He would have to take on satan himself... but as a human.

So in the form of a person, Jesus Christ, he exposed the character and nature of God, His Love for people, compassion for their situations, power over all of creation, and ability to resist all temptations, He was born of a virgin by the name of Mary.

Mary was a highly favoured woman to have had this opportunity to be used by God. To place an emphasis on Mary, Jesus' earthly mother, who was human and not to place that emphasis on Jesus Christ, the Mighty Son of God, as the means to receiving favour with God, is obviously a means to distract you, ever so slightly, but sufficiently, to ensure that you miss receiving what God provided for you...

Escape from eternal Death.

Jesus Christ fulfilled every single prophecy regarding the Jewish Messiah, which, according to chance, is impossible for one person to achieve in a lifetime. He fought the Devil on his own turf and resisted every temptation satan could throw at Him. Eventually He was crucified on a cross and the final prophecies were fulfilled at His resurrection.

Why did God raise Jesus from the dead?

Jesus Christ had carried with Him to Hell, all the sins that were to be forgiven, past, present and future until the end of time, but He Himself had committed no Sin and therefore satan was not entitled to keep Him.

Jesus is now seated on a throne in Heaven at the Right Hand of God. He is waiting for the appointed time, the end of the countdown, and very soon, when we will all have to appear before Him and be judged by Him, whether we die our earthly death before then or are still alive when the time of the end comes.

The penalty for sin had now been paid. God is now able to forgive those who ask Him to forgive them. I am still studying the subject of those born prior to Jesus death on the cross, but so far I am convinced that for us who live after the penalty for sin was paid by Jesus Christ, there remains only one path open to Heaven.

God cannot save those who hear and understand the message and yet still choose to throw away God's gift of a means of escape from eternal death. Not because He does not want to, but simply because He will never interfere in your free will. He gave you your free will and for some reason he chooses to respect your choice to exercise it in whatever manner you choose. There is no doubt that He is distressed when a person chooses to reject the escape route, He has provided at so great a price, to so undeserving a species.

Scripture tells us that God does not want any of us to be lost (2 Peter 3:9). And in fact we know that when just one person accepts the escape route and is saved then there is great joy in Heaven (Luke 15:7).

But at the end of the day there will be those who choose to go to their own destruction through obstinacy, despite all that God does to try and save them, and these, even God cannot save.

If you are one of those who has heard this message of Jesus Christ, which by reading this you have, and for any reason still choose to ignore His call (God appointed this day and time for you to receive His call for you to escape) then you have judged yourself, and chosen Hell as your eternal destination. God sends no one to Hell. People choose to go there by default of not choosing the one and only path God has provided to get to Heaven.

You might just have said that you doubt that this is the one and only path?

Well let me ask you this then. If there were any other ways to get to God, then why would He suffer the pain of watching His only Son murdered to pay the price of sin, which is death (Romans 8:1-17).

So now we have seen the escape route God has created, how then do we escape through it? Jesus said that he is the door, and that no one comes to The Father but through Him. (John 14:5 - 7; John 10:9). John 3:1-36 tells us how to escape through this door. Read it for yourself at least 5 times. Study it until you understand it clearly. Then act on it. By confessing with your mouth that Jesus Christ is your Lord (Reason for your existence, your Master, and that you wish that He use you for the rest of your days on this earth) and by being Baptised (Submersed in water) where the old you is destroyed and God places a spirit which can enter Heaven within you, you will be able to enter into heaven when you die. However you have now become an enemy of satan and your life is going to be very difficult from this day on unless you ask The Holy Spirit to enter into you (Luke 11:13).

(The Holy Spirit will never force himself on you, as he will never encroach on your free will. You have to ask Him to enter you.)

You will find it an absolute necessity to have the Power of God operating from within you in the form of The Holy Spirit.

If you have done all this then you are guaranteed his presence, peace, security, and so much more He will never leave you nor forsake you.

(Hebrews 13:5 & 6; Deuteronomy 31:6,8; Joshua 1:5)

What Church did God raise up in the beginning of the Last Days?

(... for this is the Church you want to belong to.)

Firstly it should be noted that brothers and sisters of Christ are physically sexual beings being male and female. Spiritually however we are asexual and therefore there is no spiritual difference between the spirits of males and females.

Sex is required only to keep the earth populated with vessels within which God can place His Spirit and so gain children for his eternal Kingdom. Marriage only lasts as long as people are alive. Jesus taught that there is no marriage after death (Matthew 22: 23 - 30) and in fact there is separation of marriages on the death of a spouse.

Secondly Brothers and Sisters of Christ should note that it is Servant hood to God and to others, which is the key requirement of any believer (Matthew 23: 8 – 12). No emphasis should be placed on any believer in terms of Authority.

All believers are equal in authority and none are subject to another (Matthew 23: 8 - 12). All are subject to the Holy Spirit of God and are accountable to Him and to Him alone.

So then the Church is not a building, organisation, or any top- down hierarchical structure.

The Church is in fact each believer interacting with other believers where they are a servant to other believers, supplying them with whatever goods, skills, knowledge, encouragement and spiritual gifts they have wherever and whenever possible. Moreover, Believers must supply these when prompted by the Spirit of God even when it is not in line with the worldly way of doing things.

So what happened to the Church?
satan, being a finite creature, can only be in one place at one time. He relies on demons in a hierarchical reporting structure to provide him with the information he requires to cause the maximum damage to God's Church of believers.

During the first century, he attempted to wipe out all Christians. This did not work, so he infiltrated them. Not with satanists, but with people who would call themselves Christians, Ambitious people, who wanted Power and not Servant hood. These satan knew had not received the Holy Spirit within them and so were powerless to detect his presence and prompting. Demons were assigned to these "more powerful Christians" and with their influence churches were established which had a Hierarchy. Those of greater influence, who chose to be "in charge of", as apposed to "subordinate to" others, were ever so slowly and without their being aware of it, moulded to carry out satan's Plan B.

Plan B was to get all the real Christians together into a club, make everyone pleased to be there but hinder them from speaking to anyone outside of the church. To place them under such a list of rules they must obey and Things they must not do that they would spend all their time trying to be "Holy in God's sight", when in fact they were already perfectly Holy to God the moment Jesus took all their sins away.

No amount of doing good was going to make the Christians any more acceptable to God anyway, but satan kept this fact from them.

satan's plan did not completely succeed for there were still Christians who continued to talk to others about Jesus.

satan had to then come up with Plan C.

Plan C is a mixture of 3 different methods.

- Firstly kill as many of those who open their mouths, if you cannot kill them make them too busy, tired, sick, or distract them in any other way so that they will not talk.
- Secondly increase and strengthen the hold on the church hierarchies by getting people thrown out of the various churches. Using the spirits of judgement and gossip, get everyone belonging to churches to isolate these people from the church organisations.
- Thirdly turn the church into a club consisting of many who profess to be Christians but are not. People who aspire to the title of being a "good person" but never get to be children of the Most High God? - Using these people as examples get the people who are not in church to see what they do and so paint an incorrect picture of God because of what these supposed Christians are doing.

This has been his major approach since the first century AD but he has added a number of other little plans to trap and control believers. The latest is to enforce tolerance of one another and accepting of sinful practices within other believers lives and even more recently forcing the churches through

Government Legislation to endorse sinful practices such as Same-Sex Marriages.

How should the church operate?
In its current form the Church cannot function according to the actual definition of what it means to be a Christian.

A Christian is a true believer. He is a person who acts on what he sees Christ expects of him. A Christian is one who accepts the Grace Jesus bought for us by taking our sin upon the cross. We do this when we choose to accept Him as Lord and Master of every aspect of our lives). (1 John 3 : 23)

The Church of The Last Days

Well let us look at what the Church looked like in the first century, when satan could not control it.

To put this in its proper context we must first look at the relationship between the believers and Jesus Christ.

When we accept Jesus into our hearts, we are in fact marrying Him. We do not take marriage to another human being lightly and we should not take marrying Jesus lightly either. We are the Bride of Christ, Jesus is the Bride Groom (Ephesians 5:21-27)

3. We must respect and honour him.
4. We must submit to His will for our lives.

There are various marriage vows used when I married my wife Vanessa. This one was common at that time: (I have edited it a little for a better understanding of the analogy):

I (Your Name),
Take you Jesus Christ (My Bride Groom),
To be my eternal Lord and friend,
To have and to hold (in my being)
from this day forth (No turning back and no Divorce).
Whether my life gets better or worse,
Whether I get richer or poorer,
Whether I am sick or healthy,
I choose to love and to cherish You,
Forsaking all other gods and idols,
Making You my most important priority,
And this I pledge for eternity.
I give you my will as a sign that I belong to You,
With my Heart, Mind, Body and Soul I honour You,
All that I am I give to You,
      and
All that I have is Yours already,
Within the love of God, Father, Son/You and Holy Spirit,
And this is my solemn vow.

This really separates the Christ-followers from those who call themselves Christians. Read this carefully and understand all that you are giving up your right to.

There are always two sides to a marriage and in marrying Jesus it is no different. He has the following to say to you (remember, spirits are asexual, so do not think that this is about that sort of a relationship.)

I Jesus Christ,
Take you (Your Name),
To be my eternal subject and friend,
from this day forth (No turning back and no Divorce).

Whether you get better or worse,
Whether you get richer or poorer,
Whether you are sick or healthy,
I choose to love and to cherish you,
I will never leave you nor forsake you,
And this I pledge for eternity.
I give you my perfection and take all your sin away,
With my death I pay your death penalty,
All that I am I give to you,
      and
All that I have I share with you,
Within the love of God, Father, Son/Me and Holy Spirit,
And this is my solemn vow.

Now if this does not blow your mind then you still have not realised how much God has that He can share with you. How much He understands and knows that you will mess up in the future. How He will never leave you nor forsake you because He has accepted you by forgiving you, and how much, by dying for you He has made it possible to make this amazing promise to you.

I suggest you really study what these vows mean and how precious you are to God that He would offer such a promise to you. And He does because you are special. He created you because He loves you and wants you to be with Him forever (John 14:2 & 3).

Do not let satan say to you that this is not meant for you. The Bible says it is meant for you because God Almighty desires this relationship with you. You are special to Him. Even if no one else in the world thinks you are worth anything. You are worth His blood to Him (John 14: 1-31).

You might mess up, He never will, because He is perfect and keeps all His promises.

I have to stop here a while because this revelation has blown me away.

Excuse me while I take it in. Then we will look at how this relationship with Jesus affects our relationship with our Christian brothers and sisters.

Our relationship with our Christian brothers and sisters.

Well now that we have our relationship with The Son of God correctly aligned in our minds, now we can look at our relationship with our Christian brothers and sisters.

The first point to note is that you never know whether someone is your brother or sister. I am always excited to find out that someone is or has become my brother or sister. I just love knowing my family is getting bigger and there is someone else that Loves me and whom I can also Love. It is "really cool" as my children would say. I Love it.

Another thing you do not know is, what spiritual age your brother or sister, are at the moment. For example, you would never malign a baby and gossip behind their backs if they could not walk and talk at the age of 6 months would you? But Christians do that to each other all the time!

For the sake of Jesus, get your thinking straightened out.

Furthermore do not consider that because a person has been a Christian for many years that they are more spiritually mature or immature than you are. In a race, if one person starts walking and another waits a while and then starts running you cannot say which will win or who should be at which stage when. The intensity of your devotion to Jesus Christ and the Study of His Word and His Will and the speed with which you conquer temptations and evil strong holds in your life will determine the speed with which you mature spiritually. (Take the plank out of your own eye (Matt 7:1-5))

And lastly but most importantly you must understand that if someone claims to be a Christian and can say that Jesus is Lord he/she is your brother or sister (1 John 4:2). This means that no matter what they do, or say to hurt you, your loved ones, or anyone else, you have no right to hold it against them. They have been forgiven by Your Lord and Master to whom you Have to Submit your will, anger, frustration and every other negative feeling thought and emotion. Jesus chose to die for that sin they committed too. He paid a high price.

To be unforgiving when Jesus already paid the price to forgive that sin is to trample the blood of Jesus underfoot and Dishonour the very Jesus Christ you have pledged to honour. So you have to Love them and forgive them openly whether they deserve it or not, whether they continue to do it or not.

Gossipers, be warned!!! Jesus punishes those who cannot stop pouring forth filth from their mouths. Furthermore, if He has forgiven the sin that was committed which, you are gossiping about, then it has been thrown as far as the East is from the West and can be remembered no more. It never happened!!! This makes you a liar as well as a gossip. Do not be so quick to judge others, or God will judge you in the same light. (In this case on here-say, which is all that gossip is, and not on the real you) (Matt 7:1-5), (Mark 4:22-24). If others begin to Gossip, politely ask to leave the conversation or remain silently praying for all those speaking and those spoken about. If asked, boldly explain this principle to those who ask after your silence. You may be ostracised, but it would be better not to be a part of a crowd who intends to make you feel uncomfortable by continuing in your presence.

This does not mean you should remain silent. But all that is good, encouraging, pleasing, kind, whatever is of a good report, think on these things (Philippians 4:8-9). Speak these things and build up your brothers and sisters.

Give to your brothers and sisters whatever they need if you have surplus of that item, skill, talent and time. Do this at no cost, asking nothing in return and accepting whatever they choose to offer. Do not offend them by making them feel like they are poorer or less than you are, by refusing to accept an offering from them. For you will be rewarded for what you give (Luke 6:38) and you should not deny them their reward for giving to you.

Exposing satan's biggest lie & destroying his grip on mankind

Now I want to destroy one of satan's Key Lies which rules human thinking, and most likely, yours too, by exposing His ultimate stronghold on, not just you, but also the church and in fact the whole world. Once you understand this properly you will be free from his control in most areas of your life, as were the early Christians. (Ezekiel 28 : 11 – 19)

Ezekiel is sent to give a message to the king of Tyre, which he delivers in Ezekiel 26:1 – 28:26. But then strangely, he suddenly receives another message for the King of Tyre, which he delivers in chapter 28: 11 - 19

Now this blew my mind wide open. The second message was clearly not for any human being. Read it!! (Ezekiel 28 : 11 – 19) It is directed straight at satan himself who must have taken up temporary residence in the king of Tyre for Ezekiel to deliver the message to him.

The key sentence, tucked away in the Bible that explains what satan has always hidden from us is this: - satan was thrown out of heaven because of his Trade. So what was his Trade? God ascribes the creation of the principle of "Trade" to satan.

In heaven there is no Trade.

What????

Yes my friend in Heaven there is no Buying or Selling. No Barter.

The reason is that these remove the need for the giving out of Love for one another. You see both Trade and Barter have one prerequisite.

No one gets anything unless the values of the Trade or Barter Items are the same.

For example I cannot barter my old car for a new one and I cannot buy a new car for 5 cents. This is the System satan had introduced into Heaven. God however, knowing all things, seeing all things and knowing the future of all things, having wisdom beyond measure, could see that the minute you took Love out of giving and receiving you were heading for all kinds of evil consequences.

<u>Now Put down this book and think about this carefully, because satan will steal this revelation from you if you even give him the slightest chance.</u>

In fact, if you find yourself scoffing at this now, later, tomorrow, next week, next month or whenever, you can be sure he has succeeded in locking you up and stealing this one key.

I challenge you to find one evil thing that cannot be traced back to the principle of ... Trade.

My personal encounter with God on this matter:

On my journey to discovering this, I came across Ezekiel 28:11-18 and I asked the Holy Spirit to reveal to me what Trade satan had done, because whatever it was I did not want to do the same thing. Well He did not answer me immediately – about three months later He caught me in the shower and asked me to explain "Trade" to Him. So I said the following:

I assumed the role of the buyer and said:

- I go to the shop
- I collect what I want to buy
- I go to the paypoint
- I pay the money
- And walk out with my goods

He said that I was correct and asked me to reverse the process.

So, assuming that I was the buyer again, I said:

- I go to the shop
- I go to the paypoint
- I pay the money
- I collect what I want to buy
- And walk out with my goods

He said that I was correct again and then asked me, so what do you do if you do not have the money?

So I said "well I suppose I cannot buy what wanted to"

He said, "Correct again. Now let's reverse the roles. Let's make you the shop owner. Let us say that a poor person comes into your shop and asks for a glass of water, but does not have any money to pay for it. What do you do?"

So I said, "Well, I have compassion on him and give him the glass of water."

He said, "No, you are not allowed to do that. According to the principle of Trade, this poor person must give you something of equal value in return, otherwise he cannot have the glass of water."

Now very seldom have I heard such a deep bitter anger in God's voice, but He went on to say the following which when I reread the Bible, I (for the first time, after reading it cover to cover many times, saw this theme and battle between God and satan running like a thread right throughout History, and also for the first time understood why Jesus does not charge for salvation, and hates anyone who does.

God, clearly and plainly, and audibly said to me, "In fact Trade dictates, to you the shopkeeper, that not only may you not give him the glass of water, but that you will watch him and his family die of thirst, but he will not get this water unless he gives you something of equal value in return." And the God added, "NOW WHERE IS MY LOVE IN THAT!!"

Freely, freely give...

Now that you've thought this through a bit let us continue.

So God never intended Trade or Barter to be on earth. What did he intend?

What did the early Christians discover that was so devastatingly dangerous to satan's Kingdom.

The lie
Well they discovered a simple truth: - Most people have more than they need of one thing and not enough of another. They also discovered that if they found out what their Christian brothers and sisters needed, they would all be able to meet one another's needs without actually running out themselves. (Acts 2 : 44 - 47), (Acts 4 : 34 & 35)

satan has the answer to your brother'/sister' needs locked away in your cupboard, store room, garage or somewhere else you tend to dump stuff. You may have a skill/talent that could solve a brother'/sister' need. So why do we not do anything about it?

Here is the crux!

Someone, somewhere, told someone a long time ago that to discuss your problems and needs with your brothers and sisters in Christ was to become a social outcast. It is to put yourself at the mercy of the Gossipers. "It is just not right to burden other people with my problems" some would say. Others would say, "It's just not done!"

Well I have news for you... I know who started this thing off. And I know the real reason some of you subscribe to this way of thinking.

satan started this off a long time ago and held it in motion by introducing social norms and rules commonly known that would ensure that those who did not subscribe to these rules would be ostracised. He introduced Gossipers to humiliate and keep the mouths of those who would confide in brothers and sisters shut. If no one knows your problems then no one can help you and that is exactly where he wants you. If a loving brother or sister starts to help you, satan loses control over you. Imagine if all the brothers and sisters shared their needs, belongings, talents, skills and time. Well, He would be back to the days of the early Church where he would have to persecute them in every possible way to stop them from destroying his control over the planet, which is centred on ..... Wait for it .... Trade... where Love is not required to transact.

If you cannot accept this and change, then you are too proud of yourself, your standing in society, and your situation. You think, "How can I stoop to that level?"

Well actually you are swimming upside down reaching for the bottom of hell. You need to turn yourself around. Start reaching for Heaven. Throw away all your pride, your concern about your social standing, and your need for power over other people. Throw it all away. It's all an illusion.

Jesus was never concerned about His social standing.
Why did he disrespect it so much? He knew the lie. And He knew the Liar. And He knew Heaven. And He knew how it really is. (Romans 12:2)

Until you get past this issue you will never operate according to the pattern of the Church as laid down by Jesus Christ. Do not play with this idea; do not con yourself that you are doing it.

DO IT!!! (Romans 12:1-21)

And then you will be free, to operate in the Love of God.

YOU WILL BE FREE - Because the Truth will set you free (John 8 : 31 - 34).

There is a lot more to come on this subject but I need to recover. As much as this is new to you the way it has come out on paper, it is new to me too and I need to meditate on it a while and take stock of my own situation and where I stand on this issue.

So what could we do about this?
We could transform our churches to do what the 1st century churches did

Here follows a template that you can take to your church leaders to introduce a ministry which can assist in developing the re-institution of Love-based transactions instead of Trade-based transactions.

A 1st Century Church Ministry for our Church today

Primary Purpose:
To Care – Expose needs and hurts of those within our church or those who visit our church, which brings compassion and a desire to resolve.

Secondary Purpose:
To Educate – Teach the church members how God taught and sustained the early church to meet the needs of those around them without having needs themselves.

To Demonstrate – Show how we can solve other peoples problems by that which God has already given us and so Demonstrate that Where the world and the devil say you can have if... God says you can have freely

To communicate – The good news to the poor.

Our Primary Target:

Committed Membership

Secondary Target:

Core, Congregation, Community & Crowd

The Needs this ministry focuses on
The needs this ministry focuses on is the need for a mechanism whereby the Holy Spirit can prompt the church to meet one another's needs.

The Mechanism is so designed as to make known the needs of the individuals within the church in such a way as to keep anonymous those who are in need. This information is made known to the Church so that the church members can respond and assist as they are lead by the Holy Spirit.

The needs met may start off as physical needs, move to things like lift clubs, house sitting, Legal & Financial advice and eventually all the practitioners who normally charge for their services would assist church members in difficulty for nothing, simply because they recognise they are their brothers and sisters in Christ and that they love them as such.

One suggestion of how the mechanism could work (Please note that the Holy Spirit will prompt you to use one or more mechanisms in different situations so this is just an idea from which to start discussing what will work for you in your church

Description of Mechanism?
Cards people can fill in with their needs that they can drop into the offering basket

4. Collect cards and place on the board (Wall). The card has two identical numbers. One can be torn off and kept by the member in need and the other remains on the card.
   OR

5. Collect cards and enter them on a central database of needs. email or contact people that may provide for each particular need
   OR

6. Website could have a needs page and anyone could add their need or answer to it

How to make this ministry reality?
We would need to test this on the small group initially

Board (Wall) design (Where cards will be put up on)

Card design (Cards/papers on which people can write their needs)

Printing Cards

If the Cards option is successful in the small groups then implement it in the church. Continuously pray so that the Holy Spirit can show you other ways to make this work in other parts of the church too.

The person(s) who should lead this ministry should be
Be Spirit Lead, Humble, Compassionate and desire mercy, They should not be one who gossips, But they should be empathetic, enthusiastic, patient, have leadership ability, be able to do administration (manage the needs and the meeting of these needs), Should be able to deal with people in a loving way (even when they are angry)

How do we expand this ministry?
Find people with compassion/mercy gifts (If anyone wants to serve in this ministry evaluate them according to the above criteria)

Give them an introductory training.

Give them hands on training.

The Primary type of work is
Administrative mostly....Some people skills required.

There is a completely flat structure of those who would operate in this ministry. The leader is only a coach and has no authority other than the Bible. If the leader cannot find scripture with which to guide a person to a different behaviour then the leader must re-evaluate his/her attitude on the subject. If a person does not wish to change their behaviour after the Word of God on the matter has been made known to them, then make this known to all of those who are working in this ministry that they should all try to dissuade the offender and assist them to change. If the offender still refuses then at a meeting the leader is to remain silent and all those in the ministry are to individually agree that the offender must leave the ministry until such time as he/she mends his/her ways. At no time is the leader to say a word about it, it is a matter of the Holy Spirit's Authority, and not the leader. The leader however remains accountable first to the Holy Spirit and then to the Church as a whole and finally to the Church Leadership.

Training Needed
Read this book

Understand the mechanism your ministry has chosen to put in place and understand the part you are to play in it.

Regularly update their score cards for all to see

What will it cost to start this ministry?
It depends on the route....Cards...Website...phone calls ... It really should cost very little to start. A book would be used to record the needs, and when they were met.

What are the budget/financial needs to sustain our ministry?
It should not cost much at all. You will need some storage space and some volunteers. A book, pre-printed cards (or blank cards and a rubber stamp).

How can we (the Ministry team) find the money needed to support this ministry?
Pray for it and follow the prompting of the Holy Spirit. He will guide each of us in ways best for each of us.

Communication amongst one another could take place in some of these ways
- <u>With each other?</u>
  Cell Phone and Telephone and e-mail

- <u>With its leadership?</u>
  As above

- <u>With other ministries?</u>
  As above

- <u>With church staff?</u>
  As above

- <u>With the church at large?</u>
  Via weekly leaflet and from the Pulpit, quarterly magazine, email, sms, etc..

- <u>With whom is it trying to serve?</u>
  Those whose needs are met will be contacted through a leaflet specifying which needs were met, unless contact details were left on the card (transcribed into the book but not publicised) in which case a message can be left for them.

Monitoring how well this ministry is doing?

Firstly bear in mind that there is often an adoption curve where slowly & cautiously those who have needs will use this ministry. So do not expect that suddenly everyone will respond. it will take time to grow.

Measure the ministry on whether people are getting there needs to us and are they being met, I.E. It is very measurable with stats.

Stats i.e. Mr. Bloggs needs a lift...Mr. Smith met the need. This will be documented but not publicised as to who needed the lift or who met the need. A certain amount of discretion is required for example it may not be prudent to simply say lift required. But the Holy Spirit will guide you as to what to write.

The Ministry's success could be measured in some of the following ways

The growing maturity in Jesus Christ of those who serve in this ministry

Are people making needs known and are they being met...Physical needs.

Anyone in the church leadership confirmed to have integrity within the church and who has not been found to be a gossip may check the books of requests made versus those met and those collected.

How do you measure someone who needed shoes for their child getting them and someone needing a lift and getting it? These must remain stories and not be reduced to 5 needs this month 6 the following. (We publicise stories not statistics. God is far more glorified in a story than he is in a set of numbers.)

The Ministry team's success would be enhanced by?
Prayer, Prayer and more Prayer. Pray for the Ministry team, and those in need and those who will give daily. An additional suggestion, that the group can meet periodically for Bible study is also a good one.

The Ministry team members would form a family unit?
We will all shepherd one another as brothers and sisters equal to each other before God as Jesus instructed.

The leader takes responsibility for his Ministry team and their growth

The Needs Board (Wall) will be available to the Ministry team members & church leadership too.

Negotiate the following between the leader and each individual Ministry team member.
One-on-one meetings to determine:

- Time commitment
- Family matters
- Quiet Time
- Vocation vs. Ministry demands
- Small Groups/Accountability Relationships

Support within the Ministry team:
- Praying for each other
- Group devotionals
- Ministry team Fellowships

The Vision for growth of this Ministry

One vision could be that God would grow this bigger than your church and use it as a means of outreach to your surrounding communities.

In all likelihood, God will put within the Ministry team and its leadership the passion for what he wants to achieve through them.

The purpose & dream (+ - 5 years from now)

The church of the days of Acts had 0 needs. We can achieve that. The needs board (Wall) disappearing and being replaced by people who can openly confess their needs and not feel that they are open to ridicule and at the mercy of the gossipers would be the ultimate goal

After about 3 years the ministry would ideally be

Needs board (Wall), fully functional and all needs within the membership being met.

Expanding this ministry is at the discretion of the Holy Spirit

The Holy Spirit will direct – We will not dictate His direction or limit his direction to the finite knowledge of our here and now.

Concerns some people have raised as to practicalities.

How do we minimise People abusing the system for their own gain?

(We needed to make it difficult enough so that those who are really in need will follow the process (at the same time making provision for problems like cultural differences, illiteracy, disability etc). The process must also be a bit of a pain so that those, not in real need will not bother to do it.)

The Church Leadership has certain Responsibilities

Proof of what we do with whose resources is an essential

(A record of needs publicized & Needs met must be kept by the Church)

Proof that negligence is at least mitigated is also essential

(A Needs Analysis on the situation & person should be done and some form of due diligence should be assured before needs are met.)

How will we ensure that mistakes made cause the least problems?

9. This should be started on a small scale with dedicated Church Members (Preferably Cell Leaders).
10. Explain the entire concept (Best to let them read it for themselves and decide for themselves if they feel at peace starting this)
11. Select 5 of the cell leaders that volunteer.
12. Meet with the Cell Groups & explain the entire concept (Best to let the Cell Group work through the book.)
13. Ask that the cell group members submit one or more needs.)
14. The Cell Members can use the Needs Analysis Template below (Make Copies) to evaluate each others real needs.

15. *Draw up these needs and put them on the "Needs Wall". (NB No Names or identification of the person needing should be given on the need publicized on the Needs Wall)*
16. *The Needs Wall should be in a prominent place for the whole church to see.*

Is this God's work?

Proceed only when you have peace in your hearts that you have discovered God's Will in this matter.

A Needs Analysis Template

Below is a Needs Analysis Template that you could use (and adjust as the Holy Spirit dictates) which will assist you in finding and answering the real needs of people and not just their wants. Or what they think they need.

Name of your Need
Need Number
(Church to supply)

Original request - details of the need to be met.

All Information is treated as strictly confidential and all persons that will be handling your information are bound by Trust and Non-Disclosure Agreements.

Please note that the process requires a fair amount of effort on the part of the Ministry Consultant (You who filled in this card) It is therefore essential that you provide valid contact details for day and night.

Description of The Person in Need
(Names if possible)

Ministry Consultant:
Contact Details   (day)   :
Contact Details   (Night)   :
Contact Details   (Cell)   :

Description of the Need   :

Who (if any) amongst the Church Leaders &/or its members have you spoken to about this need?

NAME	FUNCTION	OUTCOME OF DISCUSSION	COMMENT

TAKE NOTE:

At no time will any consideration be given to even mentioning the person/business meeting the need.

All the Glory goes to God.

We do not Trade fame (advertising space) for that which should come naturally for God's Children.

Who is involved in this need?
Ministry Team Administrator to Complete:

Name	Function	Expected responsibility in the team	Contact no
	Ministry Consultant	Explain the Need and provide any proof of the Need if necessary.	
	Representative of the Church	To Counsel where necessary and to oversee the Church's Responsibilities	
	Ministry Team Administrator	To ensure that all Administration surrounding a Need is processed	
	Ministry Team – Leader	To ensure continuity throughout the process	
	Needs Analyst	To meet with the Needs Representative and to determine the exact nature of the need & to document it	
	Needs Supplier	The one who eventually Supplies the need	

What is the progress of this need being met?
Ministry Team - Leader to Complete:

STEP	RESPONSIBLE	START DATE	COMPLETION DATE
Need Fulfilment requested	Ministry Consultant		
Need Crystallised	Ministry Consultant		
Analyse the Need	Needs Analyst		
Request Supporting Information	Needs Analyst and Ministry Consultant		
Church Input	Representative of the Church		
Needs Request Draft	Needs Analyst		

What is the progress of this need being met? (Continued)

Ministry Team - Leader to Complete:

STEP	RESPONSIBLE	START DATE	COMPLETION DATE
QA of Needs Request Draft	Ministry Team – Leader		
Posting of Need on the Wall	Ministry Team Administrator		
Needs Provision received	Ministry Team Administrator		
Church Counsel for providers	Representative of the Church		
Permission to Witness	Ministry Team – Leader and Ministry Consultant		
Provide Need	Ministry Team – Leader and Ministry Consultant		
Witness Write up (if permitted by Needy)	Ministry Team – Leader and Ministry Consultant		
Witness Publication	Representative of the Church		
Needs Follow Up (1 Week after)	Ministry Team – Leader and Ministry Consultant		
Needs Follow Up (1 Month after)	Ministry Team – Leader and Ministry Consultant		
Needs Follow Up (3 Months after)	Ministry Team – Leader and Ministry Consultant		
Needs Follow Up (1 Year after)	Ministry Team – Leader and Ministry Consultant		

Why should you (Ministry Consultant) complete this?

Firstly

It is a need you are attempting to have satisfied that is being discussed. Only you really know the details of the real situation. The Church will bring your needs before the Body of Christ in such a way as to not mention your name or contact information publicly.

To do this without you personally standing up and telling the Church, the Body of Christ needs to know the details of what the real need is.

As an example:

If your real need is a lift to and from work, then you do not need a car. The car is one of many means to have your need met. Other ways would be a lift from a fellow Christian, or the ability to work from home, or a completely different way that the Holy Spirit wishes to meet your need.

If you need to have a safe place to stay then you do not need a house or money to rent a house. You need a safe place to stay. So remember to say it that way.

It is the purpose of this Guide to separate your real needs from how you think your needs should be met. God Almighty usually chooses ways that we do not see or expect to resolve our real needs. Our Church wants to free the Holy Spirit to deal with you and your need in the way that He chooses to, and not according to what you want done.

Secondly

> The Church Leadership has a responsibility to God Almighty to act responsibly with the Resources God puts in their hands. There may be situations where the Church itself has a solution to the need. In such a case the Church Leadership must be a good steward of these.
>
> > <u>Please note right up front that the Church will not be providing money to buy something to meet a need.</u>

Thirdly

> The Church is also a meeting place for the Body of Christ. Christians will be able to see these needs on the Needs Wall and they may be lead by the Holy Spirit to resolve the need.
>
> > <u>Once again no money will be used to buy something to meet your need</u>.
>
> The Church is therefore responsible for making sure that there is no abuse of the Body of Christ that frequent this church community.

Fourthly

> If you really need to have this need met, you will be prepared to make the effort to have your needs met.
>
> May Almighty God lead you and guide you.
>
> Church Leadership

__Identifying the real need__

Explain the current situation that is being faced

(Ministry Consultant to ask those in Need the questions & then fills in the boxes below)

What was the situation before this need arose?

```

```

What happened to cause this need?

```

```

What other problems are making this worse?

Unforgiveness, Bitterness, Physical or Mental Abuse, Divorce, Substance Abuse, Accident,

Sickness, Injury, Loss of Loved One(s), Death, Loss of Income, Ex Prisoner, Depression, Other

Circle those that are/have recently occurred.

(Please give details of each in the box below)

(You will not be disqualified based on the above – It is to ensure that we understand the nature of the Need in its context)

<u>What is the exact nature of the needs you have?</u>

(Ministry Consultant to discuss with those in Need & then Document)

<u>What, besides money, do you think would meet your needs?</u>

<u>What do you expect of the church needs wall?</u>

An example of Useful Questioning Techniques

The Person in Need	: "I need a car"
Ministry Consultant	: "Why do you need the car?"
The Person in Need	: "I need to take my children to School"
Ministry Consultant	: "Which School do you need to take them to?"
The Person in Need	: "I need to take my children to xxxxxx School"
Ministry Consultant	: "Is there someone you know who can take them to School for you?"
The Person in Need	: "No"
Ministry Consultant	: "So you need to get your children to School and Back?"
The Person in Need	: "Yes"
Ministry Consultant	: "Do you want us to find a way to get them to School for you?" (A)

Possible Responses:

One Response could be:
(A) Ministry Consultant: "Do you want us to find a way to get them to School for you?"

The Person in Need	: "Yes"
Ministry Consultant	: "So you want someone to help you get them to School?"
The Person in Need	: "Yes I do."
Ministry Consultant	: "Are there any special requests you have about this need?"
The Person in Need	: "Yes."
Ministry Consultant	: "What special requests do you have for this need?"
The Person in Need	: "I must be able to go with to drop off & pick up my children."
Ministry Consultant	: "Ok, Anything else?"
The Person in Need	: "No."

You have identified a Real Need and you know what the criteria for the need being met are.

Then Identify any other reasons for the person believing the car is the solution to the problem - Start from the beginning again

Ministry Consultant   : "What else do you need the car for?"

Another Response could be:
(A) Ministry Consultant: "Do you want us to find a way to get them to School for you?"
The Person in Need   : "No"
Ministry Consultant   : "So you do not need a car for this?"
The Person in Need   : "I need the car"
Ministry Consultant   : "If not for this then what?"
    This is Not the Real Need – Start from the beginning again.

Another Response could be:
(A) Ministry Consultant: "Do you want us to find a way to get them to School for you?"
The Person in Need   : "No"
Ministry Consultant   : "So you do not need a car for this?"
The Person in Need   : "I need the car"
Ministry Consultant   : "If not for this then what?"
The Person in Need   : "I need the car to go to coffee with my friends"

NB Do not write this off as not being a real need. Ask questions and let them decide if it is or is not a need. There may be other reasons why they go to the Coffee Shop that they do not want to disclose. Gently tell them that you can only give the needs you can explain in full to the Church.

Actual needs to be met:

(Ministry Consultant to discuss with those in Need & then Document)

Take a Specific Need and describe the real need not the solution (See Example discussion above)

Need # _____

Solution Detail:

Reason for this Solution:

Why would this solution solve the problem

Need Number _____

What is the real Need to be met

What will you <u>no longer</u> be able to do/have if this need is met by someone else? (Consider the effect of this solution).

The way you plan to do/get this – Are there possibly better ways of doing /getting this that will cause you less loss?

What problems could come from someone else meeting your need?

Special request when this need is met:
(This should also find a way around the problems)

Make extra copies of this page if necessary

Take another Specific Need and describe the real need not the solution

Actual needs to be met:
(Ministry Consultant to discuss with those in Need & then complete the form)

Take a Specific Need and describe the real need not the solution (See Example discussion above)

Need # _____

Solution Detail:

Reason for this Solution:

Why would this solution solve the problem

To be posted on the Needs Wall

Need Number _____

What is the real Need to be met

What will you <u>no longer</u> be able to do/have if this need is met by someone else? (Consider the effect of this solution).

The way you plan to do/get this – Are there possibly better ways of doing /getting this that will cause you less loss?

What problems could come from someone else meeting your need?

Special request when this need is met:
(This should also find a way around the problems)

Make extra copies of this page if necessary

Take another Specific Need and describe the real need not the solution

Actual needs to be met:
(Ministry Consultant to discuss with those in Need & then complete the form)

Take a Specific Need and describe the real need not the solution (See Example discussion above)

Need # _____

Solution Detail:
Reason for this Solution:
Why would this solution solve the problem

Need Number _____

What is the real Need to be met

What will you <u>no longer</u> be able to do/have if this need is met by someone else? (Consider the effect of this solution).

The way you plan to do/get this – Are there possibly better ways of doing /getting this that will cause you less loss?

What problems could come from someone else meeting your need?

Special request when this need is met:
(This should also find a way around the problems)

Make extra copies of this page if necessary

Return this to the church and put it in the Offering for your Needs to be presented & prayed for.

The Ministry Consultant must get this completed document back to the Church and hand it in to the person who will get it to the right Person to review and pray through.

The person will then check if there is more information required and they will contact the Ministry Consultant for more information if necessary.

The Need will be posted on the Needs Wall. Only the Ministry Team will have your name and contact details. From then on you will need to pray that the Holy Spirit sends someone to meet your need. You have now done what is required of you, leave the rest to God.

God Almighty may choose to meet your need another way. If so, please let us know that your needs have been met so that we can take your need off the Wall.

Human Needs

Background
I would like to now explore the needs of all Humans first and how we are made up.

Think of yourself as a set of 3 spheres one inside the other.

1. The **Spiritual** area of your life is the centre sphere.
2. The **Emotional** is your middle sphere within which the spiritual sphere resides.
3. The **Physical** area of your life is the outer sphere or layer, which is that area of your life through which you experience this physical world.

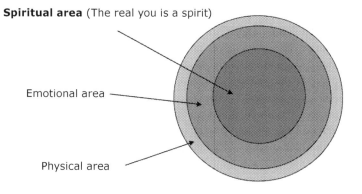

Spiritual area (The real you is a spirit)

Emotional area

Physical area

A Table showing you and your needs.

Your	Centre	Middle Layer	Outer Layer
Needs	Spiritual	Emotional	Physical
Survival	- Eternal Salvation, - Prayer, - Quite Time with God, - Indwelling of the Holy Spirit, - Forgiving all others	- Ability to cry & laugh, - Ability to forgive yourself, - Someone to talk to, - Someone who loves you, - Someone to love.	- Air, - Food, - Water, - Sunlight, - Shelter.
Basic	- Encouragement, - Prayer Partners, - Group Bible Study, - Problems for spiritual exercise, - Understanding God's Will for you.	- A Clear Conscience, - Encouragement, - Someone who will listen without judging, - Someone who lovingly shows you your faults, - Someone who accepts you exactly as you are.	- Clothing, - Health, - Exercise, - Sound Mind, - Working Body.
General	- Friends, - Desires, - Understanding the spiritual world, - Being in constant dialogue with Jesus, - A Ministry	- A listening ear to which you can unload, - Peaceful environment to recharge, - Someone you can help, - Ability to control your emotions, - Ability to detect the spiritual atmosphere through your emotions.	- Friends, - Desires met, - Knowledge, - Intelligence, - Areas to still grow in.

These are just some of these needs, what is important to note is that you are a complex creation.

Why should we show your needs at 3 different layers

In answering this we must refer to the table above. (The block where "Survival" (heading on the left of the table above) and "Outer Layer Physical" (heading on the top of the table above) meet is the minimum requirement for existence). A balloon can be popped easily because it has a thin outer layer. So too your physical layer can easily be penetrated. If that person has nothing in any of their emotional and spiritual blocks they are just like this balloon, having nothing but hot air within it. They have nothing to fall back on when they receive a hard knock. The impact of such a hard knock is often extremely serious.

On the other hand you have people who have Solid Spiritual, Emotional, and Physical layers who can handle the most horrific of life's storms very easily. This is what we must strive to achieve.

Self test
Test yourself and see if you are living at Survival, Basic or General Need's level. Test yourself in each of the areas of your life (physical, emotional and spiritual) The ideal is that all three should be balanced. If you are surviving in one area and General in another then you will be suffering.

The principle of testing yourself and measuring your progress is extremely important. To test yourself you need to measure yourself against a standard. The Standard is what the Bible says about each of these areas: You need to then take this standard and measure yourself according to it.

What is essential for your growth is that you make a commitment to repeat this exercise at regular intervals throughout your life.

You need to measure yourself at least once every 6 months to see how you are progressing. You will need to keep blank copies of the scoring sheets so that you can re-evaluate yourself.

Read the scripture References in your Bible and the measure yourself against these standards.

The first Criteria – an example of how to score on your sheet
Each of the 5 spiritual needs should be scored out of 10.

1. Pray before reading further:

   "Holy Spirit, You have been sent to teach me, guide and counsel me. Open my eyes to The Words of God for my life right now. Help me to see myself through Your eyes and to honestly judge where I am currently. Show me what I need to do to become what You want me to be. In the Name of Jesus Christ of Nazareth who bled and died to take away my sin and who I have accepted as the sole payment for my sin and who is my Lord and Saviour. Amen"

2. Read the Bible references for that one criterion. (Provided below)

   E.g. Survival Eternal Salvation. (See Exercise 1 below).

3. It is important to remember that the self test table provides some scripture references but you can grow even further by using a Concordance and finding other scriptures to which you can also apply the criteria. I do not want to limit God Almighty in His walk with you by restricting you to the list in this book. So see this as a training ground upon which you will grow even more once the principles taught

in this book have been entrenched in to your daily living.

4. Read one scripture passage right through. Write on a card, or underline in your Bible the verse(s) that speak about this criterion. Read these verses a few times over and write down whatever The Holy Spirit puts into your mind. Perhaps you are already doing or partly doing what The Holy Spirit has put in your mind and He might want you to learn to do it in another way. Perhaps you are not doing what The Holy Spirit has put in your mind at all. In almost every situation where you must change there will be something you will have to stop doing, people you should no longer associate with or a change that must come in the work you do or something similar. Write these down on your card or in the column in your Bible.

5. Score yourself on this Scripture.

   a. You are given a total of 10 points before you start evaluating a part of your life.
   b. If you are not doing, or only partly doing what The Holy Spirit has put in your mind score a minus 1 to be taken off the total of 10 for this criterion. (You will need to apply a bit more effort here)
   c. If you are doing what The Holy Spirit has put in your mind or are doing it and see an opportunity to do even better then score a 0 to be taken off this criterion. (Well Done!!!!)

6. Read the next scripture and repeat points 4 & 5 until done. One Scripture reference a day is normally sufficient unless the Holy Spirit

prompts you otherwise. Make this a habit as part of your daily schedule. And think about it regularly during the day.

Psalms 1:1 – 1:6 (KJV)

Psa 1:1 Blessed *is* the man that walketh not in the counsel of the ungodly, nor standeth in the way of sinners, nor sitteth in the seat of the scornful.

Psa 1:2 But his delight *is* in the law of the LORD; and in his law doth he meditate day and night.

Psa 1:3 And he shall be like a tree planted by the rivers of water, that bringeth forth his fruit in his season; his leaf also shall not wither; and whatsoever he doeth shall prosper.

Psa 1:4 The ungodly *are* not so: but *are* like the chaff which the wind driveth away.

Psa 1:5 Therefore the ungodly shall not stand in the judgment, nor sinners in the congregation of the righteous.

Psa 1:6 For the LORD knoweth the way of the righteous: but the way of the ungodly shall perish.

7. The Bible is a book for life, so do not expect to just read it and pack it away. Read it and re-read it and re-read it. The purpose of the book I have written is to provide an understanding of why and how you should read the Bible so that you are able to grow correctly and in strength. You will then be able to become a reliable soldier in the Army of Jesus Christ – "The Church" ... Enjoy.

I have provided the scriptures (using e-Sword Technology) for the first Spiritual Criteria in this section of the book as both an example and because it is the core to your spiritual survival.

Eternal Salvation
Return to Spiritual Survival – Eternal Salvation

Mat 24 : 3 – 51

Mat 24:3 And as he sat upon the mount of Olives, the disciples came unto him privately, saying, Tell us, when shall these things be? and what *shall be* the sign of thy coming, and of the end of the world?

Mat 24:4 And Jesus answered and said unto them, Take heed that no man deceive you.

Mat 24:5 For many shall come in my name, saying, I am Christ; and shall deceive many.

Mat 24:6 And ye shall hear of wars and rumours of wars: see that ye be not troubled: for all *these things* must come to pass, but the end is not yet.

Mat 24:7 For nation shall rise against nation, and kingdom against kingdom: and there shall be famines, and pestilences, and earthquakes, in divers places.

Mat 24:8 All these *are* the beginning of sorrows.

Mat 24:9 Then shall they deliver you up to be afflicted, and shall kill you: and ye shall be hated of all nations for my name's sake.

Mat 24:10 And then shall many be offended, and shall betray one another, and shall hate one another.

Mat 24:11 And many false prophets shall rise, and shall deceive many.

Mat 24:12 And because iniquity shall abound, the love of many shall wax cold.

Mat 24:13 But he that shall endure unto the end, the same shall be saved.

Mat 24:14 And this gospel of the kingdom shall be preached in all the world for a witness unto all nations; and then shall the end come.

Mat 24:15 When ye therefore shall see the abomination of desolation, spoken of by Daniel the prophet, stand in the holy place, (whoso readeth, let him understand:)

Mat 24:16 Then let them which be in Judaea flee into the mountains:

Mat 24:17 Let him which is on the housetop not come down to take any thing out of his house:

Mat 24:18 Neither let him which is in the field return back to take his clothes.

Mat 24:19 And woe unto them that are with child, and to them that give suck in those days!

Mat 24:20 But pray ye that your flight be not in the winter, neither on the sabbath day:

Mat 24:21 For then shall be great tribulation, such as was not since the beginning of the world to this time, no, nor ever shall be.

Mat 24:22 And except those days should be shortened, there should no flesh be saved: but for the elect's sake those days shall be shortened.

Mat 24:23 Then if any man shall say unto you, Lo, here *is* Christ, or there; believe *it* not.

Mat 24:24 For there shall arise false Christs, and false prophets, and shall shew great signs and wonders; insomuch that, if *it were* possible, they shall deceive the very elect.

Mat 24:25 Behold, I have told you before.

Mat 24:26 Wherefore if they shall say unto you, Behold, he is in the desert; go not forth: behold, *he is* in the secret chambers; believe *it* not.

Mat 24:27 For as the lightning cometh out of the east, and shineth even unto the west; so shall also the coming of the Son of man be.

Mat 24:28 For wheresoever the carcase is, there will the eagles be gathered together.

Mat 24:29 Immediately after the tribulation of those days shall the sun be darkened, and the moon shall not give her light, and the stars shall fall from heaven, and the powers of the heavens shall be shaken:

Mat 24:30 And then shall appear the sign of the Son of man in heaven: and then shall all the tribes of the earth mourn, and they shall see the Son of man coming in the clouds of heaven with power and great glory.

Mat 24:31 And he shall send his angels with a great sound of a trumpet, and they shall gather together his elect from the four winds, from one end of heaven to the other.

Mat 24:32 Now learn a parable of the fig tree; When his branch is yet tender, and putteth forth leaves, ye know that summer *is* nigh:

Mat 24:33 So likewise ye, when ye shall see all these things, know that it is near, *even* at the doors.

Mat 24:34 Verily I say unto you, This generation shall not pass, till all these things be fulfilled.

Mat 24:35 Heaven and earth shall pass away, but my words shall not pass away.

Mat 24:36 But of that day and hour knoweth no *man,* no, not the angels of heaven, but my Father only.

Mat 24:37 But as the days of Noe *were,* so shall also the coming of the Son of man be.

Mat 24:38 For as in the days that were before the flood they were eating and drinking, marrying and giving in marriage, until the day that Noe entered into the ark,

Mat 24:39 And knew not until the flood came, and took them all away; so shall also the coming of the Son of man be.

Mat 24:40 Then shall two be in the field; the one shall be taken, and the other left.

Mat 24:41 Two *women shall be* grinding at the mill; the one shall be taken, and the other left.

Mat 24:42 Watch therefore: for ye know not what hour your Lord doth come.

Mat 24:43 But know this, that if the goodman of the house had known in what watch the thief would come, he would have watched, and would not have suffered his house to be broken up.

Mat 24:44 Therefore be ye also ready: for in such an hour as ye think not the Son of man cometh.

Mat 24:45 Who then is a faithful and wise servant, whom his lord hath made ruler over his household, to give them meat in due season?

Mat 24:46 Blessed *is* that servant, whom his lord when he cometh shall find so doing.

Mat 24:47 Verily I say unto you, That he shall make him ruler over all his goods.

Mat 24:48 But and if that evil servant shall say in his heart, My lord delayeth his coming;

Mat 24:49 And shall begin to smite *his* fellowservants, and to eat and drink with the drunken;

Mat 24:50 The lord of that servant shall come in a day when he looketh not for *him,* and in an hour that he is not aware of,

Mat 24:51 And shall cut him asunder, and appoint *him* his portion with the hypocrites: there shall be weeping and gnashing of teeth.

Return to Spiritual Survival – Eternal Salvation

Mar 10 : 23 – 31

Mar 10:23 And Jesus looked round about, and saith unto his disciples, How hardly shall they that have riches enter into the kingdom of God!

Mar 10:24 And the disciples were astonished at his words. But Jesus answereth again, and saith unto them, Children, how hard is it for them that trust in riches to enter into the kingdom of God!

Mar 10:25 It is easier for a camel to go through the eye of a needle, than for a rich man to enter into the kingdom of God.

Mar 10:26 And they were astonished out of measure, saying among themselves, Who then can be saved?

Mar 10:27 And Jesus looking upon them saith, With men *it is* impossible, but not with God: for with God all things are possible.

Mar 10:28 Then Peter began to say unto him, Lo, we have left all, and have followed thee.

Mar 10:29 And Jesus answered and said, Verily I say unto you, There is no man that hath left house, or brethren, or sisters, or father, or mother, or wife, or children, or lands, for my sake, and the gospel's,

Mar 10:30 But he shall receive an hundredfold now in this time, houses, and brethren, and sisters, and mothers, and children, and lands, with persecutions; and in the world to come eternal life.

Mar 10:31 But many *that are* first shall be last; and the last first.

Return to Spiritual Survival – Eternal Salvation

Mar 16 : 14 – 16

Mar 16:14 Afterward he appeared unto the eleven as they sat at meat, and upbraided them with their unbelief and hardness of heart, because they believed not them which had seen him after he was risen.

Mar 16:15 And he said unto them, Go ye into all the world, and preach the gospel to every creature.

Mar 16:16 He that believeth and is baptized shall be saved; but he that believeth not shall be damned.

Return to Spiritual Survival – Eternal Salvation

Luk 13 : 23 – 30

Luk 13:23 Then said one unto him, Lord, are there few that be saved? And he said unto them,

Luk 13:24 Strive to enter in at the strait gate: for many, I say unto you, will seek to enter in, and shall not be able.

Luk 13:25 When once the master of the house is risen up, and hath shut to the door, and ye begin to stand without, and to knock at the door, saying, Lord, Lord, open unto us; and he shall answer and say unto you, I know you not whence ye are:

Luk 13:26 Then shall ye begin to say, We have eaten and drunk in thy presence, and thou hast taught in our streets.

Luk 13:27 But he shall say, I tell you, I know you not whence ye are; depart from me, all *ye* workers of iniquity.

Luk 13:28 There shall be weeping and gnashing of teeth, when ye shall see Abraham, and Isaac, and Jacob, and all the prophets, in the kingdom of God, and you *yourselves* thrust out.

Luk 13:29 And they shall come from the east, and *from* the west, and from the north, and *from* the south, and shall sit down in the kingdom of God.

Luk 13:30 And, behold, there are last which shall be first, and there are first which shall be last.

Return to Spiritual Survival – Eternal Salvation

Luk 18 : 18 – 30

Luk 18:18 And a certain ruler asked him, saying, Good Master, what shall I do to inherit eternal life?

Luk 18:19 And Jesus said unto him, Why callest thou me good? none *is* good, save one, *that is,* God.

Luk 18:20 Thou knowest the commandments, Do not commit adultery, Do not kill, Do not steal, Do not bear false witness, Honour thy father and thy mother.

Luk 18:21 And he said, All these have I kept from my youth up.

Luk 18:22 Now when Jesus heard these things, he said unto him, Yet lackest thou one thing: sell all that thou hast, and distribute unto the poor, and thou shalt have treasure in heaven: and come, follow me.

Luk 18:23 And when he heard this, he was very sorrowful: for he was very rich.

Luk 18:24 And when Jesus saw that he was very sorrowful, he said, How hardly shall they that have riches enter into the kingdom of God!

Luk 18:25 For it is easier for a camel to go through a needle's eye, than for a rich man to enter into the kingdom of God.

Luk 18:26 And they that heard *it* said, Who then can be saved?

Luk 18:27 And he said, The things which are impossible with men are possible with God.

Luk 18:28 Then Peter said, Lo, we have left all, and followed thee.

Luk 18:29 And he said unto them, Verily I say unto you, There is no man that hath left house, or parents, or brethren, or wife, or children, for the kingdom of God's sake,

Luk 18:30 Who shall not receive manifold more in this present time, and in the world to come life everlasting.

Return to Spiritual Survival – Eternal Salvation

Mat 25 : 1 – 46

Mat 25:1 Then shall the kingdom of heaven be likened unto ten virgins, which took their lamps, and went forth to meet the bridegroom.

Mat 25:2 And five of them were wise, and five *were* foolish.

Mat 25:3 They that *were* foolish took their lamps, and took no oil with them:

Mat 25:4 But the wise took oil in their vessels with their lamps.

Mat 25:5 While the bridegroom tarried, they all slumbered and slept.

Mat 25:6 And at midnight there was a cry made, Behold, the bridegroom cometh; go ye out to meet him.

Mat 25:7 Then all those virgins arose, and trimmed their lamps.

Mat 25:8 And the foolish said unto the wise, Give us of your oil; for our lamps are gone out.

Mat 25:9 But the wise answered, saying, *Not so;* lest there be not enough for us and you: but go ye rather to them that sell, and buy for yourselves.

Mat 25:10 And while they went to buy, the bridegroom came; and they that were ready went in with him to the marriage: and the door was shut.

Mat 25:11 Afterward came also the other virgins, saying, Lord, Lord, open to us.

Mat 25:12 But he answered and said, Verily I say unto you, I know you not.

Mat 25:13 Watch therefore, for ye know neither the day nor the hour wherein the Son of man cometh.

Mat 25:14 For *the kingdom of heaven is* as a man travelling into a far country, *who* called his own servants, and delivered unto them his goods.

Mat 25:15 And unto one he gave five talents, to another two, and to another one; to every man according to his several ability; and straightway took his journey.

Mat 25:16 Then he that had received the five talents went and traded with the same, and made *them* other five talents.

Mat 25:17 And likewise he that *had received* two, he also gained other two.

Mat 25:18 But he that had received one went and digged in the earth, and hid his lord's money.

Mat 25:19 After a long time the lord of those servants cometh, and reckoneth with them.

Mat 25:20 And so he that had received five talents came and brought other five talents, saying, Lord, thou deliveredst unto me five talents: behold, I have gained beside them five talents more.

Mat 25:21 His lord said unto him, Well done, *thou* good and faithful servant: thou hast been faithful over a few things, I will make thee ruler over many things: enter thou into the joy of thy lord.

Mat 25:22 He also that had received two talents came and said, Lord, thou deliveredst unto me two talents: behold, I have gained two other talents beside them.

Mat 25:23 His lord said unto him, Well done, good and faithful servant; thou hast been faithful over a few things, I will make thee ruler over many things: enter thou into the joy of thy lord.

Mat 25:24 Then he which had received the one talent came and said, Lord, I knew thee that thou art an hard man, reaping where thou hast not sown, and gathering where thou hast not strawed:

Mat 25:25 And I was afraid, and went and hid thy talent in the earth: lo, *there* thou hast *that is* thine.

Mat 25:26 His lord answered and said unto him, *Thou* wicked and slothful servant, thou knewest that I reap where I sowed not, and gather where I have not strawed:

Mat 25:27 Thou oughtest therefore to have put my money to the exchangers, and *then* at my coming I should have received mine own with usury.

Mat 25:28 Take therefore the talent from him, and give *it* unto him which hath ten talents.

Mat 25:29 For unto every one that hath shall be given, and he shall have abundance: but from him that hath not shall be taken away even that which he hath.

Mat 25:30 And cast ye the unprofitable servant into outer darkness: there shall be weeping and gnashing of teeth.

Mat 25:31 When the Son of man shall come in his glory, and all the holy angels with him, then shall he sit upon the throne of his glory:

Mat 25:32 And before him shall be gathered all nations: and he shall separate them one from another, as a shepherd divideth *his* sheep from the goats:

Mat 25:33 And he shall set the sheep on his right hand, but the goats on the left.

Mat 25:34 Then shall the King say unto them on his right hand, Come, ye blessed of my Father, inherit the kingdom prepared for you from the foundation of the world:

Mat 25:35 For I was an hungred, and ye gave me meat: I was thirsty, and ye gave me drink: I was a stranger, and ye took me in:

Mat 25:36 Naked, and ye clothed me: I was sick, and ye visited me: I was in prison, and ye came unto me.

Mat 25:37 Then shall the righteous answer him, saying, Lord, when saw we thee an hungred, and fed *thee?* or thirsty, and gave *thee* drink?

Mat 25:38 When saw we thee a stranger, and took *thee* in? or naked, and clothed *thee?*

Mat 25:39 Or when saw we thee sick, or in prison, and came unto thee?

Mat 25:40 And the King shall answer and say unto them, Verily I say unto you, Inasmuch as ye have done *it* unto one of the least of these my brethren, ye have done *it* unto me.

Mat 25:41 Then shall he say also unto them on the left hand, Depart from me, ye cursed, into everlasting fire, prepared for the devil and his angels:

Mat 25:42 For I was an hungred, and ye gave me no meat: I was thirsty, and ye gave me no drink:

Mat 25:43 I was a stranger, and ye took me not in: naked, and ye clothed me not: sick, and in prison, and ye visited me not.

Mat 25:44 Then shall they also answer him, saying, Lord, when saw we thee an hungred, or athirst, or a stranger, or naked, or sick, or in prison, and did not minister unto thee?

Mat 25:45 Then shall he answer them, saying, Verily I say unto you, Inasmuch as ye did *it* not to one of the least of these, ye did *it* not to me.

Mat 25:46 And these shall go away into everlasting punishment: but the righteous into life eternal.

Return to Spiritual Survival – Eternal Salvation

Joh 3 : 1 – 18

Joh 3:1 There was a man of the Pharisees, named Nicodemus, a ruler of the Jews:

Joh 3:2 The same came to Jesus by night, and said unto him, Rabbi, we know that thou art a teacher come from God: for no man can do these miracles that thou doest, except God be with him.

Joh 3:3 Jesus answered and said unto him, Verily, verily, I say unto thee, Except a man be born again, he cannot see the kingdom of God.

Joh 3:4 Nicodemus saith unto him, How can a man be born when he is old? can he enter the second time into his mother's womb, and be born?

Joh 3:5 Jesus answered, Verily, verily, I say unto thee, Except a man be born of water and *of* the Spirit, he cannot enter into the kingdom of God.

Joh 3:6 That which is born of the flesh is flesh; and that which is born of the Spirit is spirit.

Joh 3:7 Marvel not that I said unto thee, Ye must be born again.

Joh 3:8 The wind bloweth where it listeth, and thou hearest the sound thereof, but canst not tell whence it cometh, and whither it goeth: so is every one that is born of the Spirit.

Joh 3:9 Nicodemus answered and said unto him, How can these things be?

Joh 3:10 Jesus answered and said unto him, Art thou a master of Israel, and knowest not these things?

Joh 3:11 Verily, verily, I say unto thee, We speak that we do know, and testify that we have seen; and ye receive not our witness.

Joh 3:12 If I have told you earthly things, and ye believe not, how shall ye believe, if I tell you *of* heavenly things?

Joh 3:13 And no man hath ascended up to heaven, but he that came down from heaven, *even* the Son of man which is in heaven.

Joh 3:14 And as Moses lifted up the serpent in the wilderness, even so must the Son of man be lifted up:

Joh 3:15 That whosoever believeth in him should not perish, but have eternal life.

Joh 3:16 For God so loved the world, that he gave his only begotten Son, that whosoever believeth in him should not perish, but have everlasting life.

Joh 3:17 For God sent not his Son into the world to condemn the world; but that the world through him might be saved.

Joh 3:18 He that believeth on him is not condemned: but he that believeth not is condemned already, because he hath not believed in the name of the only begotten Son of God.

Return to Spiritual Survival – Eternal Salvation

Joh 3 : 34 – 36

Joh 3:34 For he whom God hath sent speaketh the words of God: for God giveth not the Spirit by measure *unto him.*

Joh 3:35 The Father loveth the Son, and hath given all things into his hand.

Joh 3:36 He that believeth on the Son hath everlasting life: and he that believeth not the Son shall not see life; but the wrath of God abideth on him.

Return to Spiritual Survival – Eternal Salvation

Joh 4 : 30 – 38

Joh 4:30 Then they went out of the city, and came unto him.

Joh 4:31 In the mean while his disciples prayed him, saying, Master, eat.

Joh 4:32 But he said unto them, I have meat to eat that ye know not of.

Joh 4:33 Therefore said the disciples one to another, Hath any man brought him *ought* to eat?

Joh 4:34 Jesus saith unto them, My meat is to do the will of him that sent me, and to finish his work.

Joh 4:35 Say not ye, There are yet four months, and *then* cometh harvest? behold, I say unto you, Lift up your eyes, and look on the fields; for they are white already to harvest.

Joh 4:36 And he that reapeth receiveth wages, and gathereth fruit unto life eternal: that both he that soweth and he that reapeth may rejoice together.

Joh 4:37 And herein is that saying true, One soweth, and another reapeth.

Joh 4:38 I sent you to reap that whereon ye bestowed no labour: other men laboured, and ye are entered into their labours.

Return to Spiritual Survival – Eternal Salvation

Joh 5:19 Then answered Jesus and said unto them, Verily, verily, I say unto you, The Son can do nothing of himself, but what he seeth the Father do: for what things soever he doeth, these also doeth the Son likewise.

Joh 5:20 For the Father loveth the Son, and sheweth him all things that himself doeth: and he will shew him greater works than these, that ye may marvel.

Joh 5:21 For as the Father raiseth up the dead, and quickeneth *them;* even so the Son quickeneth whom he will.

Joh 5:22 For the Father judgeth no man, but hath committed all judgment unto the Son:

Joh 5:23 That all *men* should honour the Son, even as they honour the Father. He that honoureth not the Son honoureth not the Father which hath sent him.

Joh 5:24 Verily, verily, I say unto you, He that heareth my word, and believeth on him that sent me, hath everlasting life, and shall not come into condemnation; but is passed from death unto life.

Joh 5:25 Verily, verily, I say unto you, The hour is coming, and now is, when the dead shall hear the voice of the Son of God: and they that hear shall live.

Joh 5:26 For as the Father hath life in himself; so hath he given to the Son to have life in himself;

Joh 5:27 And hath given him authority to execute judgment also, because he is the Son of man.

Joh 5:28 Marvel not at this: for the hour is coming, in the which all that are in the graves shall hear his voice,

Joh 5:29 And shall come forth; they that have done good, unto the resurrection of life; and they that have done evil, unto the resurrection of damnation.

Joh 5:30 I can of mine own self do nothing: as I hear, I judge: and my judgment is just; because I seek not mine own will, but the will of the Father which hath sent me.

Return to Spiritual Survival – Eternal Salvation

Joh 6 : 27 – 40

Joh 6:27 Labour not for the meat which perisheth, but for that meat which endureth unto everlasting life, which the Son of man shall give unto you: for him hath God the Father sealed.

Joh 6:28 Then said they unto him, What shall we do, that we might work the works of God?

Joh 6:29 Jesus answered and said unto them, This is the work of God, that ye believe on him whom he hath sent.

Joh 6:30 They said therefore unto him, What sign shewest thou then, that we may see, and believe thee? what dost thou work?

Joh 6:31 Our fathers did eat manna in the desert; as it is written, He gave them bread from heaven to eat.

Joh 6:32 Then Jesus said unto them, Verily, verily, I say unto you, Moses gave you not that bread from heaven; but my Father giveth you the true bread from heaven.

Joh 6:33 For the bread of God is he which cometh down from heaven, and giveth life unto the world.

Joh 6:34 Then said they unto him, Lord, evermore give us this bread.

Joh 6:35 And Jesus said unto them, I am the bread of life: he that cometh to me shall never hunger; and he that believeth on me shall never thirst.

Joh 6:36 But I said unto you, That ye also have seen me, and believe not.

Joh 6:37 All that the Father giveth me shall come to me; and him that cometh to me I will in no wise cast out.

Joh 6:38 For I came down from heaven, not to do mine own will, but the will of him that sent me.

Joh 6:39 And this is the Father's will which hath sent me, that of all which he hath given me I should lose nothing, but should raise it up again at the last day.

Joh 6:40 And this is the will of him that sent me, that every one which seeth the Son, and believeth on him, may have everlasting life: and I will raise him up at the last day.

Return to Spiritual Survival – Eternal Salvation

Joh 6 : 43 – 48

Joh 6:43 Jesus therefore answered and said unto them, Murmur not among yourselves.

Joh 6:44 No man can come to me, except the Father which hath sent me draw him: and I will raise him up at the last day.

Joh 6:45 It is written in the prophets, And they shall be all taught of God. Every man therefore that hath heard, and hath learned of the Father, cometh unto me.

Joh 6:46 Not that any man hath seen the Father, save he which is of God, he hath seen the Father.

Joh 6:47 Verily, verily, I say unto you, He that believeth on me hath everlasting life.

Joh 6:48 I am that bread of life.

Return to Spiritual Survival – Eternal Salvation

Joh 6 : 53 – 69

Joh 6:53 Then Jesus said unto them, Verily, verily, I say unto you, Except ye eat the flesh of the Son of man, and drink his blood, ye have no life in you.

Joh 6:54 Whoso eateth my flesh, and drinketh my blood, hath eternal life; and I will raise him up at the last day.

Joh 6:55 For my flesh is meat indeed, and my blood is drink indeed.

Joh 6:56 He that eateth my flesh, and drinketh my blood, dwelleth in me, and I in him.

Joh 6:57 As the living Father hath sent me, and I live by the Father: so he that eateth me, even he shall live by me.

Joh 6:58 This is that bread which came down from heaven: not as your fathers did eat manna, and are dead: he that eateth of this bread shall live for ever.

Joh 6:59 These things said he in the synagogue, as he taught in Capernaum.

Joh 6:60 Many therefore of his disciples, when they had heard *this,* said, This is an hard saying; who can hear it?

Joh 6:61 When Jesus knew in himself that his disciples murmured at it, he said unto them, Doth this offend you?

Joh 6:62 *What* and if ye shall see the Son of man ascend up where he was before?

Joh 6:63 It is the spirit that quickeneth; the flesh profiteth nothing: the words that I speak unto you, *they* are spirit, and *they* are life.

Joh 6:64 But there are some of you that believe not. For Jesus knew from the beginning who they were that believed not, and who should betray him.

Joh 6:65 And he said, Therefore said I unto you, that no man can come unto me, except it were given unto him of my Father.

Joh 6:66 From that *time* many of his disciples went back, and walked no more with him.

Joh 6:67 Then said Jesus unto the twelve, Will ye also go away?

Joh 6:68 Then Simon Peter answered him, Lord, to whom shall we go? thou hast the words of eternal life.

Joh 6:69 And we believe and are sure that thou art that Christ, the Son of the living God.

Return to Spiritual Survival – Eternal Salvation

Joh 10 : 24 – 30

Joh 10:24 Then came the Jews round about him, and said unto him, How long dost thou make us to doubt? If thou be the Christ, tell us plainly.

Joh 10:25 Jesus answered them, I told you, and ye believed not: the works that I do in my Father's name, they bear witness of me.

Joh 10:26 But ye believe not, because ye are not of my sheep, as I said unto you.

Joh 10:27 My sheep hear my voice, and I know them, and they follow me:

Joh 10:28 And I give unto them eternal life; and they shall never perish, neither shall any *man* pluck them out of my hand.

Joh 10:29 My Father, which gave *them* me, is greater than all; and no *man* is able to pluck *them* out of my Father's hand.

Joh 10:30 I and *my* Father are one.

Return to Spiritual Survival – Eternal Salvation

Joh 12 : 23 – 50

Joh 12:23 And Jesus answered them, saying, The hour is come, that the Son of man should be glorified.

Joh 12:24 Verily, verily, I say unto you, Except a corn of wheat fall into the ground and die, it abideth alone: but if it die, it bringeth forth much fruit.

Joh 12:25 He that loveth his life shall lose it; and he that hateth his life in this world shall keep it unto life eternal.

Joh 12:26 If any man serve me, let him follow me; and where I am, there shall also my servant be: if any man serve me, him will *my* Father honour.

Joh 12:27 Now is my soul troubled; and what shall I say? Father, save me from this hour: but for this cause came I unto this hour.

Joh 12:28 Father, glorify thy name. Then came there a voice from heaven, *saying,* I have both glorified *it,* and will glorify *it* again.

Joh 12:29 The people therefore, that stood by, and heard *it,* said that it thundered: others said, An angel spake to him.

Joh 12:30 Jesus answered and said, This voice came not because of me, but for your sakes.

Joh 12:31 Now is the judgment of this world: now shall the prince of this world be cast out.

Joh 12:32 And I, if I be lifted up from the earth, will draw all *men* unto me.

Joh 12:33 This he said, signifying what death he should die.

Joh 12:34 The people answered him, We have heard out of the law that Christ abideth for ever: and how sayest thou, The Son of man must be lifted up? who is this Son of man?

Joh 12:35 Then Jesus said unto them, Yet a little while is the light with you. Walk while ye have the light, lest darkness come upon you: for he that walketh in darkness knoweth not whither he goeth.

Joh 12:36 While ye have light, believe in the light, that ye may be the children of light. These things spake Jesus, and departed, and did hide himself from them.

Joh 12:37 But though he had done so many miracles before them, yet they believed not on him:

Joh 12:38 That the saying of Esaias the prophet might be fulfilled, which he spake, Lord, who hath believed our report? and to whom hath the arm of the Lord been revealed?

Joh 12:39 Therefore they could not believe, because that Esaias said again,

Joh 12:40 He hath blinded their eyes, and hardened their heart; that they should not see with *their* eyes, nor understand with *their* heart, and be converted, and I should heal them.

Joh 12:41 These things said Esaias, when he saw his glory, and spake of him.

Joh 12:42 Nevertheless among the chief rulers also many believed on him; but because of the Pharisees they did not confess *him,* lest they should be put out of the synagogue:

Joh 12:43 For they loved the praise of men more than the praise of God.

Joh 12:44 Jesus cried and said, He that believeth on me, believeth not on me, but on him that sent me.

Joh 12:45 And he that seeth me seeth him that sent me.

Joh 12:46 I am come a light into the world, that whosoever believeth on me should not abide in darkness.

Joh 12:47 And if any man hear my words, and believe not, I judge him not: for I came not to judge the world, but to save the world.

Joh 12:48 He that rejecteth me, and receiveth not my words, hath one that judgeth him: the word that I have spoken, the same shall judge him in the last day.

Joh 12:49 For I have not spoken of myself; but the Father which sent me, he gave me a commandment, what I should say, and what I should speak.

Joh 12:50 And I know that his commandment is life everlasting: whatsoever I speak therefore, even as the Father said unto me, so I speak.

Return to Spiritual Survival – Eternal Salvation

Joh 17 : 1 – 26

Joh 17:1 These words spake Jesus, and lifted up his eyes to heaven, and said, Father, the hour is come; glorify thy Son, that thy Son also may glorify thee:

Joh 17:2 As thou hast given him power over all flesh, that he should give eternal life to as many as thou hast given him.

Joh 17:3 And this is life eternal, that they might know thee the only true God, and Jesus Christ, whom thou hast sent.

Joh 17:4 I have glorified thee on the earth: I have finished the work which thou gavest me to do.

Joh 17:5 And now, O Father, glorify thou me with thine own self with the glory which I had with thee before the world was.

Joh 17:6 I have manifested thy name unto the men which thou gavest me out of the world: thine they were, and thou gavest them me; and they have kept thy word.

Joh 17:7 Now they have known that all things whatsoever thou hast given me are of thee.

Joh 17:8 For I have given unto them the words which thou gavest me; and they have received *them,* and have known surely that I came out from thee, and they have believed that thou didst send me.

Joh 17:9 I pray for them: I pray not for the world, but for them which thou hast given me; for they are thine.

Joh 17:10 And all mine are thine, and thine are mine; and I am glorified in them.

Joh 17:11 And now I am no more in the world, but these are in the world, and I come to thee. Holy Father, keep through thine own name those whom thou hast given me, that they may be one, as we *are.*

Joh 17:12 While I was with them in the world, I kept them in thy name: those that thou gavest me I have kept, and none of them is lost, but the son of perdition; that the scripture might be fulfilled.

Joh 17:13 And now come I to thee; and these things I speak in the world, that they might have my joy fulfilled in themselves.

Joh 17:14 I have given them thy word; and the world hath hated them, because they are not of the world, even as I am not of the world.

Joh 17:15 I pray not that thou shouldest take them out of the world, but that thou shouldest keep them from the evil.

Joh 17:16 They are not of the world, even as I am not of the world.

Joh 17:17 Sanctify them through thy truth: thy word is truth.

Joh 17:18 As thou hast sent me into the world, even so have I also sent them into the world.

Joh 17:19 And for their sakes I sanctify myself, that they also might be sanctified through the truth.

Joh 17:20 Neither pray I for these alone, but for them also which shall believe on me through their word;

Joh 17:21 That they all may be one; as thou, Father, *art* in me, and I in thee, that they also may be one in us: that the world may believe that thou hast sent me.

Joh 17:22 And the glory which thou gavest me I have given them; that they may be one, even as we are one:

Joh 17:23 I in them, and thou in me, that they may be made perfect in one; and that the world may know that thou hast sent me, and hast loved them, as thou hast loved me.

Joh 17:24 Father, I will that they also, whom thou hast given me, be with me where I am; that they may behold my glory, which thou hast given me: for thou lovedst me before the foundation of the world.

Joh 17:25 O righteous Father, the world hath not known thee: but I have known thee, and these have known that thou hast sent me.

Joh 17:26 And I have declared unto them thy name, and will declare *it:* that the love wherewith thou hast loved me may be in them, and I in them.

Return to Spiritual Survival – Eternal Salvation

1Jo 5 : 1 - 20

1Jn 5:1 Whosoever believeth that Jesus is the Christ is born of God: and every one that loveth him that begat loveth him also that is begotten of him.

1Jn 5:2 By this we know that we love the children of God, when we love God, and keep his commandments.

1Jn 5:3 For this is the love of God, that we keep his commandments: and his commandments are not grievous.

1Jn 5:4 For whatsoever is born of God overcometh the world: and this is the victory that overcometh the world, *even* our faith.

1Jn 5:5 Who is he that overcometh the world, but he that believeth that Jesus is the Son of God?

1Jn 5:6 This is he that came by water and blood, *even* Jesus Christ; not by water only, but by water and blood. And it is the Spirit that beareth witness, because the Spirit is truth.

1Jn 5:7 For there are three that bear record in heaven, the Father, the Word, and the Holy Ghost: and these three are one.

1Jn 5:8 And there are three that bear witness in earth, the Spirit, and the water, and the blood: and these three agree in one.

1Jn 5:9 If we receive the witness of men, the witness of God is greater: for this is the witness of God which he hath testified of his Son.

1Jn 5:10 He that believeth on the Son of God hath the witness in himself: he that believeth not God hath made him a liar; because he believeth not the record that God gave of his Son.

1Jn 5:11 And this is the record, that God hath given to us eternal life, and this life is in his Son.

1Jn 5:12 He that hath the Son hath life; *and* he that hath not the Son of God hath not life.

1Jn 5:13 These things have I written unto you that believe on the name of the Son of God; that ye may know that ye have eternal life, and that ye may believe on the name of the Son of God.

1Jn 5:14 And this is the confidence that we have in him, that, if we ask any thing according to his will, he heareth us:

1Jn 5:15 And if we know that he hear us, whatsoever we ask, we know that we have the petitions that we desired of him.

1Jn 5:16 If any man see his brother sin a sin *which is* not unto death, he shall ask, and he shall give him life for them that sin not unto death. There is a sin unto death: I do not say that he shall pray for it.

1Jn 5:17 All unrighteousness is sin: and there is a sin not unto death.

1Jn 5:18 We know that whosoever is born of God sinneth not; but he that is begotten of God keepeth himself, and that wicked one toucheth him not.

1Jn 5:19 *And* we know that we are of God, and the whole world lieth in wickedness.

1Jn 5:20 And we know that the Son of God is come, and hath given us an understanding, that we may know him that is true, and we are in him that is true, *even* in his Son Jesus Christ. This is the true God, and eternal life.

Return to Spiritual Survival – Eternal Salvation

Ezekiel 33: 8 – 9

Eze 33:8 When I say unto the wicked, O wicked *man,* thou shalt surely die; if thou dost not speak to warn the wicked from his way, that wicked *man* shall die in his iniquity; but his blood will I require at thine hand.

Eze 33:9 Nevertheless, if thou warn the wicked of his way to turn from it; if he do not turn from his way, he shall die in his iniquity; but thou hast delivered thy soul..

Return to Spiritual Survival – Eternal Salvation

How to Score:

1. Start with a score of 10. for the criterion (in this case "Spiritual Survival - Eternal Salvation")

2. As you read through the scriptures associated with a particular criterion, The Holy Spirit will drop situations into your mind. If the Holy Spirit calls to mind one or more situation(s) where you did not do one of the things in the scripture you read, subtract 1 point. (Do not subtract more than 1 point per scripture.)

3. As you think of these things ask The Father, in the Name of The Lord Jesus Christ to forgive you. Write down what you will do next time on a sheet of paper and find opportunities to do the right thing.

4. You will probably only come back to that scripture quite some time in the future so keep the paper pasted in a book, on a card or written next to the scripture in your Bible so that you can see what you decided to practice when you read these scriptures again.

Completing your score card

I pray, and ask you to pray that the Holy Spirit will give you the wisdom and the understanding to use the table below – It is quite simple actually.

Let's assume I scored on spiritual survival as follows:

Eternal Salvation	10	out of 10
Prayer	7	out of 10
Quite Time with God	0	out of 10
Indwelling of the Holy Spirit,	10	out of 10
Forgiving all others	9	out of 10

If you add these up: 10+7+0+10+9 = **36**
Total for Spiritual Survival is therefore **36**.

We know that each need area is split up into Survival, Basic and General needs. Above we have calculated the Survival needs. Let us assume that in the same way I scored **22** for the Spiritual (Basic Needs) and **5** for the Spiritual (General Needs).

Referring to the table below we find how to calculate our scorecard. Multiply the figures as follows **1** (in the block marked "Survival" as shown in the table below), multiplied by **36** (which is the number calculated above), times **3** (in the block marked "Spiritual" as shown in the table below).

That is **1** x **36** x **3** = **108** points of a possible 150 which is **72%**. This means that my Spiritual Survival is not where it should be and I am not walking as right as I should be. I would therefore have to address those areas I marked myself as -1.

Repeat this process for the Basic and General Spiritual scores

	Spiritual (**3**)	Emotional (**2**)	Physical (**1**)	Total	%
Survival (**1**)	**36**			**1**x**36**x**3** = **108**/150	**72**%
Basic(**2**)	22			2x22x3 = 132/300	44%
General (**3**)	05			3x5x3 = 45/450	10%
Total				285/900 =	31.6%

Let us assume someone has completed their self-assessment and has come up with the following results:

	Spiritual (3)	Emotional (2)	Physical (1)	Total	%
Survival (1)	33	42	50	(1x33x3) + (1x42x2) + (1x50x1) = 99+84+50 = <u>233</u> 300	77.6%
Basic (2)	21	28	44	(2x21x3) + (2x28x2) + (2x44x1) = 126+112+88 = <u>326</u> 600	54.3%
General (3)	8	13	38	(3x8x3) + (3x12x2) + (3x38x1) = 72+72+114 = <u>258</u> 900	28.6%
Total				233 + 326 + 258 = <u>817</u> 1800	45.3%

You can now see for yourself how far you are from 100%.

What is the purpose of this exercise then?
You need to know how vulnerable you are to satan's attacks. You need to know where your weaknesses are so that you can identify brothers and sisters in Christ who can help you strengthen these areas.

This is how satan attacks you:
He causes situations, which you must face in the physical area of your life. This will, create within you a fear factor. (Fear, confusion, lies, distrust are some of

satan's most powerful traps – We need to stay away / reject these out of our lives.)

But to get back to it, this fear attacks your thinking and penetrates your being. If you are strong at an emotional level you may rebuff this fear. If your emotional level is not strong enough, the fear turns to panic. The problem is then perceived as very serious.

The panic will penetrate through your emotional layer and to your spiritual layer. If this is not strong enough you will be vulnerable to serious hurt and recovery can be a long and difficult process.

Another purpose of this exercise is to identify where you are strong. If you are strong spiritually, help those who are week spiritually. If you are strong emotionally, help those who are week emotionally, and if you are strong physically, help those who are weak physically.

Here is a blank Table for you to complete yourself:
(Make Copies to test yourself regularly)

	Spiritual (3)	Emotional (2)	Physical (1)	Total	%
Survival (1)	a. ___ /10 + b. ___ /10 + c. ___ /10 + d. ___ /10 + e. ___ /10 = _____ (SS)	a. ___ /10 + b. ___ /10 + c. ___ /10 + d. ___ /10 + e. ___ /10 = _____ (ES)	a. ___ /10 + b. ___ /10 + c. ___ /10 + d. ___ /10 + e. ___ /10 = _____ (PS)	((1 x [_____ SS] x 3) + (1 x [_____ ES] x 2) + (1 x [_____ PS] x 1))= = _____ + _____ + _____ = _____ (Sur) =[_____ Sur] / 300 =	Ability to Survive is Currently is at _____%
Basic (2)	a. ___ /10 + b. ___ /10 + c. ___ /10 + d. ___ /10 + e. ___ /10 = _____ (SB)	a. ___ /10 + b. ___ /10 + c. ___ /10 + d. ___ /10 + e. ___ /10 = _____ (EB)	a. ___ /10 + b. ___ /10 + c. ___ /10 + d. ___ /10 + e. ___ /10 = _____ (PB)	((1 x [_____ SB] x 3) + (1 x [_____ EB] x 2) + (1 x [_____ PB] x 1))= = _____ + _____ + _____ = _____ (Bas) =[_____ Bas] / 600 =	Ability to Scrape through is at _____%
General (3)	a. ___ /10 + b. ___ /10 + c. ___ /10 + d. ___ /10 + e. ___ /10 = _____ (SG)	a. ___ /10 + b. ___ /10 + c. ___ /10 + d. ___ /10 + e. ___ /10 = _____ (EG)	a. ___ /10 + b. ___ /10 + c. ___ /10 + d. ___ /10 + e. ___ /10 = _____ (PG)	((1 x [_____ SG] x 3) + (1 x [_____ EG] x 2) + (1 x [_____ PG] x 1))= = _____ + _____ + _____ = _____ (Bas) =[_____ Bas] / 900 =	Ability to Enjoy Life is at _____%
Sub Total	[___SS]x3 + [___SB]x3 + [___SG]x3= (_____ + _____ + _____) = _____ / 450	[___ES]x2 + [___EB]x2 + [___EG]x2 = (_____ + _____ + _____) = _____ / 300	[___PS] + [___PB] + [___PG] = (_____ + _____ + _____) = _____ / 150	[_____ Sur] + [_____ Bas] + [_____ Gen] + = _____ (Tot) =[_____ Tot] / 1800 = = _____ %	Your Total Strength is at _____%
Your Separate Strengths	Spiritual Strength is currently at _____%	Emotional Strength is currently at _____%	Physical Strength is currently at _____%		

Now you should have a good idea that in fact you are not as strong as you thought you were, or possibly you are in fact stronger than you thought you were. In both these cases you will find that satan has been lying to you about who and what you actually are. I suggest you throw away the old picture of yourself, which he has used to keep you proud or self-defeated, respectively, and take a look at who you really are.

Real Christians are committed to being part of the Real Body of Jesus Christ.

The next step is to identify what you can do about those areas in your life where you could not score yourself 10 out of 10, so that you can reach 100%. Starting with survival (spiritual, emotional and physical) then address Basic needs for all three and then general needs for all three. If you achieve this then redo this excercise using a concordance/e-sword looking for more scriptures to test yourself against.

Reaching 100% does not mean you will no longer be attacked. It simply means you will find it easier to stand when satan does attack you. You also cannot say that because you did not score well on this self-test that you are not a Christian. Giving your Heart to Jesus Christ, asking Him to forgive you, forgiving those who sin against you and being Baptised in the Name of the Father, the Son and the Holy Spirit is all you require to be a Christian. But if you want to walk in the Spirit and be strong in the Lord, you need to keep growing in these other areas of your life.

I have provided the actual Scriptures for the Spiritual Survival section but the balance you will need to look up in your own Bible.

You can download Bible Software for free from www.e-sword.net (If you feel lead to donate to supporting the distribution of this free software and God's Word, please do – details are on the web site. In fact all references in this book are directly copied from this software and are correct according to the written versions.)

Spiritual Development Measurement

1.1 Measuring your Spiritual Survival Strength

Needs	Criteria	Scripture Ref.	My Score
Spiritual Survival (SS)	**(SSa.) Eternal Salvation,**	**Total Possible Score** Mat 24: 12 - 13; Mar 10: 23 – 31; Mar 16: 14 – 16; Luk 13: 23 – 30; Luk 18: 25 – 30; Mat 25: 1 - 46; Joh 3: 1 – 18; Joh 3: 34 - 36; Joh 4: 30 – 38; Joh 5: 19 – 30; Joh 6: 27 – 40; Joh 6: 43 – 48; Joh 6: 53 – 69; Joh 10: 24 – 30; Joh 12: 23 – 50; Joh 17: 1 – 26; 1Jo 5: 1 – 20; Ezekiel 33: 8 – 9 **Current Score**	**10** Circle your score - 1 / + 0 - 1 / + 0 - 1 / + 0 - 1 / + 0 - 1 / + 0 - 1 / + 0 - 1 / + 0 - 1 / + 0 - 1 / + 0 - 1 / + 0 - 1 / + 0 - 1 / + 0 - 1 / + 0 - 1 / + 0 - 1 / + 0 - 1 / + 0 - 1 / + 0 - 1 / + 0 =_____(SSa.)

Needs	Criteria	Scripture Ref.	My Score
Spiritual Survival (SS)	**(SSb.) Prayer,**	**Total Possible Score** Gen 24:12 – 22;_	**10** Circle your score
		Gen 30:1 – 2;_	- 0.5 / + 0
		Exo 9:27 - 35;	- 0.5 / + 0
		1Ki 8:22 – 61;	- 0.5 / + 0
		1Ki 17:17 – 24;	- 0.5 / + 0
		2Ki 6:15 – 23;	- 0.5 / + 0
		2Ki 22:19 – 20;	- 0.5 / + 0
		2Ch 30:17 – 20;	- 0.5 / + 0
		2Ch 33:10 – 13;	- 0.5 / + 0
		Neh 1:4 – 2:8;	- 0.5 / + 0
		Neh 9:1 – 6;	- 0.5 / + 0
		Job 1: 6 – 12	- 0.5 / + 0
		& - Job 2:1 - 7	- 0.5 / + 0
		& - Job 2:9 & 10	- 0.5 / + 0
		&_- Job 6:8 – 15	- 0.5 / + 0
		& - Job 42:1 - 5;_	- 0.5 / + 0
		Psa 4:1 & 6 – 8;	- 0.5 / + 0
		Psa 5:1 – 3;	- 0.5 / + 0
		Psa 25:1; Psa	- 0.5 / + 0
		55:15 – 18,	- 0.5 / + 0
		22 & 23; Psa	- 0.5 / + 0
		66:17 – 20; Isa	
		1:11 – 20; Isa	- 0.5 / + 0
		37:9&14–20&36;_	- 0.5 / + 0
		Isa 38:1 – 6;	- 0.5 / + 0
		Dan 10:11 – 13;	
		Hos 14: 2 & 8;	- 0.5 / + 0
		Mal 1:6 – 9; Mat	- 0.5 / + 0
		21:13, 21 & 22;	- 0.5 / + 0
		Mat 26:26 – 28;	- 0.5 / + 0
		Mar 9: 23 – 25 &	- 0.5 / + 0
		29;_Luk 22:39 –	- 0.5 / + 0
		46; Act 4:23 –	- 0.5 / + 0
		31; Act 6:3 & 4;	
		Act 10:1 – 23;	- 0.5 / + 0
		1Co 7:5; 1Co	- 0.5 / + 0
		14:13 – 17;	- 0.5 / + 0
		Eph 6:10 – 19;	- 0.5 / + 0
		Col 4:1 – 4;	- 0.5 / + 0
		1Ti 4:3 – 5;	- 0.5 / + 0
		Phm 1:6; Jam	- 0.5 / + 0
		5:13 – 18;	- 0.5 / + 0
			- 0.5 / + 0
			- 0.5 / + 0
			- 0.5 / + 0
			=_____(SSb.)
		Current Score	

Needs	Criteria	Scripture Ref.	My Score
Spiritual Survival (SS)	**(SSc.) Quite Time with God,**	**Total Possible Score** Job 37:14;_Psa 77:12 - 19; Psa 107:31 & 32; Psa 119:144 – 149; Isa 46:8; Mat 14:13; Mar 6:46; Luk 6:12; Act 10:9; Rom 8:26 & 27; 1Pe 4:7; Luk 18:9-14;	**10** Circle your score - 1 / + 0 - 1 / + 0 - 1 / + 0 - 1 / + 0 - 1 / + 0 - 1 / + 0 - 1 / + 0 - 1 / + 0 - 1 / + 0 - 1 / + 0 - 1 / + 0 - 1 / + 0
		Current Score	**=**_____(SSc.)

Needs	Criteria	Scripture Ref.	My Score
Spiritual Survival (SS)	**(SSd.) Indwelling of the Holy Spirit,**	**Total Possible Score** Psa 51:11; Isa 63:10; Mat 1:18 - 20; Mat 3:11; Mat 12:30 - 32; Mar 13:11; Luk 2:25 - 27; Luk 3: 21 & 22; Luk 4:1 - 14; Luk 10:21; Luk 11:13; Joh 1:32 - 34; Joh 14:26; Joh 20:21 - 23; Act 1:8; Act 2:3 - 4; Act 2:38; Act 4:31; Act 5:3 - 5; Act 6:3 - 4; Act 8:15 – 17; Act 8:29; Act 10:44 - 47; Act 15:8-9;	**10** Circle your score -0.5 / + 0 =_____(SSd.)
		Current Score	

Needs	Criteria	Scripture Ref.	My Score
Spiritual Survival (SS)	**(Sse.) Forgiving all others**	**Total Possible Score** Pro 17:9; Mat 6:14 & 15; Mat 18:21 – 35; Mar 11:25 & 26; Luk 6:37; Luk 17:3 & 4; Joh 20:23; 2Co 2:7; 2Co 2:10; Eph 4:32; Col 3:13; 1Jo 1:9	**10** Circle your score - 1 / + 0 - 1 / + 0 - 1 / + 0 - 1 / + 0 - 1 / + 0 - 1 / + 0 - 1 / + 0 - 1 / + 0 - 1 / + 0 - 1 / + 0 - 1 / + 0 - 1 / + 0
		Current Score	=_____(Sse.)

1.2 Measuring your Basic Spiritual Growth (Refer to your own Bible)

Needs	Criteria	Scripture Ref.	My Score
Spiritual Basic (SB)	**(Sba.) Encouragement,**	**Total Possible Score** Rom 12: 8 Deut 1:38 Deut 3:28 Isa 62: 1 1 Cor 8:10 2 Cor 2: 7 1 The 4:18 1 The 5:14 2 The 2:17 2 Tim 4: 2 Titus 2:15 Jude 1: 3	**10** Circle your score - 1 / + 0 - 1 / + 0 - 1 / + 0 - 1 / + 0 - 1 / + 0 - 1 / + 0 - 1 / + 0 - 1 / + 0 - 1 / + 0 - 1 / + 0 - 1 / + 0 - 1 / + 0
		Current Score	=_____(Sba.)

Needs	Criteria	Scripture Ref.	My Score
Spiritual Basic (SB)	**(SBb.) Prayer Partners**	**Total Possible Score** Est 4:16 Psa 35:14 Psa 86: 5 Pro 15:29 Isia 58: 2 – 14 Jer 42: 3 & 4 Hos 7: 14 Mat 5:44 Mat 18:19 Act 1:14 Eph 6:18 Jam 5:16	**10** Circle your score - 1 / + 0 - 1 / + 0 - 1 / + 0 - 1 / + 0 - 1 / + 0 - 1 / + 0 - 1 / + 0 - 1 / + 0 - 1 / + 0 - 1 / + 0 - 1 / + 0 - 1 / + 0
		Current Score	=_____(SBb.)

Needs	Criteria	Scripture Ref.	My Score
Spiritual Basic (SB)	**(SBc.) Group Bible Study**	**Total Possible Score**	**10** Circle your score
		Jos 1: 8 Neh 8:13 Psa 1: 2 Psa 119:15 Ecc 12:12 – 14 Joh 5:39 Mat 22:23 – 46 Luk 10:25 – 42 Luk 24:25 – 27 Luk 24:32 -34 Luk 24: 45 Act 17:11	- 1 / + 0 - 1 / + 0 - 1 / + 0 - 1 / + 0 - 1 / + 0 - 1 / + 0 - 1 / + 0 - 1 / + 0 - 1 / + 0 - 1 / + 0 - 1 / + 0 - 1 / + 0
		Current Score	**=**_____(SBc.)

Needs	Criteria	Scripture Ref.	My Score
Spiritual Basic (SB)	**(SBd.) Problems for spiritual exercise**	**Total Possible Score** Jam 1: 2 - 5 Jam 1:12 1 Pet 1: 6 & 7 2 Pet 2: 7 - 9 2 Cor 12: 7 - 9 Phil 4: 4 – 13 Joh 9: 1 - 7 Pro 1: 20 – 33 Isiah 53: 1 – 12 Lam 1:12 – 18 Lam 3: 1 – 41 Zec 13: 9	**10** Circle your score - 1 / + 0 - 1 / + 0 - 1 / + 0 - 1 / + 0 - 1 / + 0 - 1 / + 0 - 1 / + 0 - 1 / + 0 - 1 / + 0 - 1 / + 0 - 1 / + 0 - 1 / + 0
		Current Score	=_____(SBd.)

Needs	Criteria	Scripture Ref.	My Score
Spiritual Basic (SB)	**(SBe.) Understanding God's Will for you.**	**Total Possible Score** Gen 17: 2 - 7 Gen 24: 1 – 22 Exo 7: 3 - 5 Exo 14:13 – 31 Exo 19: 5 Exo 34: 7 Lev 20: 6 Lev 20:22 Psa 143: 8 – 10 Pro 3: 1 – 35 Mat 28: 18 – 20 Mat 25: 31 – 46	**10** Circle your score - 1 / + 0 - 1 / + 0 - 1 / + 0 - 1 / + 0 - 1 / + 0 - 1 / + 0 - 1 / + 0 - 1 / + 0 - 1 / + 0 - 1 / + 0 - 1 / + 0 - 1 / + 0
		Current Score	**=**_____(SBe.)

1.3 Measuring your Spiritual Enjoyment and Satisfaction (Refer to your own Bible)

Needs	Criteria	Scripture Ref.	My Score
Spiritual General (SG)	(SGa.) Friends	**Total Possible Score** Exo 33:11 Joh 3:25-30 Rom 2: 1- 3 Job 16:21 Rom 16: 2 Jam 4: 4 Psa 119:63 3Joh 1:11 Mat 6: 1 - 4 Luk 5:20 Luk 11: 5 - 8 Luk 14: 8 - 11	**10** Circle your score - 1 / + 0 - 1 / + 0 - 1 / + 0 - 1 / + 0 - 1 / + 0 - 1 / + 0 - 1 / + 0 - 1 / + 0 - 1 / + 0 - 1 / + 0 - 1 / + 0 - 1 / + 0
		Current Score	=_____(SGa.)

Needs	Criteria	Scripture Ref.	My Score
Spiritual General (SG)	**(SGb.) Desires**	**Total Possible Score** Num 15:37 1Ch 28: 9 Psa 7: 9 Psa 63: 1 Pro 27:20 Son 7:10 Mar 4:19 Rom 7: 5 Rom 13:14 1Cor 7: 9 Col 3: 1 – 10 Heb 4:12	**10** Circle your score - 1 / + 0 - 1 / + 0 - 1 / + 0 - 1 / + 0 - 1 / + 0 - 1 / + 0 - 1 / + 0 - 1 / + 0 - 1 / + 0 - 1 / + 0 - 1 / + 0 - 1 / + 0
		Current Score	=_____(SGb.)

Needs	Criteria	Scripture Ref.	My Score
Spiritual General (SG)	**(SGc.) Understanding the spiritual world.**	**Total Possible Score** Gen 1: 1 - 3:24 Eze 28:11 – 19 Job 1: 1 - 3:10 Job 39: 1 - 42:17 Exo 1: 1 - 12:51 Gen 18: 1 - 19:29 Gen 22: 1 – 18 Mat 27: 1 - 28: 20 Isa 53: 1 – 12 Mal 3: 1 – 18 Mat 5: 1 - 7:29 Rom 8: 1 – 39 Mat 18: 1 - 26: 45	**10** Circle your score - 1 / + 0 - 1 / + 0 - 1 / + 0 - 1 / + 0 - 1 / + 0 - 1 / + 0 - 1 / + 0 - 1 / + 0 - 1 / + 0 - 1 / + 0 - 1 / + 0 - 1 / + 0 - 1 / + 0
		Current Score	**=**_____**(SGc.)**

Needs	Criteria	Scripture Ref.	My Score
	(SGd.) Being in constant dialogue with Jesus	**Total Possible Score** Gen 2:15 – 25 Gen 5:22 – 24 Gen 17: 1 - 9 Gen 31: 5 – 13 1Sa 23: 4 & 30: 8 2Sa 2: 1 & 5:19 – 25 2Sa 7: 1 – 29 Mat 7:22 – 27 Mar 16:19 1Co 14:29 Psa 86: 3 1Tim 5: 5	**10** Circle your score - 1 / + 0 - 1 / + 0 - 1 / + 0 - 1 / + 0 - 1 / + 0 - 1 / + 0 - 1 / + 0 - 1 / + 0 - 1 / + 0 - 1 / + 0 - 1 / + 0 - 1 / + 0
			=_____(SGd.)
		Current Score	

Needs	Criteria	Scripture Ref.	My Score
Spiritual General (SG)	**(SGe.) A Ministry**	**Total Possible Score** Jam 1: 27 Mat 25: 1 – 46 1Co 12: 3 – 12 Rev 22: 17 Tit 1: 6 - 9 1Ti 4: 1 – 11 Joh 13: 2 – 17 Luk 22: 25 – 27 Mat 23: 1 – 29 Joh 15: 1 – 26 Luk 6: 12 – 49 Joh 21: 15 - 19	**10** Circle your score - 1 / + 0 - 1 / + 0 - 1 / + 0 - 1 / + 0 - 1 / + 0 - 1 / + 0 - 1 / + 0 - 1 / + 0 - 1 / + 0 - 1 / + 0 - 1 / + 0 - 1 / + 0
		Current Score	=_____(SGe.)

2). Emotional

(Self Study – Use a concordance / e-Sword Search facility to search up the scriptures that relate to these Criteria. Evaluate yourself as you have done spiritually and enter the references and scores in here.)

(Self Study – Use a concordance and your own Bible or the "e-Sword" Search facility)

Needs	Criteria	Scripture Ref.	My Score
Emotional Survival (ES)	(ESa.) Ability to Laugh & Cry	Total Possible Score	10 Circle your score
		: ;	- 1 / + 0
		: ;	- 1 / + 0
		: ;	- 1 / + 0
		: ;	- 1 / + 0
		: ;	- 1 / + 0
		: ;	- 1 / + 0
		: ;	- 1 / + 0
		: ;	- 1 / + 0
		: ;	- 1 / + 0
		: ;	- 1 / + 0
		Current Score	=_____(ESa.)

(Self Study – Use a concordance and your own Bible or the "e-Sword" Search facility)

Needs	Criteria	Scripture Ref.	My Score
Emotional Survival (ES)	**(ESb.) Ability to forgive yourself**	**Total Possible Score** : ; : ; : ; : ; : ; : ; : ; : ; : ; : ;	**10** Circle your score - 1 / + 0 - 1 / + 0 - 1 / + 0 - 1 / + 0 - 1 / + 0 - 1 / + 0 - 1 / + 0 - 1 / + 0 - 1 / + 0 - 1 / + 0
		Current Score	**=_____(ESb.)**

(Self Study – Use a concordance and your own Bible or the "e-Sword" Search facility)

Needs	Criteria	Scripture Ref.	My Score
Emotional Survival (ES)	**(ESc.) Someone to talk to**	**Total Possible Score** : ; : ; : ; : ; : ; : ; : ; : ; : ; : ;	**10** Circle your score **- 1 / + 0** **- 1 / + 0** **- 1 / + 0** **- 1 / + 0** **- 1 / + 0** **- 1 / + 0** **- 1 / + 0** **- 1 / + 0** **- 1 / + 0** **- 1 / + 0**
		Current Score	**=_____(ESc.)**

(Self Study – Use a concordance and your own Bible or the "e-Sword" Search facility)

Needs	Criteria	Scripture Ref.	My Score
Emotional Survival (ES)	**(ESd.) Someone who loves you**	**Total Possible Score** : ; : ; : ; : ; : ; : ; : ; : ; : ;	**10** Circle your score **- 1 / + 0** **- 1 / + 0** **- 1 / + 0** **- 1 / + 0** **- 1 / + 0** **- 1 / + 0** **- 1 / + 0** **- 1 / + 0** **- 1 / + 0**
		Current Score	**=_____(ESd.)**

(Self Study – Use a concordance and your own Bible or the "e-Sword" Search facility)

Needs	Criteria	Scripture Ref.	My Score
Emotional Survival (ES)	**(ESe.) Someone to love**	**Total Possible Score** : ; : ; : ; : ; : ; : ; : ; : ; : ; : ;	**10** Circle your score **- 1 / + 0** **- 1 / + 0** **- 1 / + 0** **- 1 / + 0** **- 1 / + 0** **- 1 / + 0** **- 1 / + 0** **- 1 / + 0** **- 1 / + 0** **- 1 / + 0**
		Current Score	**=_____(ESe.)**

2.2 Measuring your Basic Emotional Growth

(Self Study – Use a concordance and your own Bible or the "e-Sword" Search facility)

Needs	Criteria	Scripture Ref.	My Score
Emotional Basic (EB)	(EBa.) A Clear Conscience,	Total Possible Score	10 Circle your score
		: ;	- 1 / + 0
		: ;	- 1 / + 0
		: ;	- 1 / + 0
		: ;	- 1 / + 0
		: ;	- 1 / + 0
		: ;	- 1 / + 0
		: ;	- 1 / + 0
		: ;	- 1 / + 0
		: ;	- 1 / + 0
		: ;	- 1 / + 0
		Current Score	=_____(EBa.)

(Self Study – Use a concordance and your own Bible or the "e-Sword" Search facility)

Needs	Criteria	Scripture Ref.	My Score
Emotional Basic (EB)	**(EBb.) Encouragement**	**Total Possible Score**	**10** Circle your score
		: ;	- 1 / + 0
		: ;	- 1 / + 0
		: ;	- 1 / + 0
		: ;	- 1 / + 0
		: ;	- 1 / + 0
		: ;	- 1 / + 0
		: ;	- 1 / + 0
		: ;	- 1 / + 0
		: ;	- 1 / + 0
		: ;	- 1 / + 0
		Current Score	=_____(EBb.)

(Self Study – Use a concordance and your own Bible or the "e-Sword" Search facility)

Needs	Criteria	Scripture Ref.	My Score
Emotional Basic (EB)	**(EBc.) Someone who will listen without judging**	**Total Possible Score** : ; : ; : ; : ; : ; : ; : ; : ; : ; : ;	**10** Circle your score **- 1 / + 0** **- 1 / + 0** **- 1 / + 0** **- 1 / + 0** **- 1 / + 0** **- 1 / + 0** **- 1 / + 0** **- 1 / + 0** **- 1 / + 0** **- 1 / + 0**
		Current Score	**=_____(EBc.)**

(Self Study – Use a concordance and your own Bible or the "e-Sword" Search facility)

Needs	Criteria	Scripture Ref.	My Score
Emotional Basic (EB)	**(EBd.) Someone who lovingly shows you your faults**	**Total Possible Score** : ; : ; : ; : ; : ; : ; : ; : ; : ; : ;	**10** Circle your score **- 1 / + 0** **- 1 / + 0** **- 1 / + 0** **- 1 / + 0** **- 1 / + 0** **- 1 / + 0** **- 1 / + 0** **- 1 / + 0** **- 1 / + 0** **- 1 / + 0**
		Current Score	**=_____(EBd.)**

(Self Study – Use a concordance and your own Bible or the "e-Sword" Search facility)

Needs	Criteria	Scripture Ref.	My Score
Emotional Basic (EB)	(EBe.) Someone who accepts you exactly as you are	Total Possible Score : ; : ; : ; : ; : ; : ; : ; : ; : ; : ;	**10** Circle your score - 1 / + 0 - 1 / + 0 - 1 / + 0 - 1 / + 0 - 1 / + 0 - 1 / + 0 - 1 / + 0 - 1 / + 0 - 1 / + 0
		Current Score	=_____(EBe.)

2.3 Measuring your Emotional Enjoyment and Satisfaction

(Self Study – Use a concordance and your own Bible or the "e-Sword" Search facility)

Needs	Criteria	Scripture Ref.	My Score
Emotional Basic (EG)	(EGa.) A listening ear to which you can unload	Total Possible Score : ; : ; : ; : ; : ; : ; : ; : ; : ; : ;	**10** Circle your score - 1 / + 0 - 1 / + 0 - 1 / + 0 - 1 / + 0 - 1 / + 0 - 1 / + 0 - 1 / + 0 - 1 / + 0 - 1 / + 0
		Current Score	=_____(EGa.)

(Self Study – Use a concordance and your own Bible or the "e-Sword" Search facility)

Needs	Criteria	Scripture Ref.	My Score
Emotional Basic (EG)	**(EGb.) Peaceful environment to recharge**	**Total Possible Score** : ; : ; : ; : ; : ; : ; : ; : ; : ; : ;	**10** Circle your score - 1 / + 0 - 1 / + 0 - 1 / + 0 - 1 / + 0 - 1 / + 0 - 1 / + 0 - 1 / + 0 - 1 / + 0 - 1 / + 0 - 1 / + 0
		Current Score	**=**_____**(EGb.)**

(Self Study – Use a concordance and your own Bible or the "e-Sword" Search facility)

Needs	Criteria	Scripture Ref.	My Score
Emotional Basic (EG)	(EGc.) Someone you can help	Total Possible Score : ; : ; : ; : ; : ; : ; : ; : ; : ; : ;	**10** Circle your score - 1 / + 0 - 1 / + 0 - 1 / + 0 - 1 / + 0 - 1 / + 0 - 1 / + 0 - 1 / + 0 - 1 / + 0 - 1 / + 0 - 1 / + 0
		Current Score	=_____(EGc.)

(Self Study – Use a concordance and your own Bible or the "e-Sword" Search facility)

Needs	Criteria	Scripture Ref.	My Score
Emotional Basic (EG)	**(EGd.) Ability to control your emotions**	**Total Possible Score** : ; : ; : ; : ; : ; : ; : ; : ; : ; : ;	**10** Circle your score **- 1 / + 0** **- 1 / + 0** **- 1 / + 0** **- 1 / + 0** **- 1 / + 0** **- 1 / + 0** **- 1 / + 0** **- 1 / + 0** **- 1 / + 0** **- 1 / + 0**
		Current Score	**=_____(EGd.)**

(Self Study – Use a concordance and your own Bible or the "e-Sword" Search facility)

Needs	Criteria	Scripture Ref.	My Score
Emotional Basic (EG)	**(EGe.) Ability to detect the spiritual atmosphere through your emotions.**	**Total Possible Score** : ; : ; : ; : ; : ; : ; : ; : ; : ; : ;	**10** Circle your score **- 1 / + 0** **- 1 / + 0** **- 1 / + 0** **- 1 / + 0** **- 1 / + 0** **- 1 / + 0** **- 1 / + 0** **- 1 / + 0** **- 1 / + 0** **- 1 / + 0**
		Current Score	**=_____(EGe.)**

3). Physical

(Self Study – Use a concordance / e-Sword Search facility to search up the scriptures that relate to these Criteria. Evaluate yourself as you have done spiritually and emotionally and enter the references and scores in here. You will be greatly surprised what you find God's Word says about these.)

(Self Study – Use a concordance and your own Bible or the "e-Sword" Search facility)

Needs	Criteria	Scripture Ref.	My Score
Physical Survival (PS)	(PSa.) Air	Total Possible Score	10 Circle your score
		: ;	- 1 / + 0
		: ;	- 1 / + 0
		: ;	- 1 / + 0
		: ;	- 1 / + 0
		: ;	- 1 / + 0
		: ;	- 1 / + 0
		: ;	- 1 / + 0
		: ;	- 1 / + 0
		: ;	- 1 / + 0
		: ;	- 1 / + 0
		Current Score	=_____(PSa.)

(Self Study – Use a concordance and your own Bible or the "e-Sword" Search facility)

Needs	Criteria	Scripture Ref.	My Score
Physical Survival (PS)	**(PSb.) Food**	**Total Possible Score** : ; : ; : ; : ; : ; : ; : ; : ; : ; : ;	**10** Circle your score - 1 / + 0 - 1 / + 0 - 1 / + 0 - 1 / + 0 - 1 / + 0 - 1 / + 0 - 1 / + 0 - 1 / + 0 - 1 / + 0 - 1 / + 0
		Current Score	**=_____(PSb.)**

(Self Study – Use a concordance and your own Bible or the "e-Sword" Search facility)

Needs	Criteria	Scripture Ref.	My Score
Physical Survival (PS)	**(PSc.) Water**	**Total Possible Score**	**10** Circle your score
		: ;	**- 1 / + 0**
		: ;	**- 1 / + 0**
		: ;	**- 1 / + 0**
		: ;	**- 1 / + 0**
		: ;	**- 1 / + 0**
		: ;	**- 1 / + 0**
		: ;	**- 1 / + 0**
		: ;	**- 1 / + 0**
		: ;	**- 1 / + 0**
		: ;	**- 1 / + 0**
		Current Score	**=_____(PSc.)**

(Self Study – Use a concordance and your own Bible or the "e-Sword" Search facility)

Needs	Criteria	Scripture Ref.	My Score
Physical Survival (PS)	**(PSd.) Light**	**Total Possible Score**	**10** Circle your score
		: ;	– 1 / + 0
		: ;	– 1 / + 0
		: ;	– 1 / + 0
		: ;	– 1 / + 0
		: ;	– 1 / + 0
		: ;	– 1 / + 0
		: ;	– 1 / + 0
		: ;	– 1 / + 0
		: ;	– 1 / + 0
		: ;	– 1 / + 0
		Current Score	=_____(PSd.)

(Self Study – Use a concordance and your own Bible or the "e-Sword" Search facility)

Needs	Criteria	Scripture Ref.	My Score
Physical Survival (PS)	**(PSe.) Shelter**	**Total Possible Score**	**10** Circle your score
		: ;	**- 1 / + 0**
		: ;	**- 1 / + 0**
		: ;	**- 1 / + 0**
		: ;	**- 1 / + 0**
		: ;	**- 1 / + 0**
		: ;	**- 1 / + 0**
		: ;	**- 1 / + 0**
		: ;	**- 1 / + 0**
		: ;	**- 1 / + 0**
		: ;	**- 1 / + 0**
		Current Score	**=_____(PSe.)**

6.2 Measuring your Basic Physical Growth

(Self Study – Use a concordance and your own Bible or the "e-Sword" Search facility)

Needs	Criteria	Scripture Ref.	My Score
Physical Basic (PB)	(PBa.) Clothing	Total Possible Score	10 Circle your score
		: ;	- 1 / + 0
		: ;	- 1 / + 0
		: ;	- 1 / + 0
		: ;	- 1 / + 0
		: ;	- 1 / + 0
		: ;	- 1 / + 0
		: ;	- 1 / + 0
		: ;	- 1 / + 0
		: ;	- 1 / + 0
		: ;	- 1 / + 0
		Current Score	=_____(PBa.)

(Self Study – Use a concordance and your own Bible or the "e-Sword" Search facility)

Needs	Criteria	Scripture Ref.	My Score
Physical Basic (PB)	**(PBb.) Health**	**Total Possible Score**	**10** Circle your score
		: ;	- 1 / + 0
		: ;	- 1 / + 0
		: ;	- 1 / + 0
		: ;	- 1 / + 0
		: ;	- 1 / + 0
		: ;	- 1 / + 0
		: ;	- 1 / + 0
		: ;	- 1 / + 0
		: ;	- 1 / + 0
		: ;	- 1 / + 0
		Current Score	=_____(PBb.)

(Self Study – Use a concordance and your own Bible or the "e-Sword" Search facility)

Needs	Criteria	Scripture Ref.	My Score
Physical Basic (PB)	**(PBc.) Exercise**	**Total Possible Score** : ; : ; : ; : ; : ; : ; : ; : ; : ; : ;	**10** Circle your score **- 1 / + 0** **- 1 / + 0** **- 1 / + 0** **- 1 / + 0** **- 1 / + 0** **- 1 / + 0** **- 1 / + 0** **- 1 / + 0** **- 1 / + 0** **- 1 / + 0**
		Current Score	**=_____(PBc.)**

(Self Study – Use a concordance and your own Bible or the "e-Sword" Search facility)

Needs	Criteria	Scripture Ref.	My Score
Physical Basic (PB)	(PBd.) Sound Mind	**Total Possible Score**	**10** Circle your score
		: ;	- 1 / + 0
		: ;	- 1 / + 0
		: ;	- 1 / + 0
		: ;	- 1 / + 0
		: ;	- 1 / + 0
		: ;	- 1 / + 0
		: ;	- 1 / + 0
		: ;	- 1 / + 0
		: ;	- 1 / + 0
		Current Score	=_____(PBd.)

(Self Study – Use a concordance and your own Bible or the "e-Sword" Search facility)

Needs	Criteria	Scripture Ref.	My Score
Physical Basic (PB)	(PBe.) Your body works properly	Total Possible Score : ; : ; : ; : ; : ; : ; : ; : ; : ; : ;	10 Circle your score - 1 / + 0 - 1 / + 0 - 1 / + 0 - 1 / + 0 - 1 / + 0 - 1 / + 0 - 1 / + 0 - 1 / + 0 - 1 / + 0
		Current Score	=_____(PBe.)

3.3 Measuring your Physical Enjoyment and Satisfaction

(Self Study – Use a concordance and your own Bible or the "e-Sword" Search facility)

Needs	Criteria	Scripture Ref.	My Score
Physical Basic (PG)	(PGa.) Friends	**Total Possible Score**	**10** Circle your score
		: ;	- 1 / + 0
		: ;	- 1 / + 0
		: ;	- 1 / + 0
		: ;	- 1 / + 0
		: ;	- 1 / + 0
		: ;	- 1 / + 0
		: ;	- 1 / + 0
		: ;	- 1 / + 0
		: ;	- 1 / + 0
		: ;	- 1 / + 0
		Current Score	=_____(PGa.)

(Self Study – Use a concordance and your own Bible or the "e-Sword" Search facility)

Needs	Criteria	Scripture Ref.	My Score
Physical Basic (PG)	**(PGb.) Desires met**	**Total Possible Score** : ; : ; : ; : ; : ; : ; : ; : ; : ; : ;	**10** Circle your score - 1 / + 0 - 1 / + 0 - 1 / + 0 - 1 / + 0 - 1 / + 0 - 1 / + 0 - 1 / + 0 - 1 / + 0 - 1 / + 0 - 1 / + 0
		Current Score	=_____(PGb.)

(Self Study – Use a concordance and your own Bible or the "e-Sword" Search facility)

Needs	Criteria	Scripture Ref.	My Score
Physical Basic (PG)	**(PGc.) Knowledge**	**Total Possible Score** : ; : ; : ; : ; : ; : ; : ; : ; : ; : ;	**10** Circle your score **- 1 / + 0** **- 1 / + 0** **- 1 / + 0** **- 1 / + 0** **- 1 / + 0** **- 1 / + 0** **- 1 / + 0** **- 1 / + 0** **- 1 / + 0** **- 1 / + 0**
		Current Score	**=_____(PGc.)**

(Self Study – Use a concordance and your own Bible or the "e-Sword" Search facility)

Needs	Criteria	Scripture Ref.	My Score
Physical Basic (PG)	**(PGd.) Intelligence**	**Total Possible Score** : ; : ; : ; : ; : ; : ; : ; : ; : ;	**10** Circle your score **- 1 / + 0** **- 1 / + 0** **- 1 / + 0** **- 1 / + 0** **- 1 / + 0** **- 1 / + 0** **- 1 / + 0** **- 1 / + 0** **- 1 / + 0**
		Current Score	**=**_____**(PGd.)**

(Self Study – Use a concordance and your own Bible or the "e-Sword" Search facility)

Needs	Criteria	Scripture Ref.	My Score
Physical Basic (PG)	**(PGe.) Areas to still grow in**	**Total Possible Score** : ; : ; : ; : ; : ; : ; : ; : ; : ; : ;	**10** Circle your score **- 1 / + 0** **- 1 / + 0** **- 1 / + 0** **- 1 / + 0** **- 1 / + 0** **- 1 / + 0** **- 1 / + 0** **- 1 / + 0** **- 1 / + 0** **- 1 / + 0**
		Current Score	**=**_____**(PGe.)**

How to grow Spiritually

Now we will look at each one of the Spiritual Needs and at how to address each of them.

Emotional and Physical issues should be addressed by the relevant specialists in their fields but always ensure they align with what you have discovered in God's Word.

Spiritual - Survival Needs:

Eternal Salvation,
You will need to come to the saving knowledge of Jesus Christ spelled out in the section titled "**Escape from Eternal Death**" earlier in this book which covers your relationship with Jesus Christ.

Prayer,

> You need to spend time communicating with God. You do not need to say fancy words, simply talk to Jesus as though He were right in front of you, because in fact that is exactly where He is. (Looking into your eyes, every second of the day He cares deeply about you.)

> Share everything with Him, your worries and fears, your happiness and success, your friends and family members' situations. Bring all these to Him, by telling Him. Tell it from your heart and do not hide anything. He sees right into your deepest thoughts and desires, so share these with Him, because He wants you to.

Speak to Him and thank Him for what you have asked for. Thank Him everyday, even when you see no change in the situation.

Trust Him to the end. He will come through for you. Pray that He will show you His Will for your life.

The most powerful prayer is to pray the Prayer Jesus Taught us while reverently understanding each word (Matthew 6:9 - 13)

Quite Time with God,

Set aside a time where you do not ask for anything, do not really talk to Him about anything. Just ask Him to be present with you to sit with you and talk to you through your thoughts.

Any emotions and thoughts which suggest you do evil indicate the presence of evil. Tell the evil one that you are covered by the Blood of Jesus and that they have no right to interfere when you are busy with Jesus. Tell them that in the Name of Jesus they have to leave you, and they will (James 4:7)

The presence of God is characterised by pure peace. Confirm whatever you hear from God through discussions with others and by finding supporting, in-context, verses in the Bible (God's Word) before acting on it.

Often we try to get God to approve of our desired way of having our prayers answered, Do not do this. God has an even better plan for you than you can imagine. Do not limit Him by praying for how

He should solve your problem. Let Him surprise you, because He loves to do that.

Indwelling of the Holy Spirit,

Jesus made it clear to the disciples that they had to wait in Jerusalem for the gift of The Holy Spirit that would give them power, (Acts 1:8) encouragement, be there teacher, comforter and guide. (John 14:26)

Trying to operate behind 'enemy lines' satan's kingdom, this earth, without The Holy Spirit living within you, will lock you into religion and will not free you to enjoy Jesus in this life.

If you do not feel fulfilled, then you have either never asked The Holy Spirit into your life or you have offended Him so much He has left you. You will still go to Heaven if you accepted the Free Gift of Jesus Christ as this can only be lost if you openly declare that you do not serve Jesus Christ. But the Holy Spirit will leave your presence when He sees you are not listening anymore.

But even if you ask Him back a million times He will always return, because He loves you and wants to help you, provided you want to listen to His words and change.

Naturally, anything he asks you to do will never contradict anything in the Bible because the Bible is the Word of God. This is why you must get to know the Bible well. It is a sure-Fire differentiator between satan's trying to mislead you and God's trying to help you through His Holy Spirit.

Forgiving all others

This issue has been so fought by satan. he has hidden it, even from members of the Church

There is only one offence according to the Bible that Jesus promises his children will be punished through torture and torment on this Earth. It is so evil in God's sight that it carries with it the highest penalty second only to spiritual death.

You will be tormented until you forgive others (Matthew 18:21-35), (Matthew 18:34 & 35), (Matthew 6:14-15). satan wants to torment you and because of this he does not want you to discover you can 'legally' get out of his hands and live a beautiful life free from this torment.

Forgiving others is not easy to do, especially when forgiving means giving up the right to revenge, and even to the point of forgetting that it happened.

Jesus Christ is the only judge, not you. He may have died for that particular situation for which you hold someone else responsible. You no longer have any right to it. Jesus goes so far as to say that if you do not forgive others, then not only will you be tormented on earth, but God will also not forgive you after your death.

This means that a condition of Jesus' forgiveness to you is that you must forgive everyone who has wronged you.

Now I know, and you know, that there are situations that you got mad about and then buried in the back of your mind. You cannot remember them, but The Holy Spirit searches the innermost parts of you (1 Corinthians 2:10) and can see each and every one. If you ask Him, He will show you each one, and He will help you to forgive them from your heart.

When I did this 6 years ago, I did not think there were more than 10 or so people that I needed to forgive. Well about 3 hours later, a lot of tears, much wrestling with myself, often not wanting to forgive people for what they had done to me, my friends, loved ones, etc... (since then I do not let a day go by where I do not clean up the forgiveness problems of the day – in fact I Forgive as I or those I love am wronged – people do not understand it, but then again, that is not surprising – They do not understand God, how can they understand forgiving).

The revelation brought me to a crossroads.

If I wanted Jesus to forgive me when I did not deserve it from Him, I needed to forgive these people, from my heart, giving up the right to dislike them. I had to then approach them, and lovingly tell them what they had done that had hurt me and then to forgive them openly. (Some of them did not even know that they had even hurt me, but were thankful that our relationship was restored afterwards. satan wasn't.)

<u>I do not promise</u> you freedom from sickness, pain, psychological, physical and every other problem on this planet that is caused by the tormentor, the devil, <u>God does!!!</u> (<u>Provided you forgive everyone, everything that you are hurting about. Even those you have forgotten hurt you.</u>)

He will place a 'hedge' (protective barrier) around you and protect you (<u>Job 1: 10</u>) "Hast not thou made an hedge about him, and about his house, and about all that he hath on every side? ...". But if you have unforgiveness, which becomes bitterness, which becomes hatred, which can spill over into actions then satan the tormenter has the Biblical right to hurt and torment you until you forgive everyone else.

Of course being the sneak, and a whole bunch of words I would like to use but won't, he has hidden this truth from you – until now ...

DO IT!!!

FORGIVE THEM!!!

ALL OF THEM!!!

The way Jesus has forgiven you!

Do not delay forgiving others for any reason; your sanity depends on this, as does your peace, prosperity and well-being.

(Refer to the play on Salvation at the end of this book which helps with more specific directions on how to forgive everyone.)

I warn you, no, in fact God warns you (John 10:10), satan will steal this from your memory as fast as he can so that he can continue to have the right to cause you pain.

Spiritual – Basic Needs:

Encouragement,
Your Spiritual Self Image is what satan wants to destroy. Someone whose self-image is completely destroyed will end up useless to the cause of Jesus Christ. They will believe they can achieve nothing, and

even if they could do something "no one would want them to". This is a lie straight from Hell.

Paul (a great Christian in the Bible) said that he could do all things through Christ who strengthens him (Philippians 4:11-13). Christ will do the work He wants to through anyone who allows Him to. If you do not think you are worth anything you will make sure that Jesus cannot use you, because you have allowed satan to convince you of this.

Well I am afraid there is only one way out of this dilemma. Someone has to give you a good slap on the behind and tell you to stop grovelling in the mud. Pull your head out of the sand and put it in God's Word.

But alas, you are in control of your own thinking and if you do not want to change and want to stay hurting and sad, defeated and broken, there is nothing anyone, even Jesus, can do for you. You have to want to have a better life.

I said YOU HAVE TO WANT A BETTER LIFE!!!!

If deep down inside you, you do want a better life then listen carefully and do what I am telling you to do. Because, if you do, your life will get better.

You have to let Jesus take control of your life. You have to find someone, at your church, or in your Bible Study group, or a Christian friend at work (who is trustworthy and does not gossip about anyone at all, i.e. a Real Christian) that you can share your life with.

I know that this requires you to make yourself vulnerable and open to be hurt, but this is the only way to do it. You do this as follows:

1. Spend time praying to God to show you who He has singled out to be your 'encourager'.

2. The Holy Spirit is your ultimate encouragement but having human encouragement is also very important.

3. Family members, both blood relatives and spiritual relatives, <u>should</u> always encourage one another.

4. A Spiritual 'Encourager' is one who has a good understanding of the Bible, is sensitive towards people's feelings even when they have to say something the other does not want to hear. An 'encourager' is also a person who you feel good being with.

5. Such an 'Encourager' always has things to say that leave you feeling that you are beautiful and precious to Jesus and that they like you even though you have faults. 'Encourager's are humble and are painfully aware of their own faults too.

6. Ideally an encourager is the same sex as you are, because cross-sex relationships create far more options that satan can misuse and abuse. Another reason for same-sex partners as encouragers is that men understand men better and woman understand woman better, as do girls understand girls better and boys understand boys better.

7. You need to establish if the person is a gossip first. This is easy, because if you hear them talking about anyone at all in a negative or

judgemental way, they are a gossip. Have nothing to do with them.

8. Ask the person what ministry gifts they have from God. If they do not yet know, then they are unlikely to be the ones God has singled out for you. You can test this though by giving them a simple issue you are facing and see if they respond in an encouraging way (even if their answer is not what you wanted to hear). If they do encourage you, they may not realise that they have this gift, but proceed cautiously.

9. When you find someone with a gift of encouraging others, ask them if you can share your life story with them, because you know that you need encouragement.

10. Some may feel that they are over-extended. Do not hold this against them, and do not feel that you are being rejected (which is exactly what satan wants you to believe, because then he will have you back where he wants you.) Simply ask them if they can help you find someone who will be able to help you. Keep going along these lines until you find the one Jesus has singled out for you.

11. It is very important for you to learn to ask the questions. Especially when you think you should not ask any questions. (Not wanting to ask, because you might feel stupid, is a lie from the Devil, and will cause you a lot of pain if you do not ask.)

12. Understand that satan only tries to stop you from getting what God wants you to have, so that you can blame God for not giving it to you,

when God tried to get you to ask the questions but you chose to listen to satan and not to ask. The only stupid question is the one not asked.

13. Share your problems with your encourager, and especially the desires that you have for things you want to do for God.

14. Allow them to speak to your heart and accept that which they say as being from the Lord. Do not be blind though - make sure that what anyone says is an instruction from the Bible is in fact in the Bible. You are responsible for yourself, and therefore you need to check these things.

15. Be careful not to put your encourager on a pedestal, do not make of them any more than what they are – a brother/sister who loves you and helps you. Sure you can encourage them in return, but do not allow them to be seen by yourself as some great person. You may be guilty of giving the praise that is due to God who is working through them to the person, instead of to God who is using them. Many great Christians have suffered huge embarrassment because others praised them instead of God.

16. On this note, please do not see me any more than what I am. A Christian brother whom God for some unbelievable reason has chosen to use for this task. I am not worthy of it and I am definitely not capable of such great work. I give Him all the glory and honour for this work and pray that you thank Him for it and leave me out of the picture. I do not want to incur the wrath of God for stealing His praise (the

purpose behind which he created the entire universe). Our God is a jealous God, so please, please, leave me out of it.

17. Praise Him who has made all things and has given us the capacity to think and commune with Him.

18. Spend time regularly with the person who encourages you in your spiritual growth. Make sure you let them know how much they mean to you in their guidance and support. But again, do not praise them: - encourage them. (The difference between praise and encouragement is this: You Praise someone because of what they have done for example "God the message I have received is so useful and helpful, thank you for this message and your encouragement", you encourage the one who was used by God by saying "Thank you for being such a useful and obedient servant of God that you should pass on His message to me." Do you see the difference?

19. If you find that your encourager is breaking you down (simply criticising <u>without giving any direction on how to go about growing and getting better</u>) then break contact with them in a kind and understanding way and do not discuss your issues with them any longer.

20. Find someone else by following these points again.

<u>Now here I have a very serious warning for you</u>.

satan will try to make you feel that the whole world is against you.

He will try to get you to read into what someone says instead of just listening to the exact words they are saying. If you have any doubts about what someone means, do not let satan stop you from asking them what they mean. He is the master of causing misunderstanding and he does not want you to find out what was really meant by those who speak to you in love, he wants you to believe the thoughts he placed in your head.

Rather ask what someone means if you get a feeling that someone was being unkind. You will very often find that the thought you got in your head is not what the other person meant. Do not be trapped by satan because you kept your mouth closed.

Prayer Partners,

For some reason, God has chosen prayer, as the means by which His Children (Christians) have their needs met.

Non-Christians go out and fight their way through life getting what they want. Sometimes it is handed to them on a plate; sometimes they never seem to get anywhere.

One thing is certain it is more difficult for a Christian to get any problem solved than for a non-Christian. The reason is simple. We are on enemy soil, and the enemy is aware of us as well as what we need and those desires we have expressed (satan and his demons cannot read our minds).

It is important to realise that your prayers mobilise God's army of angels to deliver your needs.

Some people have often wandered why it is that God seems not to simply provide everything without us having to pray for it. The reason I see for this is that God created the entire universe so that he could be praised.

Praise is the one thing God cannot give himself. Praise comes from external sources. The angels have good reason to Praise Him. They have seen His Might and Power, His Glory and Majesty. We who have not seen these things are the only ones who can give God True Praise, which is based on having Faith in that which we cannot see until God provides it into reality for us.

Well that still does not answer why God wishes us to pray before we receive.

This answer is also simple. God wants you to know, beyond a shadow of a doubt that it was He, who provided what you needed. So He waits for you to ask, so that when you receive what you asked for, you will know it was God who has provided the answer to your prayers.

I am sorry to say that it is to our utmost shame that even some Christians still refer to 'luck' or 'coincidence' as being the cause of their receiving what they needed. They forget that they had asked God for this very thing and then give the Praise, the one thing God created us for, to everyone and everything else but God. satan laughs with delight when we serve his purposes like this.

Nevertheless, even though we hurt God so much, and succeed in assisting satan in stealing God's Praise, God remains faithful and continues to meet our needs.

I think we need to stop being concerned about what others think of the phrase "Praise God, do you know what he did for me? ..." and start thinking about the one who Loves us so much.

I hope you feel as ashamed as I do right now by these words. I am really going to have to do some work in this area.

So then why are Prayer Partners so important? God says through Jesus, that, "Wherever two or more of you agree on anything in My Name, it will be done for you by My Father in Heaven." (Matthew 18:18-20)

Why two or more? Two reasons really. The first is that there are witnesses to remind you that this was God's answer to prayer and not just pure 'luck'. The second is that it would be difficult to ask for something not allowed in the Bible or according to His will, if you are together with someone else who loves you and loves God.

I must also say something about the word 'agree' in this text. Too many people pray together and say 'Amen' at the end of their prayer, agreeing that what was prayed for will be done, when in actual fact both people had a different picture in their head of what was being agreed upon. Which picture is God supposed to provide?

It is important that you discuss what you will be praying for and the exact outcome you are seeking. As you discuss the details of the outcome you seek, the Holy Spirit will confirm within you, whether or not He will be doing this or not. You will know this by your confidence in the result you are speaking about.

For example I might pray,

"Father, please could you help me to get a car, (I have confidence),
that can go 250 Kms per hour, (No confidence),
that has an air conditioner, (I have confidence),
and black leather seats (little confidence),
and that has low Kms, (I have confidence),
and it should be a metallic colour, (I have confidence).

I should then revisit this picture and pull out the areas in which the Holy Spirit has indicated a problem (The parts where he did not make me feel confident)

WARNING!! THE ABOVE ONLY WORKS IF: you open your discussions by (all prayer partners) asking that The Holy Spirit guide you in your prayer before you begin discussing what you will agree on. If you do not do this satan will destroy tour prayers with doubt and unbelief.

Now the prayer reads:
"Father, please could you help me to get a car,
that has an air conditioner
and is a metallic colour."

Now I am in agreement with God's will. (Matthew 21:21-22) Jesus also said if you ask according to His will you will receive what you ask for. (John 15: 7-17)

Now sometimes our desires are such that we are confident in all of these but our prayer partner is not. They should be honest enough to tell us the parts where they do not feel confident (The confirmation of the Holy Spirit).

Most critical of all; if you do not conclude your prayer with "In the Name of Jesus Christ, Amen" then you have simply worded a wish. It is the "power and authority of Jesus Christ" which the Father acts on, not yours. The word "Amen" simply means "It is done", or "it is now real" or "it is now created".

Do not just say "Amen". Say it and mean it. Saying "Amen" means that the request you made in prayer is already reality, therefore you must believe it until you see it and not believe it only when you see it. Seeing is not believing. Believing will bring it into reality for you to see it.

> Prayer partners are there to pray in the hard times, rejoice when God answers our prayers and to encourage when we get despondent.
>
> Ensure that you share your answers to prayer with your prayer partners.
>
> A good idea is to make a logbook of all your prayers (Remember to give details) and date them. Read the log book from time to time and you will see how God answers these prayers (He does not answer them in order mind you, and seldom the way you expected Him to, but He answers them.)
>
> A Prayer Log book is a powerful source of encouragement when the dark clouds gather and you seem to be in trouble.
>
> Take the trouble to do make this logbook and give God the Praise and the Glory for each answered prayer.

Group Bible Study,

I would like to point out a very important point with regards to Bible Study Groups. The purpose is not for one person to try to open the scriptures to others. No. The purpose is for each person to hear what God is saying to them through the Holy Spirit for He is the only One who can reveal the scriptures (John 14:26).

Have you ever wondered why it is that non-Christians cannot understand the Bible? It is because they do not have the Holy Spirit revealing the things of Heaven, locked up in the Word of God to them.

Again, have you ever wondered why, every time you read the same scriptures in the Bible, you find a different meaning to the one you received the previous time? This is because the Holy Spirit reveals to you, the message you need for the time and situation you are in now.

You see the Bible is a Living Book to those who have the Holy Spirit, who reveals God and His will for our lives. For others, and this includes those Christians who have not asked the Holy Spirit to take over their lives, it is simply a Historical Record, with lots of good ideas and morals in it.

So then the first thing we need to recognise is that it is highly unlikely that we will all get the same revelation from the Holy Spirit in the same passage of scripture. So trying to be the Teacher is pointless.

The format of a Bible Study should be as follows:

Prayer:

That the Holy Spirit would teach each one of us what we need to know and that satan may not interfere with our thinking, nor with our communication with God and one another.

Scripture Reading:

> A few versus at a time (rotate the readers if you like) and then tell each other what you understood by these scriptures and what God was saying to each one of you individually. This can continue for as long as you choose.

Studying of themes and books:

There is not a problem with studying themes and books, provided that every scripture reference referred to is dealt with as above. Consider the theme topic or book as if it were one of the points of view, (as if an extra person were present). If a person in the group has created the theme, that is fine, but ensure that the Holy Spirit is in charge and not this person.

> It is of extreme importance that Bible Study Themes and Books being discussed should be considered as incorrect.

> The purpose of the Bible Study would then be to ascertain how accurate the writer in fact is. This is done by reading the Scripture verses provided and then using a Bible Concordance or Computer Bible Program to find other verses in the Bible to prove the points made in the theme or book as either true, partly true or false.

> Remember that Bible Study is centered around the fact that the Bible is 100% accurate

and any book or theme or statement, if it contradicts the Bible scriptures is then incorrect.

Bible Study is not about people and how well they do or do not know the scriptures. It is about allowing God to open His scriptures to you as individuals, and as a Group, and to give all an opportunity to be used to build up the others.

Written Notes:

The Bible tells us that satan comes to Kill, Steal and Destroy (John 10:10). He will do whatever he can to ensure that you cannot keep what you learn at Bible Study. He will steal it from your mind, by helping you to forget it.

The easiest way for him to do this is to get you not to write it down, so that you can look at it again later.

If you write it down satan will try to get you to write it on a piece of paper where it can get lost easily. Or he will get you to stuff it in a drawer somewhere, never to be found again.

You will find that if you have a Bible Study book (preferably A4) into which you can both write your notes and stick in pages, you will always have something of value to go back to. You should date every thing clearly, so that you know when you received each of the messages from God. Another useful addition is to write down who was present at each Bible Study.

Make a few key notes and stick these on the inside of a cupboard door you open often to remind you.

It is essential that next to each note that you make, that you also include the scripture reference(s) that you were reading when you got this message.

(The back of this book is a useful place to keep your Prayer Log because you can use this for closing prayer at the Bible Study and you can share with those at the Bible Study, the answers you have received to these prayers.)

Some people choose to make notes in the columns of their Bible. In my view there is nothing wrong with this. The problem I have encountered is that there is usually not enough space to write down a clear message, which I can understand when I come back to it.

Some people like to write dates next to the verses in the Bible that have particular significance to a situation or person they are praying for. Again there is no problem with this.

Remember to go back through this book from time to time, especially when you are experiencing tough times in the spiritual, emotional and or physical areas of your life. (but again I stress that this book is not a living book, it only points to the living book. So re-read this book from time to time but read the living book – the Bible – every day.)

Closing Prayer:

Thank God for his Holy Spirit and the insight you have received. Ask Him to help you apply what you have learnt in your life.

Pray for those who need prayer.

Have some social time afterwards:

Spend some time just talking to each other and encouraging one another before leaving the Bible Study. If you can afford it, let each person take a turn at providing something to eat and someone else can provide something to drink for those present.

Make sure you have everyone's contact details so that you can keep in touch in case someone for some reason experiences trauma or travel problems. The rest of you will be able to stand by them. And support them.

Bible Study should be informal and is best done in people's houses. Allow the children to be a part of your Bible Study if they are old enough to understand.

You will never know what spiritual age your children are at. They might even be more spiritually mature than you are.

Children might however choose to have their own Bible Study while the adults are busy with theirs in the next room.

Young Children can be taken care of together, by a different member of the Bible Study each week, so allowing ever family to always attend, and giving every person a chance to participate most of the time.

The most important thing about Bible Study is to enjoy finding out the exciting life Jesus has called us to, and to be in His presence together.

Enjoy

Problems for spiritual exercise,

No one wants to hear that they need problems in their lives; in fact, this world teaches that we should strive to have no problems. So we run around, chasing our tails, working our guts out, trying to make ends meet, when we have the wrong thinking in our head.

You need problems to grow.

I mean, you <u>really need</u> problems in your life.

Did you decide I had finally lost it?

Well consider this question first.

God, who knew the future, before creation, also knew the problems you have had to face, are facing and still will face and yet still created. Why would a loving God do such a thing, as place you in a position, where you would endure physical, mental and emotional problems?

Well the answer is only obvious when you stop looking at your problems from a physical perspective.

Once again, as is so often the case, those who do not have the Holy Spirit within them cannot see this truth. I will attempt to explain it.

A baby in its mother's womb decides that it is now too cramped, or something else has become a problem and it then fights its way out of the mother's womb into this life. It fights to take its first breath. It then has a whole life of fighting to move out of places where it is uncomfortable.

Looking at this we see a pattern. A situation arises which makes us uncomfortable. We try to ignore it and it gets worse. We try to run away from it and it gets worse. We get frustrated and angry that this situation does not want to just go away, or at least if we run away from it, that it just won't stop following us. And finally we accept that the problem will not go away and then finally...we do something about it.

But now....

This problem, that was originally a little problem, has, by our own actions of allowing it to grow, become a huge problem, and solving this huge problem requires a lot of fighting, energy and often time and sometimes money too.

What should we have done? Well I suppose it is now easy to see. Simply tackle the small problem the minute it surfaces and then it is dealt with, quickly and easily.

This is the first lesson God wants you to learn:

Do not run away from your problems. Jesus said we should be brave because he has already overcome the world (John 16:33)

Sure He will help you out of the big problems, if you are in them now, but it will take a lot more effort on your part to stick with it.

The second lesson you have to learn is that God has already provided the means to conquer every problem in your life.

What???

Yes He has.

It is not a simple formula though.

It is the guidance of the Holy Spirit, who will lead you into all Wisdom and all Knowledge (Ephesians 1:17) concerning all things (including how to tackle your problems).

God also has His own time frame for when the problem will be conquered.

Now this I know you did not want to hear.

Well I cannot help it. I did not say it. God did. You see you have things in your life, that God needs you to get rid of. God looks at all of us and sees how all of us have impure thoughts, words, actions, etc...

We are all susceptible to certain temptations. Each of us has our own weaknesses. God wants us to get rid of these, but will not interfere in our free will. He will however send problem after problem that causes you to have to fight in an area where you are weak. By fighting, you become strong in that area and eventually, you through your own free will, decide that you are going to conquer this weakness, because now you have finally had enough trouble from it.

I have yet to find a mother who does not leave her child on the ground so that it can fight and fight to crawl and then fight and fight to walk, all the while indirectly helping the child to develop strong muscles and balance. The mother is not negligent, or uncaring. She knows that she cannot do this for the child. It is not her body.

That child cries, screams, calls out to be picked up, and the mother does give the child attention and occasionally does pick up the child for a while, just long enough to comfort and encourage it. But the child will go down again, back on the floor to do some more fighting, until one day, that child can crawl and later, can walk.

We do not consider that mother a horrible person, although, if the child could talk, he/she would probably have a whole bunch of nasty things to say to their mother in the heat of their frustration.

How can we then be mad at God for doing exactly the same thing with us?

(Malachi 3:3) explains how God sits as a silver smith refining His people.

If you have not heard how silver refining is done, let me tell you.

The silver smith (God) will hold the piece of silver (you) in the hottest part of the fire (your troubles) until the silver (you) really heats up (you get uncomfortable). When the silver (you) gets very hot (unhappy) the impurities within the silver, come to the surface and burn off. (When you are under pressure, the worst of you will come out and you will see yourself as God sees you. You will not like it and you will allow that which you do not like to be changed within you.)

The bad news is that this is going to happen time and again until you shine like silver.

When the Silversmith can see his image in the silver, then his refining is complete. God knows you have been refined, when He can see His image (Jesus Christ) in you, at all times.

You need problems to be what God needs you to be for another reason too.

One of the first things God will deal with in your life is "Have Patience". The problem with this is that the only way you are going to have patience is knowing that this problem is temporary, and is there to grow you. <u>You gain patience when you give up having fear, and start trusting God no matter what.</u>

Patience is hard to grow because we want it to happen quickly. We are impatient to get it.

I can give you this promise: - God may not appear to be there when you think you can go on no longer. But you will know he is there just before you <u>really</u> cannot go on any longer.

Because between these two times (when you think you cannot, and when God knows you cannot) is the only time you grow. He is never too late and He will never let you suffer more than you can endure (<u>1 Corinthians 10:13</u>)

What I am telling you is most likely not what you want to hear, but it is the truth. James writes in <u>(James 1:2 – 4</u>) consider yourselves fortunate when all kinds of trials come your way, for once you have conquered them you will be stronger.

A child is excited at facing an obstacle course, or tackling some challenge. You need to have the same attitude to the problems in your life. Change your thinking. A child learning to swim is a little concerned when the teacher no longer holds them, but they know the arms are not far away. They also know that the teacher loves them and will not let them drown, even when their arms and legs get tired and they do not want to do it any more. The teacher has to force the child to go through the fear to realise that actually there was never any reason to fear in the first place.

This is the key to a successful life then:

Your success, lies on the other side of your fears.

In other words, satan uses the emotion of fear and the bombardment of a million "what if this happens?" or "what if that does not happen?" types of worries to get you to give up getting that which God has provided for you.

satan stands between you and God's provision. You need to get mad at him.

You need to get frustrated with the one stealing all that God has given you.

Then in prayer you need to march right through the fear.

Use your endurance.

Use your patience.

And take what God has put there for you.

Once you get this right in one area of your life, God will put you back in the fire to deal with the next area that contradicts His image.

It is not about being a goody-goody. Make no mistake; this is about getting you to be able to easily integrate into Heavenly life after your Earthly death, and also to help others to reach God before they die physically.

Paul writes (Philippians 4:11-13) I have learnt to be content in all things

Why be worried, anxious and fearful. Why want more money, land, and things than others. Only satan wants you to feel this way.

God says He has given you all that you need for today.

Tomorrow belongs to Him. He has a plan for tomorrow. Trust Him and be content with what you now have.

To worry now is to waste this one and only second you have now.

Trust Him who considers you so precious that He gave His life to save you. Trust Him!!!!

Understanding God's Will for you.

Another thing you will most likely not want to hear is that God's Will for you is not your will for yourself.

This is of course why, when you marry Jesus, you give up your right to having things your way. You have to give up your will, your dreams, and your desires and take on His will for you, His dreams for you and His desires for you.

God has made you for a particular purpose. Think of yourself as a tool (a spoon/a size 17 spanner)

Now in this analogy, God the (Baker/Mechanic) will not use you all the time. There is a time when you will be used, and a time when you will sit in the place God has created for you. We very often want to be used all the time. Many people pray, "Lord please give me a ministry", when we should be saying "Lord show me what I am and how you want to use me."

We need to understand that God will use us at the right time. His time often does not correspond with our time. For example, I know I need to write this book now, but I have to sacrifice other things to do it. Why could the Lord not have waited until I had a quiet time, on Holiday, or something like that? Well God in His infinite Wisdom, did not want me to sacrifice my Family time on Holiday, because He knows how much my Family needs me to be focused on them when I am on Holiday. No, He knows the best time and He also knows the best way.

I cannot tell you how many times in my past I used to try doing things for God. No matter how hard I tried and no matter how much time and sometimes money I spent, it never worked out right. Someone somewhere along the line got hurt and it was usually my family. Those closest to me.

I have since learned to be patient. To wait for the Sovereign Master to use me.

This does not mean that we must just sit back and do nothing. It does mean that we need to identify what kind of tool we are so that when a situation arises to which we are suited, we can ask the Holy Spirit for direction.

Well here is the BIG Question then.

How do you know what type of tool you are?

- Firstly you are best suited for situations in which you have had personal experience: For example, if you have been through a traumatic experience, then this is where God wants to use you. Counselling and Caring for others who are currently going through the same or similar experiences.

- Secondly you are well suited for situations in which you have talents, skills or knowledge. These can be used to uplift others, either through training or assisting.

- Thirdly you are well suited for situations for which you have a deep desire or a keen interest.

You see God puts the desire within you to be the tool He designed you to be. He gives you the desire to be in the place He wants you to be. (Psalm 37:4)

At this point we must define the word "desire". To desire something is not to want something passionately, it is much deeper, much stronger and lasts a long time.

To see if you desire something, ask yourself the question: "Would I be happy to spend ten years working towards getting this thing that I desire, or am I impatient to get it. Desires are not feelings, desires are pictures. You can see a picture in your mind of that which you desire.

Desires are from God. Impatience is not. A desire will last, a want (passionate or not) will not.

Be careful not to fall into satan's traps. He has an idea of what God intends you to be, because he can see what God is doing in your life. He will do all he can to stop you getting it too.

satan has 3 major forms of attack.

1. Stop you from doing what God wants you to do: He does this by making your body and mind (not you – you are the spirit) feel, tired, sick, depressed, unworthy, stupid, etc... All these are lies, but he will try to get you to believe them. He knows that once you believe these lies, you will not have the confidence to do what God wants you to do. If you are stopped in this way, you allow satan to win. satan never wins, unless you give up the right to what God has waiting for you on the other side of satan's lies. Do not believe him, keep going until you win. <u>Jesus guarantees that you will win if you do not believe the lies.</u>

2. Distract you and lead you in the same sort of direction but slightly off course: If you stand 20 feet away from your door facing it exactly straight. If you then turn ever so slightly to one side or another and then walk straight, you are guaranteed to miss the door. All satan has to do is get you to move ever so slightly off course. If you stay in tune with the Holy Spirit, you will know you are stepping out of the Will of God (off course), because you will sense

the Peace of God disappear. Use this peace as your spiritual compass. No peace, you're not on track and satan is winning. Go back to the Lord and pray, until you get the peace back. By simply picturing where you think you should be going you will either feel at peace or not. If you feel at peace, then that is the right direction, if not, do not go that way.

3. If satan cannot stop you or distract you, then he will push you: His primary means of pushing you is to place in your mind some sort of a deadline. This generates fear of missing the deadline, which generates impatience. You start barging into people's hearts and minds where the Holy Spirit is still busy preparing the way for your entrance. The person is not ready, or the situation is not yet perfectly right and your impatience ruins the chance you were about to be given. The net result is people judge you. You lose your opportunity and often you chase people away from God.

   God's timing is perfect. Trust Him and wait for Him to give you peace in your heart about what you believe He is leading you to do. A knot in your stomach is a sure sign that satan is trying to push you. Just back away, slow down and spend more time in prayer.

A child once wanted to bake a cake, so she took all the ingredients, and put them in the oven, each ingredient still in its packet. Her mother lovingly explained to her that there was a special method, or recipe to be followed when baking a cake and none of the steps could be left out.

It is the same with you.

God will be moulding you all your life. Adding new ingredients, mixing up your life, and then putting you into hot and uncomfortable situations to make you grow.

The child learnt more than the mother bargained for though. The child learnt that if she sat back and waited, her mother would do all the preparation and mixing, all she would have to do was patiently wait until she had to do her job.

Eat the cake.

Be patient.

Another picture that I can leave with you is this. God exists outside of the constraints of time. He may only choose to use you for a little part of a 500-year plan, affecting a tiny part of it. As with the cake, none of the steps can be left out and your work may appear so small and insignificant. But God needs every step to be followed and without your tiny piece, the whole plan will be in danger of failure. So if you choose not to do your little bit, God will simply get someone else to do it. You will then miss the blessing God has provided for you.

Do not become arrogant and want only the big jobs. God will give you little jobs first. If you make a success of these, He will give you bigger ones. Be patient and stay humble.

We cannot begin to imagine the amazing ability our God has to be able to co-ordinate all of creation the way He does.

Be patient.

Develop your skills and talents, patiently strive to achieve your desires and be constantly on the lookout for anything you can do to love, encourage, care for, assist, train, pray for, counsel etc... your Christian brothers and sisters.

These actions are always important to Jesus and the more you are the physical manifestation of His heartbeat towards others, which includes those without Jesus; the more He will use you.

Finally, do not be upset when it appears God has given you nothing to do for Him.

Of course we all want to show God how much we Love Him for what He has done for us, but this attitude is like not seeing the wood for the trees.

God died to save you, so that he could: (notice the order) firstly spend time with you, loving you, communicating with you, sharing with you, holding and cuddling and caring for you. The second priority (very often our first priority) is giving you things to do for Him.

Sure you must do things for God. But He died for you because He wants to spend time with you. Do not just do things for God. Spend time with Him just enjoying His presence, and loving to be with Him. For this is His Will.

In (Luke 10:38 -42) Mary and Martha were having Jesus over for supper. Mary sat at Jesus' feet, listening to Him and enjoying His Company. Martha on the other hand was running around preparing the supper. She came to Jesus and complained. She asked if it was fair that Mary should sit and do nothing, while she prepared the Master's supper.

Jesus said an amazing thing to Martha (the hard worker, serving Jesus). He said,

Mary has chosen to do the better thing.

Spend time with Jesus and then work later.

Get your priorities right.

(On this subject of priorities, they should be as follows: God first, then your spouse, then your children, then your work and your ministry are equal and share the same priority. All these should be balanced.)

Spiritual – General Needs:

Friends,

It is important to monitor your relationships with friends. They can bring out the best in you or the worst in you.

If you feel that your friends are not bringing out the best in you then you need to spend less time with them and more time with friends that bring out the character of Jesus.

By doing this your character will change and you will become stronger and able to resist allowing the worst of you to come out with friends that do not build you up.

You will come to a point in your relationships with friends who are not good for you, where you will either win them over because you refuse to compromise or they will ostracise you. If you win them over, great, if not, you have planted seeds for God to water.

Keep praying for them and always be prepared to help them legally and without compromising your Christian Values. If these values would be compromised kindly explain that you will not compromise your relationship with Jesus as He is the most important one in your life, but if they have any other areas of need you will see if you can help them there.

Do not keep providing money to someone who squanders it, rather feed him and his family and assist in this way.

You are likely to be rejected. Do not despair though, Jesus has experienced this and understands your feelings. The Holy Spirit will comfort you through this time.

Keep praying for them and yourself.

If you do not have Christian friends, you will find them at Churches, Bible Studies, and Church functions. Get involved, Jesus will provide you with the right friends if you ask him to.

Desires,

God says that He gives us the desires of our heart if we seek our happiness in Him. (Psalms 37:4).

This statement has two meanings and both are true. He places His desires within your heart, and then he provides the fulfilment of the desires He first put there.

It is important to note, that you can gauge your spiritual health by the strength of your desires to communicate with God on everything, your desire to read the Bible, your desire to serve others, your pain when you see those suffering, your desire to bring people to the saving knowledge of Jesus Christ.

Do not think this last desire is a minor issue either because Jesus says clearly that He will reject those who are not on fire for Him and His cause (saving people). If you do not care to save others, then you do not Love your Neighbour, which is a key requirement in obeying God, reinforced by Jesus' final words before His ascension into Heaven. "They will know you are my disciples by your love for one another" (John 13:34-35)

Beware of the evil one who will either try to draw you into cultist, or other religions. If he cannot get this right, he will draw you into a Church that does not actively draw people into the saving knowledge of Jesus Christ.

Understanding the spiritual world,

To understand the spiritual world you have to understand that God's main purpose in your life is to give you His Spirit, train up your spirit to be able to operate in Heaven once your earthly vessel breaks down. And then to bring you into Heaven to be with Him for eternity as His child.

This means that He is not really concerned about your physical comforts.

He will continue to place you in the fire, to burn you and mould you (Malachi 3:3) into the spiritual child He wants you to be.

Your physical problems, he expects you to overcome by the application of His Word, His handbook to spiritual growth, the Bible.

He will provide you with the Holy Spirit, to guide you and lead you, to teach you and comfort you, and finally to present you to the Father as a powerful child ready to do battle in His Army against the evil one.

Do not be surprised when all kinds of trials come against you, (James 1:2-4). Your Father will not allow you to be destroyed, but will provide a way out (1 Corinthians 10:13).

You need to use your spirit and His Word, together with the guidance and strength and confidence in the Holy Spirit. This will show you the way out of your problem – then act on it in faith.

Your war (troubles) are not physical in nature as they may appear, they are physical manifestations of a spiritual war. So put on the armour of God (Ephesians 6:10-18) and ensure that you remain confident and at peace, despite the storms. You will win and you will become stronger.

This is the truth about the world you live in: Everyone knows that it is useless to take a pain killer to remove the pain caused by a brain tumour. You need to remove the tumour, because that is the cause of the pain. In the same way it is useless to sort out the physical problem when the cause is a spiritual one.

Deal with the spiritual cause and the physical will take care of itself. Again if a fire is burning you fight the source of the flames, not the flames themselves.

With respect to those who appear to have great wealth and success without knowing Jesus, do not be surprised. satan knows these people will eventually turn to God for help if he took them out of their prosperity. For as long as they are prosperous they will not believe they need God and His salvation.

Because they belong to satan, and he owns this world (Adam handed over the Title Deeds to planet Earth, when he and Eve bowed to satan and sinned in the Garden of Eden.) satan can rightfully do as he pleases with those that do not belong to God and God has no legal right to stop him, except to plead with those who do not know the Truth because of satan's lies.

In fact satan has the right to attack God's children and God will only limit satan in the impact that he is allowed to make on their lives (Job 1:1 - 2:10).

By allowing satan to attack us and limiting the impact of that attack God is forcing us, His children to eventually get fed up with satan's abuse and both call down the protection of the Blood of Jesus and to take up the spiritual armour that He has provided us with and attack him back. To drive him away from us, our situations, and even from those who are not yet saved.

We have the full power of the Name of Jesus, who is the Word of God. (Note: God spoke the universe into being. That is the power you have access to when using The Name of Jesus – If you will only believe it, you can use it.)

Being in constant dialogue with Jesus,

I need to address a myth that exists, outside Christian circles and to some extent within the Body of Christ too.

The Myth goes like this, "Because God is a spirit - I cannot hear Him."

Well this is completely untrue!!

Very few people get to hear God with their physical ears. From time to time God may choose to speak to someone in this way. But if God has to talk to you like this it shows how weak you are spiritually.

To be honest, I personally believe, based on biblical events where God spoke audibly to people, that this was necessary because they did not have the faith to believe what he was saying to them in any other way. It was His last resort.

It is not a pointer to how great you are if you heard God audibly, but more that you need to start listening to Him the way He normally speaks with His children – By His Spirit.

So then how does God speak to you?

He speaks to your Spirit via His Holy Spirit.

Let me explain: If you have accepted Jesus into your life as Lord and Saviour, but have not asked His Holy Spirit to live within you and teach and guide you, it is unlikely you will get two-way communication with God to stay constant.

To ask the Holy Spirit to enter you is simple. Ask Him to enter you and teach and Guide you. Just ask him, he is everywhere all the time and can do everything all at once. So He is never too busy to spend time with you and is never too far away to not be able to hear you. He is also deeply interested in you and wants to talk to you, if you will just allow him in and listen to Him.

I need to relate my story to assist you in understanding how to listen to the Spirit of God. When I was 17, I was a pretty obnoxious Bible Bashing Christian. Zealous for the Lord but not doing much soul winning for Jesus, simply because I chased most of them away from me. If you are one of those I hurt in this time of my life as a very immature Christian I am really sorry. Do not judge God by His children, and especially not by me. I had a long way to go and still have.

But let's get back to the subject. One of my brothers in Christ told me that he heard God tell him something. I do not remember what it was, but I was up in arms explaining to him that he was misguided and that God only spoke through His Word. He did not argue with me nor was he condescending. He simply challenged me. His words were "How do you know God does not talk to you if you have not listened to Him."

Well I had one question. "How can I hear Him? I had been filled with the Holy Spirit, which was a prerequisite, but did not know what I needed to do. My brother said this to me, and I am suggesting the same to you.

"Go into your room or a place where you cannot be distracted. Pray to God and ask him to speak to you. Then keep very quiet. Trust Him to speak to you. Do not allow yourself to be distracted. (I found this very difficult.) Do not empty your mind completely, as this would allow anything in (including evil thoughts) which you do not want. Focus your mind on Jesus, and think about Him wanting to speak to you."

Well I did this. I waited about 20 minutes before I first heard God speak to me. It was a thought that appeared to come from within my body. This sounds strange, but in fact that is how it works. When God, through the Holy Spirit, talks to you it is accompanied by certain emotions. Firstly you will experience complete Peace, and an atmosphere of Love and Compassion. And thereafter you will hear a thought go through your mind, which you never tried to call to mind. You never tried to think it. It simply pops in. For me what God said to me simply floored me.

My brother had explained to me that there would be three types of thoughts,

- those I generate myself,
- those that the evil one gives me and
- those that the Holy Spirit gives me.

To tell the difference between these thoughts is the key.

To tell the difference between the different types of thoughts you have to understand the character of God. You have to know Him so well that you know what He would and would not say to you. For example God would never ask you to go and murder someone, because this is contrary to His nature. This type of thought would come from satan. These you throw away.

Then there are the thoughts that come from yourself and are more complicated to detect, because usually they are the ones you actually want to hear.

By reading the Bible to get confirmation on whether God would say this kind of thing and by speaking to your other brothers and sisters in Christ, you will find out if this thought is from you or from God.

As you become more in tune with your emotions (<u>not your emotions controlling you</u>, but you distancing yourself from and analysing your emotions without letting them affect you) you will begin to detect more easily when it is that the Holy Spirit is communicating with you and when satan is. You will also find out that while you are thinking, there is no "gut feeling" associated with the thoughts, they are just thoughts.

It is a hard truth to accept that not all the thoughts you have are your own but in fact, unless you are consciously trying to think about something, your thoughts are more often than not, not your own. I will prove this to you.

For example, anger is an emotion, which comes before the words satan will try to speak through you by means of putting a thought in your head when you lose control over your tongue). Anger is what you feel just before you say things which hurt others and which you know to be untrue, or only partly true or which are true but should have been said in a sensitive and tactful way. Anger destabilises your earth machines computer (your body's brain) and you (a spirit) choose not to grab the controls and force the machine and computer back into control.

If you keep watching your emotions, you can quickly identify who is about to try to speak through, or to, you. By using your mind, you can control whether you let that thought in to your mind or out of your mouth.

Alcohol, Drugs and all other types of mind control substances, as well as lack of sleep, over exertion, over excitement are tools that satan uses to destabilise your ability to control your tongue At these times it is easy for him to use miscommunication and misunderstanding to start fights and cause chaos.

The fact is that satan may only use you as a tool to destroy and hurt if you allow him to. So be very wary of your thoughts, and especially the emotions that precede your thoughts, they are a dead give-away as to who is behind what you are saying.

Now some of you are saying, so I am not responsible for what I say and do then.

Wrong!!!!

You are responsible, because you allow your tongue and actions to be controlled, when you have the ability (which must be worked at) to control yourself.

Now that I have kept you in suspense, and covered an extremely important topic, which I suggest you read again and again, I will tell you what God's first words to me were.

"I have waited 17 years to be able to tell you that I Love you."

I cried a full hour or more and even now it brings tears to my eyes. How could I have put so loving a God into a constant state of having to listen to my monologue prayers, and just when He wanted to respond, cut Him off and go about my business.

I ask you "How long must God wait to get His words of Love to you?"

God will never force your free will. If you do not ask Him to talk to you, then He will patiently and lovingly listen to you, care for you, and love you. But I promise you this. He is bursting to be able to express His Love and attention to you in this more intimate way, if you will just ask and listen.

I have had 24 years of this type of communication with God and I feel like I am in Heaven, even now and every time He talks with me.

I cannot express how my heart breaks when I hear people say that God does not speak to them, or seldom speaks to them. I speak to Him all day, every day, sometimes aloud, sometimes under my breath and sometimes just in thoughts and He always answers me.

The Holy Spirit has this two-way communication on offer to you. Jesus said, "I go to the Father that the Holy Spirit might come. And when He comes He will teach you ..." (John 14:26)

Start now and practice listening to Him and watching your emotions.

I have a message that Jesus has just asked me to tell you who cannot hear him:

"If I could, I would trade My treasures in Heaven to speak with you, but it is your free will and I respect and love you so much that I will not force you. You are too precious to me. I will never manipulate you into doing My will no matter how painful it is for Me to stand by and see your hurt, especially when I have the exact message that you need."

Wow!!!!!

A Ministry

You will find that once you really start to get close to Jesus and the Holy Spirit really starts working within you. You will no longer be able to contain the Love and Compassion you feel for those who are not saved and are running around on this planet chasing their tails with no eternal purpose. You will burn for them.

When this starts happening, you are being called to a ministry position. In most cases, it is not a permanent job as a minister.

Those who do not know about God or do not trust God or have been blinded by satan for some or other reason seldom go to Church. It is most likely that God has placed you in the job you are in and the place you are at, not so you can have your own enjoyment and satisfaction.

(remember the marriage vows? You are no longer your own person. You are now a Servant and child of the Most High God, and you have a job to do on this Earth.)

You are in the place God has put you to love, encourage, show kindness to others. To display pure motives and morals and to shine the Love Jesus has for you. Especially important is displaying the supernatural joy that is constant in your life no matter how bad your circumstances get. You will go through really tough times, so that those around you can witness this amazing God in action, providing Peace where there should be Fear, and Joy when there should be despair. You are there as an example of what God can do in their lives if they just let Him. So do not be quiet about the problems you face, but rather share them along with the way God is looking after you.

You are the seed-sower. Your behaviour is the seed that you must sow. It is unlikely that you will know the effect that your seeds have in someone's life, but you can be sure of this: you will have to accept that you will be considered strange, different and perhaps even worse. Know that you are giving the Holy Spirit something to work with in their lives. Your work is critical.

It is also imperative that you water these seeds with prayer. Pray for everyone you work with everyday. If you can, start or attend a company Bible Study group, before or after work or at lunch time (do not steal the time you are paid to work) – do it. This will be the start of your ministry.

Start with whatever God has given you and grow it. If you are faithful with the little He has given you, then He will multiply it out and continue to bless you in this area of your life.

The words "I can't" must disappear from your vocabulary. You can, because Jesus can, and He is inside you.

Do not be rash and dump everything and rush into your hearts desire. God often gives us a vision of where we will be years from now. Do not expect to get there tomorrow. He is simply showing you what direction you should go in. Keep the vision but approach everything sensibly in prayer.

If God opens a "door" then go that way. Check first though, go only after you have confirmed that this is in fact God's will. satan will let you push open any door you want to, so that He can sidetrack you from getting to where God wants you to go. You will know this is happening if you feel impatience, for impatience is not of God but of satan. Be patient and keep praying and working towards the vision he has given you.

If you have not received a vision of a ministry, then you already are where God wants you and you need to look around you and see what kind of a difference you can make for God where you are.

So, where do I fit into the Church

Now that you have a good idea of where you stand and what you need to do to become stronger, I want to address the place and purpose of the Body of Christ and more specifically where you as an individual believer in Jesus Christ fits in.

The Body of Christ, whether as a global entity consisting of all denominational churches at congregational level. These are not ruled by a Minister, Priest, Pastor, Arch Bishop, Pope or even Angelic Beings. No, the Body of Christ is ruled by Jesus Christ and by Jesus Christ alone!!! (Colossians 2:19) God has chosen to send the Holy Spirit as His representative on this earth to guide, teach and comfort Jesus' Body, of which you are a member. (1 Corinthians 12:1 – 31 & 13: 1 - 13)

If any person wants to rule over you, or tries to enforce authority over you they are misled. (Luke 22:25 - 27). All they are allowed to do is debate scripture with you to see what God says, for the Holy Spirit will never contradict Himself. God will reveal the truth as different scriptures are introduced into the debate. To get this right, you must use Bibles translated between 1611 and 1811 – all recent bibles have been corrupted. Those who do not follow the instruction of Jesus that they ought to be servants to their brothers and sisters in Christ, do not deserve to even be listened to at all. Those who seek or enforce authority over other brothers and sisters (The flock they are to feed, not trap) will all be among those who cry "Lord, Lord, but we prophesied and healed and taught in Your Name" Jesus will turn to these and say "Away from me you evil doers" (Matthew 7:21 – 23) (Matthew 25:31 - 46)

I am terrified of being among these people, and so I have determined to be a member of equal standing with my brothers and sisters and in fact consider every believer in Jesus, irrespective of how man has lifted them up to be equal to myself before God. In terms of my attitude, I consider myself a little brother to you all and a servant to both you and God Almighty.

If anyone thinks that they have "Divine Authority" among believers, they are not humble before God, and as such will be punished for it. You my friend are a team player (The body has many members (Colossians 2:19) There is only one captain, Jesus Christ, whom the Holy Spirit makes known to us on a continual basis.

I want to be very clear on this next point, as satan will try to twist this in your head.

You must listen to the word of God being preached. God has called certain people to preach, but they do not have authority over you. It is important that you draw the distinction between the authority to preach, which is a gift God gives to His servants and the authority to make you do or think things.

It works like this.

Someone preaches to you (and sometimes even quotes scripture too just like I am doing in this book.)

You then take the message and accept this message as Gospel Truth.

NO! NO! NO! A THOUSAND TIMES NO!!!!!

You do not accept it as Gospel Truth until you have studied the scriptures in their context and studied the message preached within the context of the Word of God with the guidance of the Holy Spirit. (Who is your teacher (John 14:26) and makes things known to you.) God said that His people perish because they lack knowledge. (Hosea 4:6) You do not have the right picture.

If you are one of these who simply accept what you are told instead of reading the Bible and measuring everything said against the Bible, then you will perish. You will be misled. You may even be led into Hell. And why? Pure Laziness and no Passion for reading the Word of God, and dare I say, no real love for God or your eternal salvation.

Sorry that came out so harsh, but I am not allowed to change it. I as the messenger am apologising, but Jesus Christ, is not. God sees His children being misled and is angry with them because of their complacency. In fact He has already said in the Bible, that if you are not Hot (Passionate) for His cause and His Word, He will spit you out of His mouth (Revelation 3:15 - 19). My friend, make a choice, either become as close to a Jesus fanatic (Hot) as possible, or get out of the Church, eat drink and be merry, soon you will die, and then all that awaits you is Hell.... Your choice.

So why are there people like this in the Church of Jesus Christ?

3 main reasons really:

1. People are Lazy and do not want to read the Bible themselves, or join a Bible Study. They want to be spoon-fed and do not care even if what they are fed is garbage or poison. They also do not mind going once a month.

Sometimes, the more consciencous probably go once a week. The old, sick, and those in trouble would probably go once a week, all the time searching for a quick fix to their physical condition. Wanting to get some kind of reassurance, but walking out once again unfulfilled. The preacher who "lords" it over the flock, has failed if he has not made every effort to help these people to see the truth about themselves. He will be judged very harshly for such negligence.

2. People are misled to believe that the person in charge has some special link between himself and God. They think that only the preacher has this special link. I once thought that too, many of my friends did too. I know that there are probably more than half of those in the Church of Christ who fall into this category. satan has kept so many Christians locked away from experiencing the beautiful personal relationship that Jesus, through His Holy Spirit wants to share with them. Now I know that many who preach are not aware that many of their flock may be feeling or thinking this, but their job is to make disciples. A disciple of Jesus Christ is not just someone who mindlessly follows a bunch of rules, traditions, dos and don'ts. No, a disciple is someone who has a personal relationship with God, who praises the Father, thanks the Son and has a personal relationship with Jesus, through the communication with the Holy Spirit. I have seen many who preach, lose their ministry because they never addressed this issue within their Church. Why don't they? Simple. They are too proud. Too happy with their status. Pleased that they are "making a difference". When all the while, they

are, if not consciously then subconsciously depriving God of a personal relationship with His children. Beware, my brothers and sisters who preach. If this is happening in your Church, your ministry will be taken away from you and given to someone who will preach on how to have a personal relationship with Jesus Christ. Who will preach about the fact that the Holy Spirit is our teacher and comforter, and that if they will just listen, they will hear His voice and they will follow Him.

3. Subconsciously and sometimes consciously, people think that well I will go to church, might even say a few prayers, read my Bible and be a good person. If there is a last judgement, then I will tell God that it was all my preachers fault. Well its time someone burst your happy little bubble and made you face reality. You will go to Hell because you did not do what you were supposed to do. You had no passion for God. You did not really care. For you it was just a happy little club. Your preacher may or may not be at fault. He will pay for His part in it, but you will get no lightening of your sentence.

The preacher's job is to preach, not to make your life cool and fuzzy. He has a job given to him by God Almighty. He is to preach the uncompromising word of God, the Most High, ruler and creator and destroyer of the entire universe.

Whew!!!

I feel drained now.

I was not looking forward to this message, and in fact, I have dragged my heels a bit in getting to this point. But my Fathers Will is clear. He is not willing that any should perish (2 Peter 3:9) and if you get in the way of His will, you pay the price, me included. There is no special treatment for anyone when it comes to how God treats us. (Deuteronomy 10:16 - 17)

Epilogue

My friends I write this book with a very heavy heart. You are all so precious to God and also to me. Yet I know that many will no welcome this message.

If you are the only one of all those that reads this book and is touched by the truth in it. If you have since asked Jesus to forgive you for everything you have done wrong, and asked him to be your Lord and Saviour. If you have asked the Father to give you the gift of The Holy Spirit and you have forgiven everyone who has ever done you (or those you love and care for) any harm. (For God will only forgive those who have forgiven everyone else.) Then whatever persecution I have to endure for writing this book will be worth what you will gain.

May God Almighty, (my Father YHWH, my Big Brother Jesus and my Teacher, Councillor, Consoler and best friend The Holy Spirit), touch you in the most special ways during your life and may we meet again in Heaven someday.

Some people claim that the Old English of the Old King James Bible is difficult to read. Most have never even tried to read it, they simply work on gossip. The Old English language is actually easy to understand, and there are only a handful of words you need to know that have changed their meaning over time. With a little effort we can read the True Word of God. (If we truly love God, it is really no trouble at all, neither do we forget that it is only those who seek God with ALL their heart that will find Him.)

Deuteronomy 4:29
> But if from thence thou shalt seek the LORD thy God, thou shalt find him, if thou seek him with all thy heart and with all thy soul.

You can rediscover the real truth that God brought to this world.

Another beauty about the Old King James Bible, is that where the translators chose to insert a word to make the sentence read more "clearly", these words are in italics. The true richness of the original meaning of the Hebrew comes through clearer when we omit these words in italics and wrestle with the sentence meanings that would all be true if the word was omitted. No other English version gives you the opportunity to see this clearly into the Hebrew. I will be praying that the eyes of your spirit are opened to the poison you drink in when you read the corrupted bibles, and that you treat the corrupted bibles with the disgrace and contempt they deserve. Burn them as Christians burnt the books that referred to magic, the occult, witchcraft, the esoteric, which includes all we would refer to now as New Age religious works. Burn them all. (Acts 19:19).

I praise God almighty who created everything we need. The air we breathe, the food we eat (and the substances from which our food is prepared.) The water we drink (and the substances from which what we drink is prepared), our bodies, minds and spirits. I praise our Father God for his master plan to save His Believers.

I praise Jesus for His obedience, to die in the places of those who by faith accept His free gift, whereby, in love, He offered Himself to be punished in your and my places, for what we had done wrong and in doing this He satisfied God's righteous justice which required that someone had to pay the penalty of death for sin against God. Sin that started in the Garden of Eden when Adam chose to listen to Eve rather than to God. For the punishment for sin is death.

Romans 6:23

> For the wages of sin is death; but the gift of God is eternal life through Jesus Christ our Lord.

James 1:12 - 15

> Blessed is the man that endureth temptation: for when he is tried, he shall receive the crown of life, which the Lord hath promised to them that love him. Let no man say when he is tempted, I am tempted of God: for God cannot be tempted with evil, neither tempteth he any man: But every man is tempted, when he is drawn away of his own lust, and enticed. Then when lust hath conceived, it bringeth forth sin: and sin, when it is finished, bringeth forth death.

Only those who allow Jesus to live in them and through them, and who actively transform themselves to be like Him will be saved. Sure we will fail and we will pick ourselves up and try again, but when we choose to sin wilfully, especially, if we choose to sin, believing that God will just forgive us, then we are insulting the Holy Spirit, who had to watch Jesus suffer and die to pay for the sin you and I just didn't care about. You and I are in great danger of no longer being protected by God, and being given a depraved mind, which will lead you and me away from God, and so also away from Jesus, which will lead you and me into Hell. It is easy to tell where you and I are on this slide. Can you still <u>very clearly feel</u> God's prompting not to do or say things that are not good? If you cannot hear Him, it is because you are choosing to ignore Him, and His words are getting softer and softer and harder and harder to hear. Turn back to Him with your whole heart, stop sinning wilfully, fight the spiritual battles against your flesh by praising and worshipping God, who inhabits the praises of His people, and use the Name of Jesus to cast away all evil, and then remove from your life all people and objects that draw you away from God and into these sins.

I praise the Holy Spirit for His patience and guidance (specifically with me, for I am the least worthy of this task He has given me.)

I praise the Father for using the foolish to confound the wise and the outcast to shame the accepted.

All Praise to you Almighty God, The Alpha and Omega, The Beginning and End of all things.

The Greatest Sign & Wonder - Which Bible is the only one to trust and why!

(Matthew 24:24-25)

> Mat 24:24 For there shall arise false Christs, and false prophets, and shall shew great signs and wonders; insomuch that, if *it were* possible, they shall deceive the very elect.
>
> Mat 24:25 Behold, I have told you before.

I, like so many other Christians, have discovered that the most recent Bibles have been translated off the corrupted Greek Alexandrian Codices.

All the underlined sections below contain hyperlinks to details which, if you currently use and trust any English Bible other than the Old King James 1611, you need to investigate for yourself.

It is Jesus nature to make His Word accessible to the poor so they can find Him, and so it becomes really difficult for the rich and the ruler, for they think according to the pattern of this world where expensive must be good - This is a lie.

Please note that **the cheapest Bible currently available is The Old King James 1611 Bible**.

Only those **truly diligent** in finding Jesus will **not conform** to the trade pattern of this world and will **seek out and follow God's Narrow Way**.

The Real Truth

Alexandrea was the centre of disbelief in Jesus. The two Greek scholars who translated the new bibles off these lying codices were Westcott & Hort.

These two people hated the correct source because it claims that Jesus **IS** God.

The Historical records of Westcott's & Hort's own other writings and journals prove this. Check out the YouTube series "The Battle of The Bibles" for this proof at https://www.youtube.com/watch?v=tNv-zzpIwBs

Naturally, as Westcott & Hort themselves did not believe that Jesus was God. They butchered the texts in the new "bibles", to poison the minds of those reading the Real Truth. To cause "The Falling Away" that must come just before Jesus' return.

2nd Thessalonians 2:1-4
> Now we beseech you, brethren, by the coming of our Lord Jesus Christ, and by our gathering together unto him,
> That ye be not soon shaken in mind, or be troubled, neither by spirit, nor by word, nor by letter as from us, as that the day of Christ is at hand.
> **Let no man deceive you by any means: for that day shall not come, except there come a falling away first**, and that man of sin be revealed, the son of perdition;
> Who opposeth and exalteth himself above all that is called God, or that is worshipped; so that he as God sitteth in the temple of God, shewing himself that he is God.

Current "bibles" like the NIV, Good News, RSV, ISV, etc... are among the bibles which have been poisoned. In fact ONLY Bibles translated <u>BEFORE 1881</u> are safe. For corroboration listen to the majesty of God's precise and perfect Word described in a one hour video on YouTube here: <u>https://www.youtube.com/watch?v=MSM0sclQTTg</u>

The correct source manuscript is Textus Receptus, from which the Old King James Version of 1611 was translated, which the theologians who support that Jesus is God will agree is the only reliable English version.

Please note that there are some versions that claim to be King James Bibles, but they are not. The "Modern King James Bible" and the "New King James Bible" include the corrupted Alexandrian texts as notes in the margin or in the commentary to bring confusion to the reader. These newer translations write them into more "understandable" [The Holy Spirit does NOT need any help explaining His Word to us] English, and then claim that they came from the same sources as the old King James Bible. However, in the process, they distorted God's Word to provide for a "christianity", that does not have Jesus as the only way to God. The discrepancies are glaring.

Check out the following verses which have also been removed to a greater or lesser extent depending on the translation. Every word in red is Jesus' own words. Removing these proved the translators intentions. Read some examples of what was removed from post-1939 translations to see just what evil corruption is taking place in these translations. And then choose to find an OLD King James Bible, and read the true Word of God for yourself, and born the corrupted ones.

The Scriptures quoted below are there for context, while **the scriptures in bold text are the ones removed from newer translations.**

<u>Matthew 17:21</u> **Howbeit this kind goeth not out but by prayer and fasting.**

> And when they were come to the multitude, there came to him a *certain* man, kneeling down to him, and saying,
> Lord, have mercy on my son: for he is lunatick, and sore vexed: for ofttimes he falleth into the fire, and oft into the water.
> And I brought him to thy disciples, and they could not cure him.
> Then Jesus answered and said, O faithless and perverse generation, how long shall I be with you? how long shall I suffer you? bring him hither to me.
> And Jesus rebuked the devil; and he departed out of him: and the child was cured from that very hour.
> Then came the disciples to Jesus apart, and said, Why could not we cast him out?
> And Jesus said unto them, Because of your unbelief: for verily I say unto you, If ye have faith as a grain of mustard seed, ye shall say unto this mountain, Remove hence to yonder place; and it shall remove; and nothing shall be impossible unto you.
> **Howbeit this kind goeth not out but by prayer and fasting.**

<u>Matthew 18:11</u> **For the Son of man is come to save that which was lost.**

At the same time came the disciples unto Jesus, saying, Who is the greatest in the kingdom of heaven?

And Jesus called a little child unto him, and set him in the midst of them,

And said, Verily I say unto you, Except ye be converted, and become as little children, ye shall not enter into the kingdom of heaven.

Whosoever therefore shall humble himself as this little child, the same is greatest in the kingdom of heaven.

And whoso shall receive one such little child in my name receiveth me.

But whoso shall offend one of these little ones which believe in me, it were better for him that a millstone were hanged about his neck, and *that* he were drowned in the depth of the sea.

Woe unto the world because of offences! for it must needs be that offences come; but woe to that man by whom the offence cometh!

Wherefore if thy hand or thy foot offend thee, cut them off, and cast *them* from thee: it is better for thee to enter into life halt or maimed, rather than having two hands or two feet to be cast into everlasting fire.

And if thine eye offend thee, pluck it out, and cast *it* from thee: it is better for thee to enter into life with one eye, rather than having two eyes to be cast into hell fire.

Take heed that ye despise not one of these little ones; for I say unto you, That in heaven their angels do always behold the face of my Father which is in heaven.

For the Son of man is come to save that which was lost.

<u>Matthew 21:44</u> **And whosoever shall fall on this stone shall be broken: but on whomsoever it shall fall, it will grind him to powder.**

But what think ye? A *certain* man had two sons; and he came to the first, and said, Son, go work to day in my vineyard.

He answered and said, I will not: but afterward he repented, and went.

And he came to the second, and said likewise. And he answered and said, I *go,* sir: and went not.

Whether of them twain did the will of *his* father? They say unto him, The first. Jesus saith unto them, Verily I say unto you, That the publicans and the harlots go into the kingdom of God before you.

For John came unto you in the way of righteousness, and ye believed him not: but the publicans and the harlots believed him: and ye, when ye had seen *it,* repented not afterward, that ye might believe him.

Hear another parable: There was a certain householder, which planted a vineyard, and hedged it round about, and digged a winepress in it, and built a tower, and let it out to husbandmen, and went into a far country:

And when the time of the fruit drew near, he sent his servants to the husbandmen, that they might receive the fruits of it.

And the husbandmen took his servants, and beat one, and killed another, and stoned another.

Again, he sent other servants more than the first: and they did unto them likewise.

But last of all he sent unto them his son, saying, They will reverence my son.

But when the husbandmen saw the son, they said among themselves, This is the heir; come, let us kill him, and let us seize on his inheritance.

And they caught him, and cast *him* out of the vineyard, and slew *him.*

When the lord therefore of the vineyard cometh, what will he do unto those husbandmen?

They say unto him, He will miserably destroy those wicked men, and will let out *his* vineyard unto other husbandmen, which shall render him the fruits in their seasons.

Jesus saith unto them, Did ye never read in the scriptures, The stone which the builders rejected, the same is become the head of the corner: this is the Lord's doing, and it is marvellous in our eyes?

Therefore say I unto you, The kingdom of God shall be taken from you, and given to a nation bringing forth the fruits thereof.

And whosoever shall fall on this stone shall be broken: but on whomsoever it shall fall, it will grind him to powder.

<u>Matthew 23:14</u> **Woe unto you, scribes and Pharisees, hypocrites! for ye devour widows' houses, and for a pretence make long prayer: therefore ye shall receive the greater damnation.**

But woe unto you, scribes and Pharisees, hypocrites! for ye shut up the kingdom of heaven against men: for ye neither go in *yourselves,* neither suffer ye them that are entering to go in.

Woe unto you, scribes and Pharisees, hypocrites! for ye devour widows' houses, and for a pretence make long prayer: therefore ye shall receive the greater damnation.

Woe unto you, scribes and Pharisees, hypocrites! for ye compass sea and land to make one proselyte, and when he is made, ye make him twofold more the child of hell than yourselves.

Woe unto you, *ye* blind guides, which say, Whosoever shall swear by the temple, it is nothing; but whosoever shall swear by the gold of the temple, he is a debtor!

Ye fools and blind: for whether is greater, the gold, or the temple that sanctifieth the gold?

And, Whosoever shall swear by the altar, it is nothing; but whosoever sweareth by the gift that is upon it, he is guilty.

Ye fools and blind: for whether *is* greater, the gift, or the altar that sanctifieth the gift?

Whoso therefore shall swear by the altar, sweareth by it, and by all things thereon.

And whoso shall swear by the temple, sweareth by it, and by him that dwelleth therein.

And he that shall swear by heaven, sweareth by the throne of God, and by him that sitteth thereon.

Woe unto you, scribes and Pharisees, hypocrites! for ye pay tithe of mint and anise and cummin, and have omitted the weightier *matters* of the law, judgment, mercy, and faith: these ought ye to have done, and not to leave the other undone.

Ye blind guides, which strain at a gnat, and swallow a camel.

Woe unto you, scribes and Pharisees, hypocrites! for ye make clean the outside of the cup and of the platter, but within they are full of extortion and excess.

Thou blind Pharisee, cleanse first that *which is* within the cup and platter, that the outside of them may be clean also.

Woe unto you, scribes and Pharisees, hypocrites! for ye are like unto whited sepulchres, which indeed appear beautiful outward, but are within full of dead *men's* bones, and of all uncleanness.

Even so ye also outwardly appear righteous unto men, but within ye are full of hypocrisy and iniquity.

Mark 7:16 **If any man have ears to hear, let him hear.** [By this Jesus makes clear He is not referring to the physical person and physical foods, but is separating physical and spiritual and is here teaching the spirits of the people, if they have spiritual ears to hear, that they are defiled by what comes from the mouth of their own physical body, then they will hear and understand this.]

He answered and said unto them, Well hath Esaias prophesied of you hypocrites, as it is written, This people honoureth me with *their* lips, but their heart is far from me.

Howbeit in vain do they worship me, teaching *for* doctrines the commandments of men.

For laying aside the commandment of God, ye hold the tradition of men, *as* the washing of pots and cups: and many other such like things ye do.

And he said unto them, Full well ye reject the commandment of God, that ye may keep your own tradition.

For Moses said, Honour thy father and thy mother; and, Whoso curseth father or mother, let him die the death:

But ye say, If a man shall say to his father or mother, *It is* Corban, that is to say, a gift, by whatsoever thou mightest be profited by me; *he shall be free.*

And ye suffer him no more to do ought for his father or his mother;

Making the word of God of none effect through your tradition, which ye have delivered: and many such like things do ye.

And when he had called all the people *unto him,* he said unto them, Hearken unto me every one *of you,* and understand:

There is nothing from without a man, that entering into him can defile him: but the things which come out of him, those are they that defile the man.

If any man have ears to hear, let him hear.

And if thy hand offend thee, cut it off: it is better for thee to enter into life maimed, than having two hands to go into hell, into the fire that never shall be quenched:

Mark 9:44 **Where their worm** [your spirit] **dieth not, and the fire is not quenched.**

Where their worm [your spirit] **dieth not, and the fire is not quenched.**

And if thy foot offend thee, cut it off: it is better for thee to enter halt into life, than having two feet to be cast into hell, into the fire that never shall be quenched:

Mark 9:46 **Where their worm** [your spirit] **dieth not, and the fire is not quenched.**

Where their worm [your spirit] **dieth not, and the fire is not quenched.**

And if thine eye offend thee, pluck it out: it is better for thee to enter into the kingdom of God with one eye, than having two eyes to be cast into hell fire:

Where their worm dieth not, and the fire is not quenched.

For every one shall be salted with fire, and every
sacrifice shall be salted with salt.

Salt *is* good: but if the salt have lost his saltness,
wherewith will ye season it? Have salt in
yourselves, and have peace one with another.

**Mark 11:26 But <u>if ye do not forgive,</u> <u>neither will</u>
<u>your Father which is in heaven forgive your</u>
<u>trespasses</u>.**

And on the morrow, when they were come from
Bethany, he was hungry:

And seeing a fig tree afar off having leaves, he
came, if haply he might find any thing thereon:
and when he came to it, he found nothing but
leaves; for the time of figs was not *yet.*

And Jesus answered and said unto it, No man
eat fruit of thee hereafter for ever. And his
disciples heard *it.*

And they come to Jerusalem: and Jesus went into
the temple, and began to cast out them that
sold and bought in the temple, and overthrew
the tables of the moneychangers, and the seats
of them that sold doves;

And would not suffer that any man should carry
any vessel through the temple.

And he taught, saying unto them, Is it not written,
My house shall be called of all nations the
house of prayer? but ye have made it a den of
thieves.

And the scribes and chief priests heard *it,* and
sought how they might destroy him: for
they feared him, because all the people was
astonished at his doctrine.

And when even was come, he went out of the city.

And in the morning, as they passed by, they saw
the fig tree dried up from the roots.

And Peter calling to remembrance saith unto him, Master, behold, the fig tree which thou cursedst is withered away.

And Jesus answering saith unto them, Have faith in God.

For verily I say unto you, That whosoever shall say unto this mountain, Be thou removed, and be thou cast into the sea; and shall not doubt in his heart, but shall believe that those things which he saith shall come to pass; he shall have whatsoever he saith.

Therefore I say unto you, What things soever ye desire, when ye pray, believe that ye receive *them,* and ye shall have *them.*

And when ye stand praying, forgive, if ye have ought against any: that your Father also which is in heaven may forgive you your trespasses.

But if ye do not forgive, neither will your Father which is in heaven forgive your trespasses.

Mark 15:28 **And the scripture was fulfilled, which saith, And he was numbered with the transgressors.**

And when they had crucified him, they parted his garments, casting lots upon them, what every man should take.

And it was the third hour, and they crucified him.

And the superscription of his accusation was written over, THE KING OF THE JEWS.

And with him they crucify two thieves; the one on his right hand, and the other on his left.

And the scripture was fulfilled, which saith, And he was numbered with the transgressors.

<u>Luke 17:36</u> **Two _men_ shall be in the field; the one shall be taken, and the other left.** [Note that the word "men" is not in the original Hebrew. This is another reason why I do not use another translation. I get to be able to focus on only the original text and ignore man's additions because they are highlighted as having been added.]

And he said unto the disciples, The days will come, when ye shall desire to see one of the days of the Son of man, and ye shall not see _it._

And they shall say to you, See here; or, see there: go not after _them,_ nor follow _them._

For as the lightning, that lighteneth out of the one _part_ under heaven, shineth unto the other _part_ under heaven; so shall also the Son of man be in his day.

But first must he suffer many things, and be rejected of this generation.

And as it was in the days of Noe, so shall it be also in the days of the Son of man.

They did eat, they drank, they married wives, they were given in marriage, until the day that Noe entered into the ark, and the flood came, and destroyed them all.

Likewise also as it was in the days of Lot; they did eat, they drank, they bought, they sold, they planted, they builded;

But the same day that Lot went out of Sodom it rained fire and brimstone from heaven, and destroyed _them_ all.

Even thus shall it be in the day when the Son of man is revealed.

In that day, he which shall be upon the housetop, and his stuff in the house, let him not come down to take it away: and he that is in the field, let him likewise not return back.

Remember Lot's wife.

Whosoever shall seek to save his life shall lose it; and whosoever shall lose his life shall preserve it.

I tell you, in that night there shall be two *men* in one bed; the one shall be taken, and the other shall be left.

Two *women* shall be grinding together; the one shall be taken, and the other left.

Two *men* shall be in the field; the one shall be taken, and the other left.

John 5:4 **For <u>an angel went down</u> at a certain season into the pool, and troubled the water: <u>whosoever then first after the troubling of the water stepped in was made whole of whatsoever disease he had</u>.**

After this there was a feast of the Jews; and Jesus went up to Jerusalem.

Now there is at Jerusalem by the sheep *market* a pool, which is called in the Hebrew tongue Bethesda, having five porches.

In these lay a great multitude of impotent folk, of blind, halt, withered, waiting for the moving of the water.

For an angel went down at a certain season into the pool, and troubled the water: whosoever then first after the troubling of the water stepped in was made whole of whatsoever disease he had.

And a certain man was there, which had an infirmity thirty and eight years.

When Jesus saw him lie, and knew that he had been now a long time *in that case,* he saith unto him, Wilt thou be made whole?

The impotent man answered him, Sir, I have no man, when the water is troubled, to put me into the pool: but while I am coming, another steppeth down before me.

Jesus saith unto him, Rise, take up thy bed, and walk.

And immediately the man was made whole, and took up his bed, and walked: and on the same day was the sabbath.

The Jews therefore said unto him that was cured, It is the sabbath day: it is not lawful for thee to carry *thy* bed.

He answered them, He that made me whole, the same said unto me, Take up thy bed, and walk.

Then asked they him, What man is that which said unto thee, Take up thy bed, and walk?

And he that was healed wist not who it was: for Jesus had conveyed himself away, a multitude being in *that* place.

Afterward Jesus findeth him in the temple, and said unto him, Behold, thou art made whole: sin no more, lest a worse thing come unto thee.

The man departed, and told the Jews that it was Jesus, which had made him whole.

And therefore did the Jews persecute Jesus, and sought to slay him, because he had done these things on the sabbath day.

But Jesus answered them, My Father worketh hitherto, and I work.

Therefore the Jews sought the more to kill him, because he not only had broken the sabbath, but said also that God was his Father, making himself equal with God.

Then answered Jesus and said unto them, Verily, verily, I say unto you, The Son can do nothing of himself, but what he seeth the Father do: for what things soever he doeth, these also doeth the Son likewise.

For the Father loveth the Son, and sheweth him all things that himself doeth: and he will shew him greater works than these, that ye may marvel.

For as the Father raiseth up the dead, and quickeneth *them;* even so the Son quickeneth whom he will.

For the Father judgeth no man, but hath committed all judgment unto the Son:

That all *men* should honour the Son, even as they honour the Father. He that honoureth not the Son honoureth not the Father which hath sent him.

Verily, verily, I say unto you, He that heareth my word, and believeth on him that sent me, hath everlasting life, and shall not come into condemnation; but is passed from death unto life.

Verily, verily, I say unto you, The hour is coming, and now is, when the dead shall hear the voice of the Son of God: and they that hear shall live.

For as the Father hath life in himself; so hath he given to the Son to have life in himself;

And hath given him authority to execute judgment also, because he is the Son of man.

Marvel not at this: for the hour is coming, in the which all that are in the graves shall hear his voice,

And shall come forth; they that have done good, unto the resurrection of life; and they that have done evil, unto the resurrection of damnation.

I can of mine own self do nothing: as I hear, I judge: and my judgment is just; because I seek not mine own will, but the will of the Father which hath sent me.

Acts 8:37 And Philip said, If thou believest with all thine heart, thou mayest. And he answered and said, I believe that <u>Jesus Christ is the Son of God</u>.

And the angel of the Lord spake unto Philip, saying, Arise, and go toward the south unto the way that goeth down from Jerusalem unto Gaza, which is desert.

And he arose and went: and, behold, a man of Ethiopia, an eunuch of great authority under Candace queen of the Ethiopians, who had the charge of all her treasure, and had come to Jerusalem for to worship,

Was returning, and sitting in his chariot read Esaias the prophet.

Then the Spirit said unto Philip, Go near, and join thyself to this chariot.

And Philip ran thither to *him,* and heard him read the prophet Esaias, and said, Understandest thou what thou readest?

And he said, How can I, except some man should guide me? And he desired Philip that he would come up and sit with him.

The place of the scripture which he read was this, He was led as a sheep to the slaughter; and like a lamb dumb before his shearer, so opened he not his mouth:

In his humiliation his judgment was taken away: and who shall declare his generation? for his life is taken from the earth.

And the eunuch answered Philip, and said, I pray thee, of whom speaketh the prophet this? of himself, or of some other man?

Then Philip opened his mouth, and began at the same scripture, and preached unto him Jesus.

And as they went on *their* way, they came unto a certain water: and the eunuch said, See, *here is* water; what doth hinder me to be baptized?

And Philip said, If thou believest with all thine heart, thou mayest. And he answered and said, I believe that Jesus Christ is the Son of God.

And he commanded the chariot to stand still: and they went down both into the water, both Philip and the eunuch; and he baptized him.

And when they were come up out of the water, the Spirit of the Lord caught away Philip, that the eunuch saw him no more: and he went on his way rejoicing.

But Philip was found at Azotus: and passing through he preached in all the cities, till he came to Caesarea.

Acts 28:29 And when he had said these words, the Jews departed, and had great reasoning among themselves.

And when they had appointed him a day, there came many to him into *his* lodging; to whom he expounded and testified the kingdom of God, persuading them concerning Jesus, both out of the law of Moses, and *out of* the prophets, from morning till evening.

And some believed the things which were spoken, and some believed not.

And when they agreed not among themselves, they departed, after that Paul had spoken one word, Well spake the Holy Ghost by Esaias the prophet unto our fathers,

Saying, Go unto this people, and say, Hearing ye shall hear, and shall not understand; and seeing ye shall see, and not perceive:

For the heart of this people is waxed gross, and their ears are dull of hearing, and their eyes have they closed; lest they should see with *their* eyes, and hear with *their* ears, and understand with *their* heart, and should be converted, and I should heal them.

Be it known therefore unto you, that the salvation of God is sent unto the Gentiles, and *that* they will hear it.

And when he had said these words, the Jews departed, and had great reasoning among themselves.

And Paul dwelt two whole years in his own hired house, and received all that came in unto him,

Preaching the kingdom of God, and teaching those things which concern the Lord Jesus Christ, with all confidence, no man forbidding him.

Romans 16:24 **The grace of our <u>Lord Jesus Christ</u> *be* with you all. Amen.**

The grace of our Lord Jesus Christ *be* with you all. Amen.

Now to him that is of power to stablish you according to my gospel, and the preaching of Jesus Christ, according to the revelation of the mystery, which was kept secret since the world began,

But now is made manifest, and by the scriptures of the prophets, according to the commandment of the everlasting God, made known to all nations for the obedience of faith:

Salvation - a Play you can expand on and produce

<u>Actors:</u>

Narrator
Rob
Grant
Susan
Jackie
Frank
Thief
"God"
Extras
Mime Team

<u>Stage Lighting Suggestions</u>

Stage Lighting should have at least 2 different brightness settings. or different sets of independent lights

An Ultra-violet light is a good idea to bring out the brilliance of the white in contrast with the Black.

Spotlights that are able to weave around the stage and can shine different colours.

<u>Stage Props</u>

Large sign saying "HEAVEN, THIS WAY"
Large sign saying "HELL, THIS WAY"
One very thick piece of rope
Many, Many pieces of rope of different thickness.

Costumes

Only all Black or all white may be worn.

Each person who is to have ropes on them must be heavily laden with these ropes. The number of ropes must look like a heavy burden.

Rob should have an all-black overall that is easy to step out of without needing to remove all his ropes.

Knee and Hand Guards would be useful for the extras crawling about on the stage.

CAUTION:

1. Ensure that the rope nooses are not slip knots, with the exception of Robs and the Thief's one that he shares with Rob.
2. Care must be taken not to make these ropes so long that other people can stand on them and cause an injury. (About ankle height should be fine.)

Curtain Closed - Enter Narrator

Narrator:

"What you will see represented today/tonight is what happens to each person's spirit. You will be able, as it were, to see through the people to what is happening with their spirits.

Exit Narrator

Open Curtain: Scene One (Bare stage with a sign on the left saying 'Heaven this way', and a sign on the right saying 'Hell this way'. An entrance at the back of the stage in the centre allows actors to enter & exit while they are still alive.

Extras continue to crawl by in the direction of Hell for the full duration of the play. This must be done in such a way that they do not distract the audience from the main actors.

(I suggest knee and hand guards for these people.)

Enter Extras from back of stage
(dressed in white and black with ropes around their necks crawl by very slowly and at an even pace. beware of backstage noise when moving from the

Hell sign back to the back entrance.)

Enter Rob from back of stage

(A man dressed in black with at least a 100 nooses around his neck, of varying lengths and thickness' of rope, crawls on to the stage and sits in the middle with his legs dangling off the edge of the stage. Rob sits down.)

Enter Grant from back of stage

Grant is dressed in black also with many nooses around his neck. Grant crawls up to Rob.

Grant : "Hello Rob"

Rob : "Hi"

Grant : "How are you today?"

Rob : "I feel fine thanks and you?"

Grant : "Not as great as yesterday, but I'll do thanks"

Rob : "Sorry to hear about that, anything particular the problem?"

Grant : "Not really, just the normal pressures piled a little higher today."

Rob : "Well I hope your day gets better."

Grant : "Me too, well, see you around some time."

Rob : "Sure thing, Cheers."

Exit Grant in direction of Hell.

Enter Susan

(Susan is dressed in white and crawls up to Rob and sits next to him her feet also dangling over the stage.)

Susan : "Hi Rob"

Rob : "Hi Susie"

Susan : "What you up to?"

Rob : "Nothing particular, sitting in the sunshine and catching a few rays. Weather is great today. And you, what are you doing."

Susan : "Much the same. I sure love it when Jesus makes the sun shine, reminds me of how much he loves me."

Rob : "Hey, I didn't know you were a Jesus freak"

Susan : "Wouldn't have it any other way. I remember very clearly what my life was like before I made him my Lord and Master. I tell you this though, I wouldn't give up what he has given me for anything in the world. I don't know how he does it or what he does but I just have a completely different view of life, an extra bounce in my step. Just knowing why I am here on this earth and having someone always with me that I can count on, no matter what happens or how bad it gets."

Rob : "Are you for real Susie. Is there really something in this whole Jesus stuff?"

Susan : "You better believe it Rob. What do you believe in?"

Rob :   "Well... I believe in a God, whoever he or she, heaven forbid, might be. I am not really sure about the details though. I kind of have my own philosophy about all of this stuff. I suppose you think I am going to go to that place called Hell. You know I do a lot of good stuff, surely that must count for something in your God's eyes.

Susan : "Well not really Rob, you see if you have sinned just once in your life you will go to hell when you die...

Rob :   "Hey man that isn't fair Susie, I mean isn't your God supposed to be a God of Love. How could he send almost everyone to Hell. I mean, I do not want anything to do with a God like that! And what about all the other religions, I suppose they too are all going to go to Hell.

Susan : "Well Rob I don't make the rules, but I'll tell you this. It must be impossible for people to save themselves no matter what religions they follow if God saw it necessary to have his own Son killed and Cursed as a sacrifice to buy us back from Hell, where, as you correctly said, we were all going to end up. I figure a God that does that for those who hurt Him regularly is a God of Love, don't you.

Rob :   "I suppose, but why not simply forgive us. I mean, after all there is supposed to be no-one else he has to report to. He can make the rules any way he wants. Why have to kill someone if he sins?

Susan : "Well, actually, before the beginning of time God did make the rules, and one of them was that anyone who disobeys him has to die and be cut off from him forever. That's what Hell is you know. You probably do not realise it but you were given your five senses so that you could see the magnificence of God's handiwork. You take your five senses away and that is being removed from God. You cannot talk or hear yourself. You cannot see anything or feel anything around you. You cannot even feel yourself you know. You can't even smell anything. All you can do is think. Did you know that babies born with less than 3 senses generally lasts less than a day or two. They scream frantically because they cannot be consoled or made to feel safe. You think of all the horror movies you've seen and how real they would become if you were in Hell with that terrible fear of the unknown. No thanks. I have no intention of Going there.

But getting back to the point. God cannot break the rules he has already made. What he does with those who died in the past I do not know. But those who die after Jesus' death, who have accepted Jesus as their Lord and Master, and prove that they Believe in Jesus by what they do and how they act. Jesus pays the death penalty for them. For those who do not however, they have to pay their own death penalty. Think about how hard it must have been for God to watch his Son die such an agonising death. I do not think God will simply pardon those who actually do not even care that Jesus died for them, or those that say they care but do not prove it.

Rob : "You know Susie what you say makes a hell of a lot of sense if you'll excuse the pun. If I wanted to get Jesus to pay my death penalty, what would I have to do. How much must I pay the Church, How often must I pray and read the Bible. I really want to do this. Please wont you tell me.

Susan : "You can't buy God's forgiveness Rob. The same way as being in a garage doesn't make you a car, being in a church doesn't make you a child of God.

Making the sound of a car doesn't make you a car, reading the Bible and praying does not make you a child of God. In fact there is nothing that you can do except surrender all you have, and swap God everything you are, and want to have or be, for everything he has, and everything he wants you to have and be. That is the deal.... You have to give up."

Rob : "That's one hell of a tough request Susie. I suppose I really have to mean it hey."

Susan : "Well He knows if you mean it or not. You can be sure the swap will not take place unless you really do mean it, and live a life from then on doing your best to prove it."

Rob : "So if I really want to do this, how do I tell him."

Susan : "Well there I can help you. I'll be back later, you think about it a bit. Perhaps some of the people in the audience also want to think about it. They will not have to let anyone else around them know but silently within their hearts they can also give up, and swap with Jesus.

Rob : "Well that has given me something to think about. See you later Susie."

Susan : "Sure see you just now. I am just going to get a chocolate from the café, want something?"

Rob : "Huh, No thanks."

Susan exits through the back of the stage.

Rob gets up and moves to the side of the stage.

Curtain Closes and Opens again

A Narrator reads the Bible verses that deal with Nicodemus' visit to Jesus in the night. (John 3 :1-21)

And the story is acted out in mime on the stage.

Curtains Close and Open again and the mime team are now off stage.

Rob moves back to his place in the middle of the stage with his feet once again dangling over the edge of the stage.

Enter Susan from the back of the stage with a chocolate.

Rob :   "Hi That was quick.... I've thought about it and it all makes sense, well sort of. I have a lot of questions though."

Susan : "You ever here of the Holy Spirit Rob?"

Rob :   "Mmm bits and pieces. Why?"

Susan : "Well it's like this. When you become a true believer in Jesus something happens that no one can explain. You begin to receive insight into a world that exists, but to which you were cut off before. Well the Holy Spirit is the one who gives this insight. I could sit and argue issues with you until the cows come home. It will not help you understand anything. Only the Holy Spirit can show you these things and give you the answers to your questions. He does it in his own time mind you, so you had better learn patience. But I will tell you this. Until you have accepted Jesus as Lord and Saviour and passed from the world's side of life to God's side of life, no answers will be made clear to you. You have to accept this first step by faith, and then the Holy Spirit will start to lead you through the rest of your life. Step by step.

Rob : "Are you going to be there if I need help Susie?"

Susan : "Sure I will. you know my number, just call me."

Rob : "Ok... so lets do it.

Susan : "Just pray after me."

Rob : "But I do not know how to pray."

Susan : "Simply picture in your mind what you believe the Father looks like and talk to him."

Rob : "Oh... seems simple enough... Ok I am ready, Those of you out there that want to join me, you do not have to get up, simply pray along with me and Susie. God knows who and what you are and he loves you."

Susan : "Father Almighty,"

Rob : "Father Almighty,"

Susan : "have done so many things that are wrong,"

Rob : "I have done so many things that are wrong,"

Susan : "know now that these things,"

Rob : "I know now that these things,"

Susan : "are going to separate me from you when I die."

Rob : "are going to separate me from you when I die."

Susan : "I have seen this beautiful world you made,"

Rob : "I have seen this beautiful world you made,"

Susan : "and I want to stay with you forever."

Rob : "and I want to stay with you forever."

Susan : "You say in your Bible,"

Rob : "You say in your Bible,"

Susan : "That to be born again as your child,"

Rob : "That to be born again as your child,"

Susan : "All I need to do is truly believe in Jesus,"

Rob : "All I need to do is truly believe in Jesus,"

Susan : "And accept his death as having paid for mine,"

Rob : "And accept his death as having paid for mine,"

Susan : "And then you will cause my spirit to be born,"

Rob : "And then you will cause my spirit to be born,"

Susan : "Into your kingdom,"

Rob : "Into your kingdom,"

Susan : "And I will be made your child."

Rob : "And I will be made your child."

Susan : "I Believe what your Bible says,"

Rob : "I Believe what your Bible says,"

Susan : "And I surrender all I am and all I have,"

Rob : "And I surrender all I am and all I have,"

Susan : "In exchange for eternal life with you."

Rob : "In exchange for eternal life with you."

Susan : "Please forgive me for all the wrong things I have done."

Rob : "Please forgive me for all the wrong things I have done."

Susan : "And make me a brand new person in Jesus."

Rob : "And make me a brand new person in Jesus."

Stage dims to pitch black

Rob takes off his black clothes under which he has white clothes. Susan & Rob are still in the exact same position as when every light went out.

Stage Lights up again

Susan : "Well there you go Rob, you are now a Born again child of God."

Rob :   "But that seems too simple. Isn't there something hard that I have to do to attain this status of being a child of God?"

Susan :   "No Rob. It is easy because God has already done the hard part. Watching Jesus die in your place when you deserved to, and he did not, was very hard.

          But he did that because he loves you. You cannot attain the status of Child of God. It is a free gift given to you because God is gracious and loves you very much."

Rob :   "So what do I need to do now?"

Susan :   "Set aside a special time with God each day to tell him about what you are doing and to ask for guidance. Use this time to learn more about God from His Bible... Oh crikey look at the time, I really must fly. I will see you soon. Cheers."

Rob :   "Thanks a million Susie, Cheers."

Exit Susan in the direction of Hell dragging her ropes behind her.

Narrator: "Well, to all of you who prayed this prayer what you saw that happened to Rob is what has happened to your spirits. Congratulations and welcome to the family of God. Please can you furnish us with your details so that we can stay in touch with you. There is a register at the back of the church as well as literature to help you get started on your walk through life with Jesus."

Ensure a register is available and that the following columns can be filled in: Name, Date of re-birth, Contact Tel,. Postal Address, Name of Christian friend, Contact Tel. of Christian friend, Postal Address of Christian friend.

Suggested literature available should be Daily Prayer Guides, Bibles and Simple Tracts.

Interval

Curtain Opens

The same scene as displayed in Scene One. People dressed in White and Black with Ropes around their necks are still crawling their way to Hell in the background.

Enter Rob

Rob still dressed in white with even more ropes around his neck, once again sits in the middle of the stage with his feet dangling over the edge.

Rob picks up one of the ropes and starts to tug at the rope end tightening the noose around his neck. With a bitter voice:

Rob :   "You know that Susan, that led me to Christ, I think she is avoiding me. I never get to see her any more. I have so many questions. I thought that seeing as she helped me to become a Christian, that she would at least help me get started, and be there when I needed to talk to another Christian."

A moment of silence

Rob picks up another Rope and tugs at this one tightening the noose around his neck. In a bitter voice:

Rob :   "I was retrenched last month you know. Another guy started after I started. He should have been retrenched. Why did I have to lose my job. I am sure that the management were just against me because I no longer go out drinking until all hours of the night. Where will I find the means to support my family for this month."

A moment of silence

Rob picks up another Rope and tugs at this one tightening the noose around his neck. In a bitter voice:

Rob :   "In the supermarket the other day, Some person caused us to wait an extra 20 minutes while she and the supervisor had a massive argument over the actual cost of a security gate she had bought. As a result I was late for an interview. I probably will not get that job. I do not think the Personnel Agent believed my excuse for being late."

A moment of silence

Rob picks up by far the thickest Rope and tugs at this one tightening the noose around his neck. In a bitter voice:

Rob :   "You know it all started to go wrong with my Grade 1 teacher. She victimised me so badly. She destroyed my confidence. You know what she did the one day. She kept us all in during break because we had been running around the class. I needed to go to the toilet and she wouldn't let me. I wet my pants and everyone laughed at me. She laughed too. She was so ugly to me. I hope she has died a horrible painful death."

Enter Thief

Thief is wearing the traditional burglars mask on his face. He too has ropes around his neck and he is dressed in black The thief steals Rob's wallet and moves off a little way.

Rob jumps up and violently acts out his anger (Do not use offensive hand signals)

Rob and the thief both pick up one end of the same rope. (The audience must be able to see that this is the same rope.) As Rob is saying the following they both put the noose around their necks and pull it tight.

Rob :   "That good for nothing thief. He just stole my last hundred Rand. What am I going to do for supper tonight now. I swear if I catch him I am going to pulverise him."

Enter Narrator

Narrator: "Please be aware that although you have so far only seen people with ropes around their necks that in fact the other ends are nooses around the necks of someone else. Unforgiveness is the rope and it binds both the unforgiving as well as the unforgiven. This is the reason that God says in His Bible in Matthew Chapter 5 verses 23 & 24 that if you are presenting a gift to God at the alter and you remember that someone else has something against you, that you should leave your gift there, go and make right with that person and then return and offer your gift to God. Remember Unforgiveness binds both sides."

Enter Jackie

For the first time someone comes on stage wearing no ropes. For the first time someone is not crawling on the stage. Jackie is dressed in Black with no ropes around her neck. Jackie comes and sits next to Rob.

Jackie : "Hi Rob."

Rob :   "Hi Jackie. What are you up to this weekend?"

Jackie : "Why, what you got in mind?"

Rob : "You know our church is having a special speaker from the States to discuss the end of the world. Would you like to come."

Jackie : "Hey Rob, you know me, I don't believe in all this Jesus stuff. I believe in a different religion. Ill tell you something though. I feel so free since I have been with them. It's like a weight that was lifted off my shoulders. They are a wonderful group of people. So caring, so kind, always ready to lend a helping hand to anyone in need. I really have found freedom there. Why don't you rather come to my church this weekend?"

Rob : "You really have got me thinking Jackie. Unfortunately I have a few responsibilities at our church this weekend. I will not be able to do it this weekend. But maybe next weekend I'll join you. I can see that you are a really relaxed person. There must be something in it. I'll chat to you next week."

Jackie : "Okay then see you around Rob. Chin up Rob, it could always be worse."

Rob : "I suppose that's true. Well take care then. Bye."

Jackie : "Bye"

Jackie gets up and skips off in the direction of Hell.

Exit Jackie

Rob : "You know that girl is such an amazing person. I am really having a problem with this being a Christian thing. I see people that are not Christians more happy than the

Christians I see. (Looking Up, Hands Clasped in prayer and praying in desperation.) God I do not understand, If I have been set free, why do I not feel great and bubbly all the time. Just look at Jackie. She seems to have no worries at all. Please God tell me what I am doing wrong. I know that you love me. There must be more to being a Christian than the life I am leading now."

All the lights go off for a few seconds and come back on to indicate a time lapse.

Enter Frank

Frank is dressed in white and has no ropes around his neck. He skips in from the back entrance. He is smiling and is full of joy. Frank comes and sits next to Rob.

Frank : "Howzit Rob?"

Rob : "Could be better Frank."

Frank : "Why's that?"

Rob : "Oh well, I am just having a real rough time at the moment.

Frank : "Sounds to me like you need to find Jesus."

Rob : "What do you mean?"

Frank : "Well no matter what happens in my life Jesus just gives me a continuous bounce. Nothing gets to me any more."

Rob :　"Well Frank I've found Jesus, but there is no way I feel like you look everyday. One day I am up, the next I am down. I just seem to be being dragged down by so many situations and people. You know some good for nothing thief stole my wallet the other day. What is this world coming to Frank. Is everyone out there just a nut out to smash and grab, hit and run, destroy and kill. I think I am going to immigrate to Australia. It's much better there."

Frank :　"Well Rob, I don't know about Australia being safer or not but I will tell you this. I've been where you are now. I found the secret to the most brilliant life in Jesus. You know that story of the unforgiving servant."

Everything goes to black

Frank and Rob move to the side of the stage to join the audience in watching the parable of the unforgiving servant done in mime while the Narrator reads (Matthew 18: 21-35)

Everything goes to black again and Rob and Frank take up their original positions on the stage.

Stage is lit up again

Frank :　"Well that servant was forgiven completely. But he refused to forgive his fellow servant. So his forgiveness was taken away again. If you are harbouring any unforgiveness in your heart Rob, the forgiveness you were given by God when you accepted Jesus will be taken away from you when you die and you will still go to Hell."

Rob : "Are you telling me that I could still go to Hell after accepting Jesus as my Lord and Saviour?"

Frank : "No Rob, Jesus is telling you that unless you actually put into practice the things he has told us to do we are not actually His followers. If we are not His followers then we will go to Hell. Becoming a Christian is not a one time incident. It is an ongoing lifestyle. Jesus says a number of times Forgive others if you want the Father to forgive you. In fact when you pray the Lords Prayer. You are specifically asking God not to forgive you if you have not forgiven others.

Rob (Indignantly) "But Frank I do not hold any grudges against anyone. I forgive those who hurt me.

Frank : "Well Rob the Holy Spirit knows your heart. He also knows each and everything that you are holding against someone. I'll tell you what I did. I asked the Holy Spirit to show me each and every person and situation that I needed to forgive someone. It was not easy I might add. But Once I had forgiven everyone I was truly free."

Rob : "But Frank, I have forgiven everyone. I know. I pray every night and forgive everyone anything they have done to me."

Frank : "O..K.. Rob, are you recalling the situation and the person to mind, or are you simply doing a one prayer fits all type of I forgive everyone."

Rob : "Yes the general prayer, why is there something wrong with that?

Frank : "No, but what often happens, is that we simply say the words, and do not actually deal with the forgiving.

Rob : "So what should I do then?"

Frank : "Well lets ask the Holy Spirit to show you who you need to forgive and what for. Let him deal with each one, one at a time. Once you have been through all of these people then make sure that you forgive the moment you get angry...Oh another thing, get in touch with as many of those that you can, and tell them that you forgive them for what they did. You might find that they have forgotten what they did to you. Don't get angry with them all over again. In this way you will release them too."

The audience is invited to on an individual basis join in the prayer to have their hearts opened so that they can forgive those who have wronged them.

There should be a moment of silence to let people decide if they want to do this.

Frank : "Rob Repeat this prayer after me and the Holy Spirit will help you do the rest."

2 second pause

Frank : "Holy Spirit, you know my heart."

Rob : "Holy Spirit, you know my heart."

Frank : "You know what I have buried deep within me."

Rob : "You know what I have buried deep within me."

Frank : "If there is anyone whom I need to forgive,"

Rob : "If there is anyone whom I need to forgive,"

Frank : "Show me who it is,"

Rob : "Show me who it is,"

Frank : "and show me what they did to me, or those I love."

Rob : "and show me what they did to me, or those I love."

Frank : "Holy Spirit, please give me the strength,"

Rob : "Holy Spirit, please give me the strength,"

Frank : "to forgive them from my heart,"

Rob : "to forgive them from my heart,"

Frank : "and help me to tell them that I forgive them."

Rob : "and help me to tell them that I forgive them."

Frank : "Then Holy Spirit, help me to forget that they ever did it at all."

Rob : "Then Holy Spirit, help me to forget that they ever did it at all."

The stage is lit up as fully as possible. (a clear contrast from the whole of the performance so far.) Coloured light beams interweave and finally settle on Rob.

Rob picks up one of the ropes and loosens the noose and takes it off

Rob :   "Susan led me to Christ and is avoiding me now. Susan I forgive you from the bottom of my heart and I hold nothing against you. In the Name of Jesus Christ whose blood has set me free. Amen."

There is a moment of silence

Rob picks up another Rope and loosens the noose and takes it off

Rob :   "I was angry with the managers of my company for retrenching me. I also was angry with the guy who started after me who was not retrenched. I forgive them all from the bottom of my heart and I hold nothing against them. In the Name of Jesus Christ whose blood has set me free. Amen."

There is a moment of silence

Rob picks up another Rope and loosens the noose and takes it off.

Rob :   "That person in the Supermarket that made me late for my interview I forgive you from the bottom of my heart and I hold nothing against you. In the Name of Jesus Christ whose blood has set me free. Amen."

Everything goes to black while Rob takes off all the ropes except the thickest one.

The bright lights come back on and focus on Rob again.

Rob picks up the thickest and last Rope and starts to loosen it. He stops and tugs it tight again. In a bitter voice:

Rob : "God I cannot forgive this teacher. She was evil. She does not deserve to be forgiven. No ways. I just cannot do it. She victimised me so badly. She destroyed my confidence. You know what she did the one day. She kept us all in during break because we had been running around the class. I needed to go to the toilet and she would not let me. I wet my pants and everyone laughed at me. She laughed too. She was so ugly to me. No I cannot do it. I cannot forgive her."

There is a moment of silence

Then over a PA system set very loudly, there is the sound of a whispering voice saying.

God : "Do you deserve to be forgiven by me? Is there anything you can say or do that could earn you my forgiveness."

There is a moment of silence

Rob : "I have accepted Jesus as my Lord and Saviour"

God : "Yes you have. But you never earned it Jesus earned it and gave it to you subject to certain conditions. You need to Love me with all your heart, mind and soul. To Love Me naturally means that you must Love My son Jesus and My Holy Spirit too. Furthermore, You must love your neighbour as yourself.

Both you and that teacher are my creations and I demand that you love her. If you Love her as my creation, however badly satan has warped her, You will forgive her."

There is a moment of silence

Rob :   "I do not understand much about you Almighty God, But I do know that you have created all things and that satan is warping your whole creation to the best of his ability. In the light of this I forgive that Teacher in the Name of Jesus Christ whose blood has set me free, and I pray that you release her from satan's grasp Amen."

Rob removes the last noose from his neck and starts walking off towards Heaven.

God :   "Where are you going".

(People dressed in white and black with ropes around their necks are still crawling around on the floor in the direction of Hell.)

Rob : "Well, to Heaven of course."

God :   "Look around you. What about the rest of my creation. Do you Love yourself enough to forgive others, and do you love God's creation enough to help your neighbour out of the pit you once found yourself in. Start by telling all those you have forgiven that you have forgiven them."

There is a moment of silence.

Rob goes over to the Thief

Rob : "You stole my wallet a while back. I have forgiven you for that. Even if you reject my forgiveness, you stand forgiven by me. What is between you and God is between you and God. May God heal you my friend."

The thief tugs in vain at the noose to try to loosen it.

There is a moment of silence.

Thief : "I am sorry that I stole your wallet."

The thief removes the noose with ease.

Rob picks up one of those dressed in black with ropes around his neck and leads him to the front of the stage where they both sit down with their legs dangling over the edge of the stage.

Rob : "My friend have you heard how much God Almighty loves you?" Go to black

Close the curtains.

Enter Narrator

Narrator: "May God Almighty be your guide through this process. He knows where you are now. He can guide you home. This is the narrow road that leads to Heaven. You need to accept the forgiveness God Almighty offers because his justice has been satisfied by the blood of His own Son. You need to forgive others form your heart, or your forgiveness will be withdrawn when you die. This is the narrow road ---- Follow it."

Author & Script Writer – Rick Evans (Author of this book)

Scriptures Quoted

All biblical quotes in red text are God's own words, pay very special attention to each word!!

Scriptures quoted are copied and pasted as-is from the KJV (Old King James Version) using the e-sword program, with permission from Rick Meyers.

Ref 1 Corinthians 02:10

The Holy Spirit searches the innermost parts of you

1Co 2:10 But God hath revealed *them* unto us by his Spirit: for the Spirit searcheth all things, yea, the deep things of God.

Ref 1 Corinthians 05:1-13

ALL THE MEMBERS OF THE CHURCH had to treat him/her as one who does not know Christ.

1Co 5:1 It is reported commonly *that there is* fornication among you, and such fornication as is not so much as named among the Gentiles, that one should have his father's wife.

1Co 5:2 And ye are puffed up, and have not rather mourned, that he that hath done this deed might be taken away from among you.

1Co 5:3 For I verily, as absent in body, but present in spirit, have judged already, as though I were present, *concerning* him that hath so done this deed,

1Co 5:4 In the name of our Lord Jesus Christ, when ye are gathered together, and my spirit, with the power of our Lord Jesus Christ,

1Co 5:5 To deliver such an one unto Satan for the destruction of the flesh, that the spirit may be saved in the day of the Lord Jesus.

1Co 5:6 Your glorying *is* not good. Know ye not that a little leaven leaveneth the whole lump?

1Co 5:7 Purge out therefore the old leaven, that ye may be a new lump, as ye are unleavened. For even Christ our passover is sacrificed for us:

1Co 5:8 Therefore let us keep the feast, not with old leaven, neither with the leaven of malice and wickedness; but with the unleavened *bread* of sincerity and truth.

1Co 5:9 I wrote unto you in an epistle not to company with fornicators:

1Co 5:10 Yet not altogether with the fornicators of this world, or with the covetous, or extortioners, or with idolaters; for then must ye needs go out of the world.

1Co 5:11 But now I have written unto you not to keep company, if any man that is called a brother be a fornicator, or covetous, or an idolater, or a railer, or a drunkard, or an extortioner; with such an one no not to eat.

1Co 5:12 For what have I to do to judge them also that are without? do not ye judge them that are within?

1Co 5:13 But them that are without God judgeth. Therefore put away from among yourselves that wicked person.

Ref 1 Corinthians 06:1-10

The Church members appointed judges to rule on issues.

1Co 6:1 Dare any of you, having a matter against another, go to law before the unjust, and not before the saints?

1Co 6:2 Do ye not know that the saints shall judge the world? and if the world shall be judged by you, are ye unworthy to judge the smallest matters?

1Co 6:3 Know ye not that we shall judge angels? how much more things that pertain to this life?

1Co 6:4 If then ye have judgments of things pertaining to this life, set them to judge who are least esteemed in the church.

1Co 6:5 I speak to your shame. Is it so, that there is not a wise man among you? no, not one that shall be able to judge between his brethren?

1Co 6:6 But brother goeth to law with brother, and that before the unbelievers.

1Co 6:7 Now therefore there is utterly a fault among you, because ye go to law one with another. Why do ye not rather take wrong? why do ye not rather *suffer yourselves to* be defrauded?

1Co 6:8 Nay, ye do wrong, and defraud, and that *your* brethren.

1Co 6:9 Know ye not that the unrighteous shall not inherit the kingdom of God? Be not deceived: neither fornicators, nor idolaters, nor adulterers, nor effeminate, nor abusers of themselves with mankind,

1Co 6:10 Nor thieves, nor covetous, nor drunkards, nor revilers, nor extortioners, shall inherit the kingdom of God.

1Co 6:11 And such were some of you: but ye are washed, but ye are sanctified, but ye are justified in the name of the Lord Jesus, and by the Spirit of our God.

Ref 1 Corinthians 06:12-20

Does your Church Condone or treat as normal, accept or tolerate, Same Sex Marriages, or Sex before Marriage, or Divorce?

1Co 6:12 All things are lawful unto me, but all things are not expedient: all things are lawful for me, but I will not be brought under the power of any.

1Co 6:13 Meats for the belly, and the belly for meats: but God shall destroy both it and them. Now the body *is* not for fornication, but for the Lord; and the Lord for the body.

1Co 6:14 And God hath both raised up the Lord, and will also raise up us by his own power.

1Co 6:15 Know ye not that your bodies are the members of Christ? shall I then take the members of Christ, and make *them* the members of an harlot? God forbid.

1Co 6:16 What? know ye not that he which is joined to an harlot is one body? for two, saith he, shall be one flesh.

1Co 6:17 But he that is joined unto the Lord is one spirit.

1Co 6:18 Flee fornication. Every sin that a man doeth is without the body; but he that committeth fornication sinneth against his own body.

1Co 6:19 What? know ye not that your body is the temple of the Holy Ghost *which is* in you, which ye have of God, and ye are not your own?

1Co 6:20 For ye are bought with a price: therefore glorify God in your body, and in your spirit, which are God's.

Ref 1 Corinthians 07:2-5

God's design for a family is a Man and a Woman joined in Holy Matrimony that God joins together in some unknown and supernatural way.

Does your Church Condone or treat as normal, accept or tolerate, Same Sex Marriages, or Sex before Marriage, or Divorce?

1Co 7:2 Nevertheless, *to avoid* fornication, let every man have his own wife, and let every woman have her own husband.

1Co 7:3 Let the husband render unto the wife due benevolence: and likewise also the wife unto the husband.

1Co 7:4 The wife hath not power of her own body, but the husband: and likewise also the husband hath not power of his own body, but the wife.

1Co 7:5 Defraud ye not one the other, except *it be* with consent for a time, that ye may give yourselves to fasting and prayer; and come together again, that Satan tempt you not for your incontinency.

Ref 1 Corinthians 10:13

He will never let you suffer more than you can endure

Your Father will not allow you to be destroyed, but will provide a way out

1Co 10:13 There hath no temptation taken you but such as is common to man: but God *is* faithful, who will not suffer you to be tempted above that ye are able; but will with the temptation also make a way to escape, that ye may be able to bear *it.*

Ref 1 Corinthians 12:1-31 & 13:1-13

to guide, teach and comfort Jesus' Body, of which you are a member

1Co 12:1 Now concerning spiritual *gifts,* brethren, I would not have you ignorant.

1Co 12:2 Ye know that ye were Gentiles, carried away unto these dumb idols, even as ye were led.

1Co 12:3 Wherefore I give you to understand, that no man speaking by the Spirit of God calleth Jesus accursed: and *that* no man can say that Jesus is the Lord, but by the Holy Ghost.

1Co 12:4 Now there are diversities of gifts, but the same Spirit.

1Co 12:5 And there are differences of administrations, but the same Lord.

1Co 12:6 And there are diversities of operations, but it is the same God which worketh all in all.

1Co 12:7 But the manifestation of the Spirit is given to every man to profit withal.

1Co 12:8 For to one is given by the Spirit the word of wisdom; to another the word of knowledge by the same Spirit;

1Co 12:9 To another faith by the same Spirit; to another the gifts of healing by the same Spirit;

1Co 12:10 To another the working of miracles; to another prophecy; to another discerning of spirits; to another *divers* kinds of tongues; to another the interpretation of tongues:

1Co 12:11 But all these worketh that one and the selfsame Spirit, dividing to every man severally as he will.

1Co 12:12 For as the body is one, and hath many members, and all the members of that one body, being many, are one body: so also *is* Christ.

1Co 12:13 For by one Spirit are we all baptized into one body, whether *we be* Jews or Gentiles, whether *we be* bond or free; and have been all made to drink into one Spirit.

1Co 12:14 For the body is not one member, but many.

1Co 12:15 If the foot shall say, Because I am not the hand, I am not of the body; is it therefore not of the body?

1Co 12:16 And if the ear shall say, Because I am not the eye, I am not of the body; is it therefore not of the body?

1Co 12:17 If the whole body *were* an eye, where *were* the hearing? If the whole *were* hearing, where *were* the smelling?

1Co 12:18 But now hath God set the members every one of them in the body, as it hath pleased him.

1Co 12:19 And if they were all one member, where *were* the body?

1Co 12:20 But now *are they* many members, yet but one body.

1Co 12:21 And the eye cannot say unto the hand, I have no need of thee: nor again the head to the feet, I have no need of you.

1Co 12:22 Nay, much more those members of the body, which seem to be more feeble, are necessary:

1Co 12:23 And those *members* of the body, which we think to be less honourable, upon these we bestow more abundant honour; and our uncomely *parts* have more abundant comeliness.

1Co 12:24 For our comely *parts* have no need: but God hath tempered the body together, having given more abundant honour to that *part* which lacked:

1Co 12:25 That there should be no schism in the body; but *that* the members should have the same care one for another.

1Co 12:26 And whether one member suffer, all the members suffer with it; or one member be honoured, all the members rejoice with it.

1Co 12:27 Now ye are the body of Christ, and members in particular.

1Co 12:28 And God hath set some in the church, first apostles, secondarily prophets, thirdly teachers, after that miracles, then gifts of healings, helps, governments, diversities of tongues.

1Co 12:29 *Are* all apostles? *are* all prophets? *are* all teachers? *are* all workers of miracles?

1Co 12:30 Have all the gifts of healing? do all speak with tongues? do all interpret?

1Co 12:31 But covet earnestly the best gifts: and yet shew I unto you a more excellent way.

1Co 13:1 Though I speak with the tongues of men and of angels, and have not charity, I am become *as* sounding brass, or a tinkling cymbal.

1Co 13:2 And though I have *the gift of* prophecy, and understand all mysteries, and all knowledge; and though I have all faith, so that I could remove mountains, and have not charity, I am nothing.

1Co 13:3 And though I bestow all my goods to feed *the poor,* and though I give my body to be burned, and have not charity, it profiteth me nothing.

1Co 13:4 Charity suffereth long, *and* is kind; charity envieth not; charity vaunteth not itself, is not puffed up,

1Co 13:5 Doth not behave itself unseemly, seeketh not her own, is not easily provoked, thinketh no evil;

1Co 13:6 Rejoiceth not in iniquity, but rejoiceth in the truth;

1Co 13:7 Beareth all things, believeth all things, hopeth all things, endureth all things.

1Co 13:8 Charity never faileth: but whether *there be* prophecies, they shall fail; whether *there be* tongues, they shall cease; whether *there be* knowledge, it shall vanish away.

1Co 13:9 For we know in part, and we prophesy in part.

1Co 13:10 But when that which is perfect is come, then that which is in part shall be done away.

1Co 13:11 When I was a child, I spake as a child, I understood as a child, I thought as a child:

but when I became a man, I put away childish things.

1Co 13:12 For now we see through a glass, darkly; but then face to face: now I know in part; but then shall I know even as also I am known.

1Co 13:13 And now abideth faith, hope, charity, these three; but the greatest of these *is* charity.

Ref 1 Corinthians 14:26-33

None of these people or functions had any authority over anyone else including the members of the church.

Does The Holy Spirit have the freedom to use whomever he wishes during the service to bless and teach the Church Members?

1Co 14:26 How is it then, brethren? when ye come together, every one of you hath a psalm, hath a doctrine, hath a tongue, hath a revelation, hath an interpretation. Let all things be done unto edifying.

1Co 14:27 If any man speak in an *unknown* tongue, *let it be* by two, or at the most *by* three, and *that* by course; and let one interpret.

1Co 14:28 But if there be no interpreter, let him keep silence in the church; and let him speak to himself, and to God.

1Co 14:29 Let the prophets speak two or three, and let the other judge.

1Co 14:30 If *any thing* be revealed to another that sitteth by, let the first hold his peace.

1Co 14:31 For ye may all prophesy one by one, that all may learn, and all may be comforted.

1Co 14:32 And the spirits of the prophets are subject to the prophets.

1Co 14:33 For God is not *the author* of confusion, but of peace, as in all churches of the saints.

Ref 1 John 02:27

The Holy Spirit is ordained to be the teacher and guide to each one of God's Children

1Jn 2:27 But the anointing which ye have received of him abideth in you, and ye need not that any man teach you: but as the same anointing teacheth you of all things, and is truth, and is no lie, and even as it hath taught you, ye shall abide in him.

Ref 1 John 03 : 23

First Jesus is our Lord, and then we love one another

1Jn 3:23 And this is his commandment, That we should believe on the name of his Son Jesus Christ, and love one another, as he gave us commandment.

Ref 1 John 04:02

he or she is your brother or sister

1Jn 4:2 Hereby know ye the Spirit of God: Every spirit that confesseth that Jesus Christ is come in the flesh is of God:

Ref 1 Timothy 03:1-7

The Church members appointed leaders in the church.

1Ti 3:1 This *is* a true saying, If a man desire the office of a bishop, he desireth a good work.

1Ti 3:2 A bishop then must be blameless, the husband of one wife, vigilant, sober, of good behaviour, given to hospitality, apt to teach;

1Ti 3:3 Not given to wine, no striker, not greedy of filthy lucre; but patient, not a brawler, not covetous;

1Ti 3:4 One that ruleth well his own house, having his children in subjection with all gravity;

1Ti 3:5 (For if a man know not how to rule his own house, how shall he take care of the church of God?)

1Ti 3:6 Not a novice, lest being lifted up with pride he fall into the condemnation of the devil.

1Ti 3:7 Moreover he must have a good report of them which are without; lest he fall into reproach and the snare of the devil.

Ref 1 Timothy 05:20

ALL THE MEMBERS OF THE CHURCH had to treat him/her as one who does not know Christ.

1Ti 5:20 Them that sin rebuke before all, that others also may fear.

Ref 2 John 01:9-11

Do not take this lightly. You no longer have any excuse

2Jn 1:9 Whosoever transgresseth, and abideth not in the doctrine of Christ, hath not God. He that abideth in the doctrine of Christ, he hath both the Father and the Son.

2Jn 1:10 If there come any unto you, and bring not this doctrine, receive him not into *your* house, neither bid him God speed:

2Jn 1:11 For he that biddeth him God speed is partaker of his evil deeds.

Ref 2 Peter 03:09

God does not want any of us to be lost
He is not willing that any should perish

2Pe 3:9 The Lord is not slack concerning his promise, as some men count slackness; but is longsuffering to us-ward, not willing that any should perish, but that all should come to repentance.

Ref 2 Timothy 03:1-5

If your church has accepted society's standards
then get out of there.

2Ti 3:1 This know also, that in the last days
perilous times shall come.

2Ti 3:2 For men shall be lovers of their own selves,
covetous, boasters, proud, blasphemers,
disobedient to parents, unthankful, unholy,

2Ti 3:3 Without natural affection, trucebreakers,
false accusers, incontinent, fierce, despisers of
those that are good,

2Ti 3:4 Traitors, heady, highminded, lovers of
pleasures more than lovers of God;

2Ti 3:5 Having a form of godliness, but denying
the power thereof: from such turn away.

Ref Acts 01:8

the gift of The Holy Spirit that would give them
power

Act 1:8 But ye shall receive power, after that the
Holy Ghost is come upon you: and ye shall
be witnesses unto me both in Jerusalem, and
in all Judaea, and in Samaria, and unto the
uttermost part of the earth.

Ref Acts 01:16-26

Act 1:16 Men *and* brethren, this scripture must
needs have been fulfilled, which the Holy Ghost
by the mouth of David spake before concerning
Judas, which was guide to them that took
Jesus.

Act 1:17 For he was numbered with us, and had
obtained part of this ministry.

Act 1:18 Now this man purchased a field with the
reward of iniquity; and falling headlong, he
burst asunder in the midst, and all his bowels
gushed out.

Act 1:19 And it was known unto all the dwellers at Jerusalem; insomuch as that field is called in their proper tongue, Aceldama, that is to say, The field of blood.

Act 1:20 For it is written in the book of Psalms, Let his habitation be desolate, and let no man dwell therein: and his bishoprick let another take.

Act 1:21 Wherefore of these men which have companied with us all the time that the Lord Jesus went in and out among us,

Act 1:22 Beginning from the baptism of John, unto that same day that he was taken up from us, must one be ordained to be a witness with us of his resurrection.

Act 1:23 And they appointed two, Joseph called Barsabas, who was surnamed Justus, and Matthias.

Act 1:24 And they prayed, and said, Thou, Lord, which knowest the hearts of all *men,* shew whether of these two thou hast chosen,

Act 1:25 That he may take part of this ministry and apostleship, from which Judas by transgression fell, that he might go to his own place.

Act 1:26 And they gave forth their lots; and the lot fell upon Matthias; and he was numbered with the eleven apostles.

Ref Acts 02:1-4

The Holy Spirit did not anoint the disciple Peter and tell the rest of the Believers to submit to Peter's authority. No! - Again Each and every single one of these Believers was anointed.

Act 2:1 And when the day of Pentecost was fully come, they were all with one accord in one place.

Act 2:2 And suddenly there came a sound from heaven as of a rushing mighty wind, and it filled all the house where they were sitting.

Act 2:3 And there appeared unto them cloven tongues like as of fire, and it sat upon each of them.

Act 2:4 And they were all filled with the Holy Ghost, and began to speak with other tongues, as the Spirit gave them utterance.

Ref Acts 02:44-47

meet one another's needs without actually running out themselves.

Act 2:44 And all that believed were together, and had all things common;

Act 2:45 And sold their possessions and goods, and parted them to all *men,* as every man had need.

Act 2:46 And they, continuing daily with one accord in the temple, and breaking bread from house to house, did eat their meat with gladness and singleness of heart,

Act 2:47 Praising God, and having favour with all the people. And the Lord added to the church daily such as should be saved.

Ref Acts 04:32 – 35

Jesus Himself repeated God's law

Act 4:32 **And the multitude of them that believed were of one heart and of one soul: neither said any *of them* that ought of the things which he possessed was his own; but they had all things common.**

Act 4:33 And with great power gave the apostles witness of the resurrection of the Lord Jesus: and great grace was upon them all.

Act 4:34 Neither was there any among them that lacked: for as many as were possessors of lands or houses sold them, and brought the prices of the things that were sold,

Act 4:35 And laid *them* down at the apostles' feet: and distribution was made unto every man according as he had need.

Ref Acts 04: 34 & 35

meet one another's needs without actually running out themselves.

Act 4:34 Neither was there any among them that lacked: for as many as were possessors of lands or houses sold them, and brought the prices of the things that were sold,

Act 4:35 And laid *them* down at the apostles' feet: and distribution was made unto every man according as he had need.

Ref Acts 06:1-4

The Apostles appointed helpers in the church.

Act 6:1 And in those days, when the number of the disciples was multiplied, there arose a murmuring of the Grecians against the Hebrews, because their widows were neglected in the daily ministration.

Act 6:2 Then the twelve called the multitude of the disciples *unto them,* and said, It is not reason that we should leave the word of God, and serve tables.

Act 6:3 Wherefore, brethren, look ye out among you seven men of honest report, full of the Holy Ghost and wisdom, whom we may appoint over this business.

Act 6:4 But we will give ourselves continually to prayer, and to the ministry of the word.

Ref Acts 19:19

Burn them as Christians did the books that referred to magic, the occult, witchcraft, the esoteric, which includes all we would refer to now as New Age religious works. Burn them.

Clear out your home and house of all that detracts from God, or is of another religion, or is of magic, or things which are not true or are misguiding.

Act 19:13 Some Jews who traveled around and drove out evil spirits also tried to use the name of the Lord Jesus to do this. They said to the evil spirits, "I command you in the name of Jesus, whom Paul preaches."

Act 19:14 Seven brothers, who were the sons of a Jewish High Priest named Sceva, were doing this.

Act 19:15 But the evil spirit said to them, "I know Jesus, and I know about Paul; but you---who are you?"

Act 19:16 The man who had the evil spirit in him attacked them with such violence that he overpowered them all. They ran away from his house, wounded and with their clothes torn off.

Act 19:17 All the Jews and Gentiles who lived in Ephesus heard about this; they were all filled with fear, and the name of the Lord Jesus was given greater honor.

Act 19:18 Many of the believers came, publicly admitting and revealing what they had done.

Act 19:19 Many of those who had practiced magic brought their books together and burned them in public. They added up the price of the books, and the total came to fifty thousand silver coins.

Act 19:20 In this powerful way the word of the Lord kept spreading and growing stronger.

Ref Colossians 2:19
God has chosen to send the Holy Spirit as His representative

There is only one captain, Jesus Christ
Col 2:19 And not holding the Head, from which all the body by joints and bands having nourishment ministered, and knit together, increaseth with the increase of God.

Ref Colossians 03:18-21

God's design for a family is a Man and a Woman joined in Holy Matrimony that God joins together in some unknown and supernatural way.

Col 3:18 Wives, submit yourselves unto your own husbands, as it is fit in the Lord.

Col 3:19 Husbands, love *your* wives, and be not bitter against them.

Col 3:20 Children, obey *your* parents in all things: for this is well pleasing unto the Lord.

Col 3:21 Fathers, provoke not your children *to anger,* lest they be discouraged.

Ref Daniel 04:33

Those who think they are high and mighty in the church or are really important in the governing body are hereby warned that their days are numbered.

Dan 4:33 The same hour was the thing fulfilled upon Nebuchadnezzar: and he was driven from men, and did eat grass as oxen, and his body was wet with the dew of heaven, till his hairs were grown like eagles' *feathers,* and his nails like birds' *claws.*

Ref Deuteronomy 05:6-21

However to get to understand how to apply these commandments, let us look at The Ten Commandments.

Deu 5:1 And Moses called all Israel, and said unto them, Hear, O Israel, the statutes and judgments which I speak in your ears this day, that ye may learn them, and keep, and do them.

Deu 5:2 The LORD our God made a covenant with us in Horeb.

Deu 5:3 The LORD made not this covenant with our fathers, but with us, *even* us, who *are* all of us here alive this day.

Deu 5:4 The LORD talked with you face to face in the mount out of the midst of the fire,

Deu 5:5 (I stood between the LORD and you at that time, to shew you the word of the LORD: for ye were afraid by reason of the fire, and went not up into the mount;) saying,

Deu 5:6 I *am* the LORD thy God, which brought thee out of the land of Egypt, from the house of bondage.

Deu 5:7 Thou shalt have none other gods before me.

Deu 5:8 Thou shalt not make thee *any* graven image, *or* any likeness *of any thing* that *is* in heaven above, or that *is* in the earth beneath, or that *is* in the waters beneath the earth:

Deu 5:9 Thou shalt not bow down thyself unto them, nor serve them: for I the LORD thy God *am* a jealous God, visiting the iniquity of the fathers upon the children unto the third and fourth *generation* of them that hate me,

Deu 5:10 And shewing mercy unto thousands of them that love me and keep my commandments.

Deu 5:11 Thou shalt not take the name of the LORD thy God in vain: for the LORD will not hold *him* guiltless that taketh his name in vain.

Deu 5:12 Keep the sabbath day to sanctify it, as the LORD thy God hath commanded thee.

Deu 5:13 Six days thou shalt labour, and do all thy work:

Deu 5:14 But the seventh day *is* the sabbath of the LORD thy God: *in it* thou shalt not do any work, thou, nor thy son, nor thy daughter, nor thy manservant, nor thy maidservant, nor thine ox, nor thine ass, nor any of thy cattle, nor thy stranger that *is* within thy gates; that thy manservant and thy maidservant may rest as well as thou.

Deu 5:15 And remember that thou wast a servant in the land of Egypt, and *that* the LORD thy God brought thee out thence through a mighty hand and by a stretched out arm: therefore the LORD thy God commanded thee to keep the sabbath day.

Deu 5:16 Honour thy father and thy mother, as the LORD thy God hath commanded thee; that thy days may be prolonged, and that it may go well with thee, in the land which the LORD thy God giveth thee.

Deu 5:17 Thou shalt not kill.

Deu 5:18 Neither shalt thou commit adultery.

Deu 5:19 Neither shalt thou steal.

Deu 5:20 Neither shalt thou bear false witness against thy neighbour.

Deu 5:21 Neither shalt thou desire thy neighbour's wife, neither shalt thou covet thy neighbour's house, his field, or his manservant, or his maidservant, his ox, or his ass, or any *thing* that *is* thy neighbour's.

Deu 5:22 These words the LORD spake unto all your assembly in the mount out of the midst of the fire, of the cloud, and of the thick darkness, with a great voice: and he added no more. And he wrote them in two tables of stone, and delivered them unto me.

Deu 5:23 And it came to pass, when ye heard the voice out of the midst of the darkness, (for the mountain did burn with fire,) that ye came near

unto me, *even* all the heads of your tribes, and
your elders;
Deu 5:24 And ye said, Behold, the LORD our God
hath shewed us his glory and his greatness,
and we have heard his voice out of the midst of
the fire: we have seen this day that God doth
talk with man, and he liveth.

Ref Deuteronomy 10:16 & 17

There is no special treatment for anyone
Deu 10:16 Circumcise therefore the foreskin of
your heart, and be no more stiffnecked.
Deu 10:17 For the LORD your God is God of gods,
and Lord of lords, a great God, a mighty, and
a terrible, which regardeth not persons, nor
taketh reward:

Ref Deuteronomy 31:06, 08

He will never leave you nor forsake you.
Deu 31:6 Be strong and of a good courage, fear
not, nor be afraid of them: for the LORD thy
God, he *it is* that doth go with thee; he will not
fail thee, nor forsake thee.
Deu 31:8 And the LORD, he *it is* that doth go
before thee; he will be with thee, he will not fail
thee, neither forsake thee: fear not, neither be
dismayed.

Ref Ephesians 01:17

the Holy Spirit, who will lead you into all Wisdom
and all Knowledge
Eph 1:17 That the God of our Lord Jesus Christ,
the Father of glory, may give unto you the spirit
of wisdom and revelation in the knowledge
of him:

Ref Ephesians 05:23

This Is True. But Jesus is still in Charge of the Church who is His Bride

Eph 5:23 For the husband is the head of the wife, even as Christ is the head of the church: and he is the saviour of the body.

Ref Ephesians 05: 21-27

We are the Bride of Christ, Jesus is the Bride Groom

Eph 5:21 Submitting yourselves one to another in the fear of God.

Eph 5:22 Wives, submit yourselves unto your own husbands, as unto the Lord.

Eph 5:23 For the husband is the head of the wife, even as Christ is the head of the church: and he is the saviour of the body.

Eph 5:24 Therefore as the church is subject unto Christ, so *let* the wives *be* to their own husbands in every thing.

Eph 5:25 Husbands, love your wives, even as Christ also loved the church, and gave himself for it;

Eph 5:26 That he might sanctify and cleanse it with the washing of water by the word,

Eph 5:27 That he might present it to himself a glorious church, not having spot, or wrinkle, or any such thing; but that it should be holy and without blemish.

Ref Ephesians 06:10 – 18

So put on the armour of God

Eph 6:10 Finally, my brethren, be strong in the Lord, and in the power of his might.

Eph 6:11 Put on the whole armour of God, that ye may be able to stand against the wiles of the devil.

Eph 6:12 For we wrestle not against flesh and blood, but against principalities, against powers, against the rulers of the darkness of this world, against spiritual wickedness in high *places.*

Eph 6:13 Wherefore take unto you the whole armour of God, that ye may be able to withstand in the evil day, and having done all, to stand.

Eph 6:14 Stand therefore, having your loins girt about with truth, and having on the breastplate of righteousness;

Eph 6:15 And your feet shod with the preparation of the gospel of peace;

Eph 6:16 Above all, taking the shield of faith, wherewith ye shall be able to quench all the fiery darts of the wicked.

Eph 6:17 And take the helmet of salvation, and the sword of the Spirit, which is the word of God:

Eph 6:18 Praying always with all prayer and supplication in the Spirit, and watching thereunto with all perseverance and supplication for all saints;

Ref Ezekiel 28:11-18

You see, long ago, satan was in charge of all of Heaven. God had given him this position

As we know, it is God who created satan

Eze 28:11 Moreover the word of the LORD came unto me, saying,

Eze 28:12 Son of man, take up a lamentation upon the king of Tyrus, and say unto him, Thus saith the Lord GOD; Thou sealest up the sum, full of wisdom, and perfect in beauty.

Eze 28:13 Thou hast been in Eden the garden of God; every precious stone *was* thy covering, the sardius, topaz, and the diamond, the beryl, the onyx, and the jasper, the sapphire, the emerald, and the carbuncle, and gold: the workmanship of thy tabrets and of thy pipes was prepared in thee in the day that thou wast created.

Eze 28:14 Thou *art* the anointed cherub that covereth; and I have set thee *so:* thou wast upon the holy mountain of God; thou hast walked up and down in the midst of the stones of fire.

Eze 28:15 Thou *wast* perfect in thy ways from the day that thou wast created, till iniquity was found in thee.

Eze 28:16 By the multitude of thy merchandise [רכלה rᵉkûllâh meaning TRADE (as *peddled*)] they have filled the midst of thee with violence, and thou hast sinned: therefore I will cast thee as profane out of the mountain of God: and I will destroy thee, O covering cherub, from the midst of the stones of fire.

Eze 28:17 Thine heart was lifted up because of thy beauty, thou hast corrupted thy wisdom by reason of thy brightness: I will cast thee to the ground, I will lay thee before kings, that they may behold thee.

Eze 28:18 Thou hast defiled thy sanctuaries by the multitude of thine iniquities, by the iniquity of thy traffick [רכלה rᵉkûllâh meaning TRADE (as *peddled*)]; therefore will I bring forth a fire from the midst of thee, it shall devour thee, and I will bring thee to ashes upon the earth in the sight of all them that behold thee.

Eze 28:19 All they that know thee [satan] among the people shall be astonished at thee: thou [satan] shalt be a terror, and never shalt thou [satan] be any more.

Ezekiel is sent to give a message to the king of Tyre

Eze 26:1 And it came to pass in the eleventh year, in the first *day* of the month, *that* the word of the LORD came unto me, saying,

Eze 26:2 Son of man, because that Tyrus hath said against Jerusalem, Aha, she is broken *that was* the gates of the people: she is turned unto me: I shall be replenished, *now* she is laid waste:

Eze 26:3 Therefore thus saith the Lord GOD; Behold, I *am* against thee, O Tyrus, and will cause many nations to come up against thee, as the sea causeth his waves to come up.

Eze 26:4 And they shall destroy the walls of Tyrus, and break down her towers: I will also scrape her dust from her, and make her like the top of a rock.

Eze 26:5 It shall be *a place for* the spreading of nets in the midst of the sea: for I have spoken *it,* saith the Lord GOD: and it shall become a spoil to the nations.

Eze 26:6 And her daughters which *are* in the field shall be slain by the sword; and they shall know that I *am* the LORD.

Eze 26:7 For thus saith the Lord GOD; Behold, I will bring upon Tyrus Nebuchadrezzar king of Babylon, a king of kings, from the north, with horses, and with chariots, and with horsemen, and companies, and much people.

Eze 26:8 He shall slay with the sword thy daughters in the field: and he shall make a fort against thee, and cast a mount against thee, and lift up the buckler against thee.

Eze 26:9 And he shall set engines of war against thy walls, and with his axes he shall break down thy towers.

Eze 26:10 By reason of the abundance of his horses their dust shall cover thee: thy walls shall shake at the noise of the horsemen, and of the wheels, and of the chariots, when he shall enter into thy gates, as men enter into a city wherein is made a breach.

Eze 26:11 With the hoofs of his horses shall he tread down all thy streets: he shall slay thy people by the sword, and thy strong garrisons shall go down to the ground.

Eze 26:12 And they shall make a spoil of thy riches, and make a prey of thy merchandise: and they shall break down thy walls, and destroy thy pleasant houses: and they shall lay thy stones and thy timber and thy dust in the midst of the water.

Eze 26:13 And I will cause the noise of thy songs to cease; and the sound of thy harps shall be no more heard.

Eze 26:14 And I will make thee like the top of a rock: thou shalt be *a place* to spread nets upon; thou shalt be built no more: for I the LORD have spoken *it,* saith the Lord GOD.

Eze 26:15 Thus saith the Lord GOD to Tyrus; Shall not the isles shake at the sound of thy fall, when the wounded cry, when the slaughter is made in the midst of thee?

Eze 26:16 Then all the princes of the sea shall come down from their thrones, and lay away their robes, and put off their broidered garments: they shall clothe themselves with trembling; they shall sit upon the ground, and shall tremble at *every* moment, and be astonished at thee.

Eze 26:17 And they shall take up a lamentation for thee, and say to thee, How art thou destroyed, *that wast* inhabited of seafaring men, the renowned city, which wast strong in the sea, she and her inhabitants, which cause their terror *to be* on all that haunt it!

Eze 26:18 Now shall the isles tremble in the day of thy fall; yea, the isles that *are* in the sea shall be troubled at thy departure.

Eze 26:19 For thus saith the Lord GOD; When I shall make thee a desolate city, like the cities that are not inhabited; when I shall bring up the deep upon thee, and great waters shall cover thee;

Eze 26:20 When I shall bring thee down with them that descend into the pit, with the people of old time, and shall set thee in the low parts of the earth, in places desolate of old, with them that go down to the pit, that thou be not inhabited; and I shall set glory in the land of the living;

Eze 26:21 I will make thee a terror, and thou *shalt be* no *more:* though thou be sought for, yet shalt thou never be found again, saith the Lord GOD.

Eze 27:1 The word of the LORD came again unto me, saying,

Eze 27:2 Now, thou son of man, take up a lamentation for Tyrus;

Eze 27:3 And say unto Tyrus, O thou that art situate at the entry of the sea, *which art* a merchant of the people for many isles, Thus saith the Lord GOD; O Tyrus, thou hast said, I *am* of perfect beauty.

Eze 27:4 Thy borders *are* in the midst of the seas, thy builders have perfected thy beauty.

Eze 27:5 They have made all thy *ship* boards of fir trees of Senir: they have taken cedars from Lebanon to make masts for thee.

Eze 27:6 *Of* the oaks of Bashan have they made thine oars; the company of the Ashurites have made thy benches *of* ivory, *brought* out of the isles of Chittim.

Eze 27:7 Fine linen with broidered work from Egypt was that which thou spreadest forth to be thy sail; blue and purple from the isles of Elishah was that which covered thee.

Eze 27:8 The inhabitants of Zidon and Arvad were thy mariners: thy wise *men*, O Tyrus, *that* were in thee, were thy pilots.

Eze 27:9 The ancients of Gebal and the wise *men* thereof were in thee thy calkers: all the ships of the sea with their mariners were in thee to occupy thy merchandise.

Eze 27:10 They of Persia and of Lud and of Phut were in thine army, thy men of war: they hanged the shield and helmet in thee; they set forth thy comeliness.

Eze 27:11 The men of Arvad with thine army *were* upon thy walls round about, and the Gammadims were in thy towers: they hanged their shields upon thy walls round about; they have made thy beauty perfect.

Eze 27:12 Tarshish *was* thy merchant by reason of the multitude of all *kind of* riches; with silver, iron, tin, and lead, they traded in thy fairs.

Eze 27:13 Javan, Tubal, and Meshech, they *were* thy merchants: they traded the persons of men and vessels of brass in thy market.

Eze 27:14 They of the house of Togarmah traded in thy fairs with horses and horsemen and mules.

Eze 27:15 The men of Dedan *were* thy merchants; many isles *were* the merchandise of thine hand: they brought thee *for* a present horns of ivory and ebony.

Eze 27:16 Syria *was* thy merchant by reason of the multitude of the wares of thy making: they occupied in thy fairs with emeralds, purple, and broidered work, and fine linen, and coral, and agate.

Eze 27:17 Judah, and the land of Israel, they *were* thy merchants: they traded in thy market wheat of Minnith, and Pannag, and honey, and oil, and balm.

Eze 27:18 Damascus *was* thy merchant in the multitude of the wares of thy making, for the multitude of all riches; in the wine of Helbon, and white wool.

Eze 27:19 Dan also and Javan going to and fro occupied in thy fairs: bright iron, cassia, and calamus, were in thy market.

Eze 27:20 Dedan *was* thy merchant in precious clothes for chariots.

Eze 27:21 Arabia, and all the princes of Kedar, they occupied with thee in lambs, and rams, and goats: in these *were they* thy merchants.

Eze 27:22 The merchants of Sheba and Raamah, they *were* thy merchants: they occupied in thy fairs with chief of all spices, and with all precious stones, and gold.

Eze 27:23 Haran, and Canneh, and Eden, the merchants of Sheba, Asshur, *and* Chilmad, *were* thy merchants.

Eze 27:24 These *were* thy merchants in all sorts *of things,* in blue clothes, and broidered work, and in chests of rich apparel, bound with cords, and made of cedar, among thy merchandise.

Eze 27:25 The ships of Tarshish did sing of thee in thy market: and thou wast replenished, and made very glorious in the midst of the seas.

Eze 27:26 Thy rowers have brought thee into great waters: the east wind hath broken thee in the midst of the seas.

Eze 27:27 Thy riches, and thy fairs, thy merchandise, thy mariners, and thy pilots, thy calkers, and the occupiers of thy merchandise, and all thy men of war, that *are* in thee, and in all thy company which *is* in the midst of thee, shall fall into the midst of the seas in the day of thy ruin.

Eze 27:28 The suburbs shall shake at the sound of the cry of thy pilots.

Eze 27:29 And all that handle the oar, the mariners, *and* all the pilots of the sea, shall come down from their ships, they shall stand upon the land;

Eze 27:30 And shall cause their voice to be heard against thee, and shall cry bitterly, and shall cast up dust upon their heads, they shall wallow themselves in the ashes:

Eze 27:31 And they shall make themselves utterly bald for thee, and gird them with sackcloth, and they shall weep for thee with bitterness of heart *and* bitter wailing.

Eze 27:32 And in their wailing they shall take up a lamentation for thee, and lament over thee, *saying,* What *city is* like Tyrus, like the destroyed in the midst of the sea?

Eze 27:33 When thy wares went forth out of the seas, thou filledst many people; thou didst enrich the kings of the earth with the multitude of thy riches and of thy merchandise.

Eze 27:34 In the time *when* thou shalt be broken by the seas in the depths of the waters thy merchandise and all thy company in the midst of thee shall fall.

Eze 27:35 All the inhabitants of the isles shall be astonished at thee, and their kings shall be sore afraid, they shall be troubled in *their* countenance.

Eze 27:36 The merchants among the people shall hiss at thee; thou shalt be a terror, and never *shalt be* any more.

Eze 28:1 The word of the LORD came again unto me, saying,

Eze 28:2 Son of man, say unto the prince of Tyrus, Thus saith the Lord GOD; Because thine heart *is* lifted up, and thou hast said, I *am* a God, I sit *in* the seat of God, in the midst of the seas; yet thou *art* a man, and not God, though thou set thine heart as the heart of God:

Eze 28:3 Behold, thou *art* wiser than Daniel; there is no secret that they can hide from thee:

Eze 28:4 With thy wisdom and with thine understanding thou hast gotten thee riches, and hast gotten gold and silver into thy treasures:

Eze 28:5 By thy great wisdom *and* by thy traffick hast thou increased thy riches, and thine heart is lifted up because of thy riches:

Eze 28:6 Therefore thus saith the Lord GOD; Because thou hast set thine heart as the heart of God;

Eze 28:7 Behold, therefore I will bring strangers upon thee, the terrible of the nations: and they shall draw their swords against the beauty of thy wisdom, and they shall defile thy brightness.

Eze 28:8 They shall bring thee down to the pit, and thou shalt die the deaths of *them that are* slain in the midst of the seas.

Eze 28:9 Wilt thou yet say before him that slayeth thee, I *am* God? but thou *shalt be* a man, and no God, in the hand of him that slayeth thee.

Eze 28:10 Thou shalt die the deaths of the uncircumcised by the hand of strangers: for I have spoken *it,* saith the Lord GOD.

Ref Ezekiel 28:11-19

destroy one of satan's Key Lies which rules human thinking

Ezekiel is sent to give a message to the king of Tyre

message was clearly not for any human being

Eze 28:11 Moreover the word of the LORD came unto me, saying,

Eze 28:12 Son of man, take up a lamentation upon the king of Tyrus, and say unto him, Thus saith the Lord GOD; Thou sealest up the sum, full of wisdom, and perfect in beauty.

Eze 28:13 Thou hast been in Eden the garden of God; every precious stone *was* thy covering, the sardius, topaz, and the diamond, the beryl, the onyx, and the jasper, the sapphire, the emerald, and the carbuncle, and gold: the workmanship of thy tabrets and of thy pipes was prepared in thee in the day that thou wast created.

Eze 28:14 Thou *art* the anointed cherub that covereth; and I have set thee *so:* thou wast upon the holy mountain of God; thou hast walked up and down in the midst of the stones of fire.

Eze 28:15 Thou *wast* perfect in thy ways from the day that thou wast created, till iniquity was found in thee.

Eze 28:16 By the multitude of thy merchandise [רכלה rᵉkûllâh meaning TRADE (as *peddled*)] they have filled the midst of thee with violence, and thou hast sinned: therefore I will cast thee as profane out of the mountain of God: and I will destroy thee, O covering cherub, from the midst of the stones of fire.

Eze 28:17 Thine heart was lifted up because of thy beauty, thou hast corrupted thy wisdom by reason of thy brightness: I will cast thee to the ground, I will lay thee before kings, that they may behold thee.

Eze 28:18 Thou hast defiled thy sanctuaries by the multitude of thine iniquities, by the iniquity of thy traffick [רכלה rᵉkûllâh meaning TRADE (as *peddled*)]; therefore will I bring forth a fire from the midst of thee, it shall devour thee, and I will bring thee to ashes upon the earth in the sight of all them that behold thee.

Eze 28:19 All they that know thee [satan] among the people shall be astonished at thee: thou [satan] shalt be a terror, and never shalt thou [satan] be any more.

Ref Galatians 01: 6-10

You have been warned. Do something about it.

Gal 1:6 I marvel that ye are so soon removed from him that called you into the grace of Christ unto another gospel:

Gal 1:7 Which is not another; but there be some that trouble you, and would pervert the gospel of Christ.

Gal 1:8 But though we, or an angel from heaven, preach any other gospel unto you than that which we have preached unto you, let him be accursed.

Gal 1:9 As we said before, so say I now again, If any *man* preach any other gospel unto you than that ye have received, let him be accursed.

Gal 1:10 For do I now persuade men, or God? or do I seek to please men? for if I yet pleased men, I should not be the servant of Christ.

Ref Galatians 05:16-26

The Holy Spirit is the source of all a Christian's supernatural strength, peace, love, forgiveness, patience, kindness, goodness, faithfulness, humility, self-control and joy.

Gal 5:16 *This* I say then, Walk in the Spirit, and ye shall not fulfil the lust of the flesh.

Gal 5:17 For the flesh lusteth against the Spirit, and the Spirit against the flesh: and these are contrary the one to the other: so that ye cannot do the things that ye would.

Gal 5:18 But if ye be led of the Spirit, ye are not under the law.

Gal 5:19 Now the works of the flesh are manifest, which are *these;* Adultery, fornication, uncleanness, lasciviousness,

Gal 5:20 Idolatry, witchcraft, hatred, variance, emulations, wrath, strife, seditions, heresies,

Gal 5:21 Envyings, murders, drunkenness, revellings, and such like: of the which I tell you before, as I have also told *you* in time past, that they which do such things shall not inherit the kingdom of God.

Gal 5:22 But the fruit of the Spirit is love, joy, peace, longsuffering, gentleness, goodness, faith,

Gal 5:23 Meekness, temperance: against such there is no law.

Gal 5:24 And they that are Christ's have crucified the flesh with the affections and lusts.

Gal 5:25 If we live in the Spirit, let us also walk in the Spirit.

Gal 5:26 Let us not be desirous of vain glory, provoking one another, envying one another.

Ref Hebrews 10:26-31

Do not take this lightly. You no longer have any excuse

Heb 10:26 For if we sin wilfully after that we have received the knowledge of the truth, there remaineth no more sacrifice for sins,

Heb 10:27 But a certain fearful looking for of judgment and fiery indignation, which shall devour the adversaries.

Heb 10:28 He that despised Moses' law died without mercy under two or three witnesses:

Heb 10:29 Of how much sorer punishment, suppose ye, shall he be thought worthy, who hath trodden under foot the Son of God, and hath counted the blood of the covenant, wherewith he was sanctified, an unholy thing, and hath done despite unto the Spirit of grace?

Heb 10:30 For we know him that hath said, Vengeance *belongeth* unto me, I will recompense, saith the Lord. And again, The Lord shall judge his people.

Heb 10:31 *It is* a fearful thing to fall into the hands of the living God.

Ref Hebrews 12:25-29

Do not take this lightly. You no longer have any excuse

Heb 12:25 See that ye refuse not him that speaketh. For if they escaped not who refused him that spake on earth, much more *shall not* we *escape,* if we turn away from him that *speaketh* from heaven:

Heb 12:26 Whose voice then shook the earth: but now he hath promised, saying, Yet once more I shake not the earth only, but also heaven.

Heb 12:27 And this *word,* Yet once more, signifieth the removing of those things that are shaken, as of things that are made, that those things which cannot be shaken may remain.

Heb 12:28 Wherefore we receiving a kingdom which cannot be moved, let us have grace, whereby we may serve God acceptably with reverence and godly fear:

Heb 12:29 For our God *is* a consuming fire.

Ref Hebrews 13:05 & 06

He will never leave you nor forsake you.

Heb 13:5 *Let your* conversation *be* without covetousness; *and be* content with such things as ye have: for he hath said, I will never leave thee, nor forsake thee.

Heb 13:6 So that we may boldly say, The Lord *is* my helper, and I will not fear what man shall do unto me.

Ref Hosea 04:6

His people perish because they lack knowledge

Hos 4:6 My people are destroyed for lack of knowledge: because thou hast rejected knowledge, I will also reject thee, that thou shalt be no priest to me: seeing thou hast forgotten the law of thy God, I will also forget thy children.

Ref James 01: 2 – 4

consider yourselves fortunate when all kinds of trials come your way

Do not be surprised when all kinds of trials come against you

Jas 1:2 My brethren, count it all joy when ye fall into divers temptations;

Jas 1:3 Knowing *this,* that the trying of your faith worketh patience.

Jas 1:4 But let patience have *her* perfect work, that ye may be perfect and entire, wanting nothing.

Ref James 02:14-26

A BELIEVER is someone who ACTS ON WHAT GOD SAYS.

Jas 2:14 What *doth it* profit, my brethren, though a man say he hath faith, and have not works? can faith save him?

Jas 2:15 If a brother or sister be naked, and destitute of daily food,

Jas 2:16 And one of you say unto them, Depart in peace, be *ye* warmed and filled;

notwithstanding ye give them not those things which are needful to the body; what *doth it* profit?

Jas 2:17 Even so faith, if it hath not works, is dead, being alone.

Jas 2:18 Yea, a man may say, Thou hast faith, and I have works: shew me thy faith without thy works, and I will shew thee my faith by my works.

Jas 2:19 Thou believest that there is one God; thou doest well: the devils also believe, and tremble.

Jas 2:20 But wilt thou know, O vain man, that faith without works is dead?

Jas 2:21 Was not Abraham our father justified by works, when he had offered Isaac his son upon the altar?

Jas 2:22 Seest thou how faith wrought with his works, and by works was faith made perfect?

Jas 2:23 And the scripture was fulfilled which saith, Abraham believed God, and it was imputed unto him for righteousness: and he was called the Friend of God.

Jas 2:24 Ye see then how that by works a man is justified, and not by faith only.

Jas 2:25 Likewise also was not Rahab the harlot justified by works, when she had received the messengers, and had sent *them* out another way?

Jas 2:26 For as the body without the spirit is dead, so faith without works is dead also.

Ref James 04:1-10

To remove The Holy Spirit from the church, satan had to create a Hierarchy within the Church.

There is no space in Heaven for those who condone or preach a standard other than that set by God Almighty.

Jas 4:1 From whence *come* wars and fightings among you? *come they* not hence, *even* of your lusts that war in your members?

Jas 4:2 Ye lust, and have not: ye kill, and desire to have, and cannot obtain: ye fight and war, yet ye have not, because ye ask not.

Jas 4:3 Ye ask, and receive not, because ye ask amiss, that ye may consume *it* upon your lusts.

Jas 4:4 Ye adulterers and adulteresses, know ye not that the friendship of the world is enmity with God? whosoever therefore will be a friend of the world is the enemy of God.

Jas 4:5 Do ye think that the scripture saith in vain, The spirit that dwelleth in us lusteth to envy?

Jas 4:6 But he giveth more grace. Wherefore he saith, God resisteth the proud, but giveth grace unto the humble.

Jas 4:7 Submit yourselves therefore to God. Resist the devil, and he will flee from you.

Jas 4:8 Draw nigh to God, and he will draw nigh to you. Cleanse *your* hands, *ye* sinners; and purify *your* hearts, *ye* double minded.

Jas 4:9 Be afflicted, and mourn, and weep: let your laughter be turned to mourning, and *your* joy to heaviness.

Jas 4:10 Humble yourselves in the sight of the Lord, and he shall lift you up.

Ref James 04:7

Tell them that in the Name of Jesus they have to leave you, and they will

Jas 4:7 Submit yourselves therefore to God. Resist the devil, and he will flee from you.

Ref Job 01:10

He will place a 'hedge' (protective barrier) around you and protect you

Job 1:10 Hast not thou made an hedge about him, and about his house, and about all that he hath on every side? thou hast blessed the work of his hands, and his substance is increased in the land.

Ref Job 01:01 – 02:10
<u>and God will only limit satan in the impact that he is allowed to make on their lives</u>

Job 1:1 There was a man in the land of Uz, whose name *was* Job; and that man was perfect and upright, and one that feared God, and eschewed evil.

Job 1:2 And there were born unto him seven sons and three daughters.

Job 1:3 His substance also was seven thousand sheep, and three thousand camels, and five hundred yoke of oxen, and five hundred she asses, and a very great household; so that this man was the greatest of all the men of the east.

Job 1:4 And his sons went and feasted *in their* houses, every one his day; and sent and called for their three sisters to eat and to drink with them.

Job 1:5 And it was so, when the days of *their* feasting were gone about, that Job sent and sanctified them, and rose up early in the morning, and offered burnt offerings *according* to the number of them all: for Job said, It may be that my sons have sinned, and cursed God in their hearts. Thus did Job continually.

Job 1:6 Now there was a day when the sons of God came to present themselves before the LORD, and Satan came also among them.

Job 1:7 And the LORD said unto Satan, Whence comest thou? Then Satan answered the LORD, and said, From going to and fro in the earth, and from walking up and down in it.

Job 1:8 And the LORD said unto Satan, Hast thou considered my servant Job, that *there is* none like him in the earth, a perfect and an upright man, one that feareth God, and escheweth evil?

Job 1:9 Then Satan answered the LORD, and said, Doth Job fear God for nought?

Job 1:10 Hast not thou made an hedge about him, and about his house, and about all that he hath on every side? thou hast blessed the work of his hands, and his substance is increased in the land.

Job 1:11 But put forth thine hand now, and touch all that he hath, and he will curse thee to thy face.

Job 1:12 And the LORD said unto Satan, Behold, all that he hath *is* in thy power; only upon himself put not forth thine hand. So Satan went forth from the presence of the LORD.

Job 1:13 And there was a day when his sons and his daughters *were* eating and drinking wine in their eldest brother's house:

Job 1:14 And there came a messenger unto Job, and said, The oxen were plowing, and the asses feeding beside them:

Job 1:15 And the Sabeans fell *upon them,* and took them away; yea, they have slain the servants with the edge of the sword; and I only am escaped alone to tell thee.

Job 1:16 While he *was* yet speaking, there came also another, and said, The fire of God is fallen from heaven, and hath burned up the sheep, and the servants, and consumed them; and I only am escaped alone to tell thee.

Job 1:17 While he *was* yet speaking, there came also another, and said, The Chaldeans made out three bands, and fell upon the camels, and have carried them away, yea, and slain the servants with the edge of the sword; and I only am escaped alone to tell thee.

Job 1:18 While he *was* yet speaking, there came also another, and said, Thy sons and thy daughters *were* eating and drinking wine in their eldest brother's house:

Job 1:19 And, behold, there came a great wind from the wilderness, and smote the four corners of the house, and it fell upon the young men, and they are dead; and I only am escaped alone to tell thee.

Job 1:20 Then Job arose, and rent his mantle, and shaved his head, and fell down upon the ground, and worshipped,

Job 1:21 And said, Naked came I out of my mother's womb, and naked shall I return thither: the LORD gave, and the LORD hath taken away; blessed be the name of the LORD.

Job 1:22 In all this Job sinned not, nor charged God foolishly.

Job 2:1 Again there was a day when the sons of God came to present themselves before the LORD, and Satan came also among them to present himself before the LORD.

Job 2:2 And the LORD said unto Satan, From whence comest thou? And Satan answered the LORD, and said, From going to and fro in the earth, and from walking up and down in it.

Job 2:3 And the LORD said unto Satan, Hast thou considered my servant Job, that *there is* none like him in the earth, a perfect and an upright man, one that feareth God, and escheweth evil? and still he holdeth fast his integrity, although thou movedst me against him, to destroy him without cause.

Job 2:4 And Satan answered the LORD, and said, Skin for skin, yea, all that a man hath will he give for his life.

Job 2:5 But put forth thine hand now, and touch his bone and his flesh, and he will curse thee to thy face.

Job 2:6 And the LORD said unto Satan, Behold, he *is* in thine hand; but save his life.

Job 2:7 So went Satan forth from the presence of the LORD, and smote Job with sore boils from the sole of his foot unto his crown.

Job 2:8 And he took him a potsherd to scrape himself withal; and he sat down among the ashes.

Job 2:9 Then said his wife unto him, Dost thou still retain thine integrity? curse God, and die.

Job 2:10 But he said unto her, Thou speakest as one of the foolish women speaketh. What? shall we receive good at the hand of God, and shall we not receive evil? In all this did not Job sin with his lips.

Ref John 03:01-36

He is the door, and that no one comes to The Father but through Him.

Joh 3:1 There was a man of the Pharisees, named Nicodemus, a ruler of the Jews:

Joh 3:2 The same came to Jesus by night, and said unto him, Rabbi, we know that thou art a teacher come from God: for no man can do these miracles that thou doest, except God be with him.

Joh 3:3 Jesus answered and said unto him, Verily, verily, I say unto thee, Except a man be born again, he cannot see the kingdom of God.

Joh 3:4 Nicodemus saith unto him, How can a man be born when he is old? can he enter the second time into his mother's womb, and be born?

Joh 3:5 Jesus answered, Verily, verily, I say unto thee, Except a man be born of water and *of* the Spirit, he cannot enter into the kingdom of God.

Joh 3:6 That which is born of the flesh is flesh; and that which is born of the Spirit is spirit.

Joh 3:7 Marvel not that I said unto thee, Ye must be born again.

Joh 3:8 The wind bloweth where it listeth, and thou hearest the sound thereof, but canst not tell whence it cometh, and whither it goeth: so is every one that is born of the Spirit.

Joh 3:9 Nicodemus answered and said unto him, How can these things be?

Joh 3:10 Jesus answered and said unto him, Art thou a master of Israel, and knowest not these things?

Joh 3:11 Verily, verily, I say unto thee, We speak that we do know, and testify that we have seen; and ye receive not our witness.

Joh 3:12 If I have told you earthly things, and ye believe not, how shall ye believe, if I tell you *of* heavenly things?

Joh 3:13 And no man hath ascended up to heaven, but he that came down from heaven, *even* the Son of man which is in heaven.

Joh 3:14 And as Moses lifted up the serpent in the wilderness, even so must the Son of man be lifted up:

Joh 3:15 That whosoever believeth in him should not perish, but have eternal life.

Joh 3:16 For God so loved the world, that he gave his only begotten Son, that whosoever believeth in him should not perish, but have everlasting life.

Joh 3:17 For God sent not his Son into the world to condemn the world; but that the world through him might be saved.

Joh 3:18 He that believeth on him is not condemned: but he that believeth not is condemned already, because he hath not believed in the name of the only begotten Son of God.

Joh 3:19 And this is the condemnation, that light is come into the world, and men loved darkness rather than light, because their deeds were evil.

Joh 3:20 For every one that doeth evil hateth the light, neither cometh to the light, lest his deeds should be reproved.

Joh 3:21 But he that doeth truth cometh to the light, that his deeds may be made manifest, that they are wrought in God.

Joh 3:22 After these things came Jesus and his disciples into the land of Judaea; and there he tarried with them, and baptized.

Joh 3:23 And John also was baptizing in Aenon near to Salim, because there was much water there: and they came, and were baptized.

Joh 3:24 For John was not yet cast into prison.

Joh 3:25 Then there arose a question between *some* of John's disciples and the Jews about purifying.

Joh 3:26 And they came unto John, and said unto him, Rabbi, he that was with thee beyond Jordan, to whom thou barest witness, behold, the same baptizeth, and all *men* come to him.

Joh 3:27 John answered and said, A man can receive nothing, except it be given him from heaven.

Joh 3:28 Ye yourselves bear me witness, that I said, I am not the Christ, but that I am sent before him.

Joh 3:29 He that hath the bride is the bridegroom: but the friend of the bridegroom, which standeth and heareth him, rejoiceth greatly because of the bridegroom's voice: this my joy therefore is fulfilled.

Joh 3:30 He must increase, but I *must* decrease.

Joh 3:31 He that cometh from above is above all: he that is of the earth is earthly, and speaketh of the earth: he that cometh from heaven is above all.

Joh 3:32 And what he hath seen and heard, that he testifieth; and no man receiveth his testimony.

Joh 3:33 He that hath received his testimony hath set to his seal that God is true.

Joh 3:34 For he whom God hath sent speaketh the words of God: for God giveth not the Spirit by measure *unto him.*

Joh 3:35 The Father loveth the Son, and hath given all things into his hand.

Joh 3:36 He that believeth on the Son hath everlasting life: and he that believeth not the Son shall not see life; but the wrath of God abideth on him.

Ref John 08:1-11

forgiveness from adultery applies only if there is repentance - Note verse 11

Joh 8:1 Jesus went unto the mount of Olives.

Joh 8:2 And early in the morning he came again into the temple, and all the people came unto him; and he sat down, and taught them.

Joh 8:3 And the scribes and Pharisees brought unto him a woman taken in adultery; and when they had set her in the midst,

Joh 8:4 They say unto him, Master, this woman was taken in adultery, in the very act.

Joh 8:5 Now Moses in the law commanded us, that such should be stoned: but what sayest thou?

Joh 8:6 This they said, tempting him, that they might have to accuse him. But Jesus stooped down, and with *his* finger wrote on the ground, *as though he heard them not.*

Joh 8:7 So when they continued asking him, he lifted up himself, and said unto them, He that is without sin among you, let him first cast a stone at her.

Joh 8:8 And again he stooped down, and wrote on the ground.

Joh 8:9 And they which heard *it,* being convicted by *their own* conscience, went out one by one, beginning at the eldest, *even* unto the last: and Jesus was left alone, and the woman standing in the midst.

Joh 8:10 When Jesus had lifted up himself, and saw none but the woman, he said unto her, Woman, where are those thine accusers? hath no man condemned thee?

Joh 8:11 She said, No man, Lord. And Jesus said unto her, Neither do I condemn thee: **go, and sin no more.**

Ref John 08: 31-34

YOU WILL BE FREE

Joh 8:31 Then said Jesus to those Jews which believed on him, If ye continue in my word, *then* are ye my disciples indeed;

Joh 8:32 And ye shall know the truth, and the truth shall make you free.

Joh 8:33 They answered him, We be Abraham's seed, and were never in bondage to any man: how sayest thou, Ye shall be made free?

Joh 8:34 Jesus answered them, Verily, verily, I say unto you, Whosoever committeth sin is the servant of sin.

Ref John 10:09

He is the door, and that no one comes to The Father but through Him.

Joh 10:9 I am the door: by me if any man enter in, he shall be saved, and shall go in and out, and find pasture.

Ref John 10:10

satan will steal this from your memory as fast as he can

satan comes to Kill, Steal and Destroy

Joh 10:10 The thief cometh not, but for to steal, and to kill, and to destroy: I am come that they might have life, and that they might have *it* more abundantly.

Ref John 13:12-17

The Most powerful example of this is when Jesus, who is The Word of Almighty God, represented to us as The Son of Almighty God, within whom is the power to create and destroy the entire Universe, knelt before the Disciples and washed their feet.

Joh 13:12 So after he had washed their feet, and had taken his garments, and was set down again, he said unto them, Know ye what I have done to you?

Joh 13:13 Ye call me Master and Lord: and ye say well; for *so* I am.

Joh 13:14 If I then, *your* Lord and Master, have washed your feet; ye also ought to wash one another's feet.

Joh 13:15 For I have given you an example, that ye should do as I have done to you.

Joh 13:16 Verily, verily, I say unto you, The servant is not greater than his lord; neither he that is sent greater than he that sent him.

Joh 13:17 If ye know these things, happy are ye if ye do them.

Ref John 13:34 & 35

He loves you and wants you to be with Him forever

They will know you are my disciples by your love for one another

Joh 13:34 A new commandment I give unto you, That ye love one another; as I have loved you, that ye also love one another.

Joh 13:35 By this shall all *men* know that ye are my disciples, if ye have love one to another.

Ref John 14:02, 03

He loves you and wants you to be with Him forever

Joh 14:2 In my Father's house are many mansions: if *it were* not *so,* I would have told you. I go to prepare a place for you.

Joh 14:3 And if I go and prepare a place for you, I will come again, and receive you unto myself; that where I am, *there* ye may be also.

Ref John 14:05-07

He is the door, and that no one comes to The Father but through Him.

Joh 14:5 Thomas saith unto him, Lord, we know not whither thou goest; and how can we know the way?

Joh 14:6 Jesus saith unto him, I am the way, the truth, and the life: no man cometh unto the Father, but by me.

Joh 14:7 If ye had known me, ye should have known my Father also: and from henceforth ye know him, and have seen him.

Ref John 14:26

be there teacher, comforter and guide.
He is the only One who can reveal the scriptures
I go to the Father that the Holy Spirit might come.

with the guidance of the Holy Spirit

Joh 14:26 But the Comforter, *which is* the Holy Ghost, whom the Father will send in my name, he shall teach you all things, and bring all things to your remembrance, whatsoever I have said unto you.

Ref John 14:01-31

You are worth His Blood to Him

Joh 14:1 Let not your heart be troubled: ye believe in God, believe also in me.

Joh 14:2 In my Father's house are many mansions: if *it were* not *so,* I would have told you. I go to prepare a place for you.

Joh 14:3 And if I go and prepare a place for you, I will come again, and receive you unto myself; that where I am, *there* ye may be also.

Joh 14:4 And whither I go ye know, and the way ye know.

Joh 14:5 Thomas saith unto him, Lord, we know not whither thou goest; and how can we know the way?

Joh 14:6 Jesus saith unto him, I am the way, the truth, and the life: no man cometh unto the Father, but by me.

Joh 14:7 If ye had known me, ye should have known my Father also: and from henceforth ye know him, and have seen him.

Joh 14:8 Philip saith unto him, Lord, shew us the Father, and it sufficeth us.

Joh 14:9 Jesus saith unto him, Have I been so long time with you, and yet hast thou not known me, Philip? he that hath seen me hath seen the Father; and how sayest thou *then,* Shew us the Father?

Joh 14:10 Believest thou not that I am in the Father, and the Father in me? the words that I speak unto you I speak not of myself: but the Father that dwelleth in me, he doeth the works.

Joh 14:11 Believe me that I *am* in the Father, and the Father in me: or else believe me for the very works' sake.

Joh 14:12 Verily, verily, I say unto you, He that believeth on me, the works that I do shall he do also; and greater *works* than these shall he do; because I go unto my Father.

Joh 14:13 And whatsoever ye shall ask in my name, that will I do, that the Father may be glorified in the Son.

Joh 14:14 If ye shall ask any thing in my name, I will do *it.*

Joh 14:15 If ye love me, keep my commandments.

Joh 14:16 And I will pray the Father, and he shall give you another Comforter, that he may abide with you for ever;

Joh 14:17 *Even* the Spirit of truth; whom the world cannot receive, because it seeth him not, neither knoweth him: but ye know him; for he dwelleth with you, and shall be in you.

Joh 14:18 I will not leave you comfortless: I will come to you.

Joh 14:19 Yet a little while, and the world seeth me no more; but ye see me: because I live, ye shall live also.

Joh 14:20 At that day ye shall know that I *am* in my Father, and ye in me, and I in you.

Joh 14:21 He that hath my commandments, and keepeth them, he it is that loveth me: and he that loveth me shall be loved of my Father, and I will love him, and will manifest myself to him.

Joh 14:22 Judas saith unto him, not Iscariot, Lord, how is it that thou wilt manifest thyself unto us, and not unto the world?

Joh 14:23 Jesus answered and said unto him, If a man love me, he will keep my words: and my Father will love him, and we will come unto him, and make our abode with him.

Joh 14:24 He that loveth me not keepeth not my sayings: and the word which ye hear is not mine, but the Father's which sent me.

Joh 14:25 These things have I spoken unto you, being *yet* present with you.

Joh 14:26 But the Comforter, *which is* the Holy Ghost, whom the Father will send in my name, he shall teach you all things, and bring all things to your remembrance, whatsoever I have said unto you.

Joh 14:27 Peace I leave with you, my peace I give unto you: not as the world giveth, give I unto you. Let not your heart be troubled, neither let it be afraid.

Joh 14:28 Ye have heard how I said unto you, I go away, and come *again* unto you. If ye loved me, ye would rejoice, because I said, I go unto the Father: for my Father is greater than I.

Joh 14:29 And now I have told you before it come to pass, that, when it is come to pass, ye might believe.

Joh 14:30 Hereafter I will not talk much with you: for the prince of this world cometh, and hath nothing in me.

Joh 14:31 But that the world may know that I love the Father; and as the Father gave me commandment, even so I do. Arise, let us go hence.

Ref John 15: 7-17

ask according to His will you will receive what you ask for.

Joh 15:7 If ye abide in me, and my words abide in you, ye shall ask what ye will, and it shall be done unto you.

Joh 15:8 Herein is my Father glorified, that ye bear much fruit; so shall ye be my disciples.

Joh 15:9 As the Father hath loved me, so have I loved you: continue ye in my love.

Joh 15:10 If ye keep my commandments, ye shall abide in my love; even as I have kept my Father's commandments, and abide in his love.

Joh 15:11 These things have I spoken unto you, that my joy might remain in you, and *that* your joy might be full.

Joh 15:12 This is my commandment, That ye love one another, as I have loved you.

Joh 15:13 Greater love hath no man than this, that a man lay down his life for his friends.

Joh 15:14 Ye are my friends, if ye do whatsoever I command you.

Joh 15:15 Henceforth I call you not servants; for the servant knoweth not what his lord doeth: but I have called you friends; for all things that I have heard of my Father I have made known unto you.

Joh 15:16 Ye have not chosen me, but I have chosen you, and ordained you, that ye should go and bring forth fruit, and *that* your fruit should remain: that whatsoever ye shall ask of the Father in my name, he may give it you.

Joh 15:17 These things I command you, that ye love one another.

Ref John 16: 7-14

The Holy Spirit is also a WHITE HOT FIRE that burns a Christian deep inside when they see or sense evil.

Joh 16:7 Nevertheless I tell you the truth; It is expedient for you that I go away: for if I go not away, the Comforter will not come unto you; but if I depart, I will send him unto you.

Joh 16:8 And when he is come, he will reprove the world of sin, and of righteousness, and of judgment:

Joh 16:9 Of sin, because they believe not on me;

Joh 16:10 Of righteousness, because I go to my Father, and ye see me no more;

Joh 16:11 Of judgment, because the prince of this world is judged.

Joh 16:12 I have yet many things to say unto you, but ye cannot bear them now.

Joh 16:13 Howbeit when he, the Spirit of truth, is come, he will guide you into all truth: for he shall not speak of himself; but whatsoever he shall hear, *that* shall he speak: and he will shew you things to come.

Joh 16:14 He shall glorify me: for he shall receive of mine, and shall shew *it* unto you.

Ref John 16: 33

he has already overcome the world

Joh 16:33 These things I have spoken unto you, that in me ye might have peace. In the world ye shall have tribulation: but be of good cheer; I have overcome the world.

Ref Joshua 01:05

He will never leave you nor forsake you.

Jos 1:5 There shall not any man be able to stand before thee all the days of thy life: as I was with Moses, *so* I will be with thee: I will not fail thee, nor forsake thee.

Ref Luke 6:17-38

Jesus Himself repeated God's law

Luk 6:17 And he came down with them, and stood in the plain, and the company of his disciples, and a great multitude of people out of all Judaea and Jerusalem, and from the sea coast of Tyre and Sidon, which came to hear him, and to be healed of their diseases;

Luk 6:18 And they that were vexed with unclean spirits: and they were healed.

Luk 6:19 And the whole multitude sought to touch him: for there went virtue out of him, and healed *them* all.

Luk 6:20 And he lifted up his eyes on his disciples, and said, Blessed *be ye* poor: for yours is the kingdom of God.

Luk 6:21 Blessed *are ye* that hunger now: for ye shall be filled. Blessed *are ye* that weep now: for ye shall laugh.

Luk 6:22 Blessed are ye, when men shall hate you, and when they shall separate you *from their company,* and shall reproach *you,* and cast out your name as evil, for the Son of man's sake.

Luk 6:23 Rejoice ye in that day, and leap for joy: for, behold, your reward *is* great in heaven: for in the like manner did their fathers unto the prophets.

Luk 6:24 But woe unto you that are rich! for ye have received your consolation.

Luk 6:25 Woe unto you that are full! for ye shall hunger. Woe unto you that laugh now! for ye shall mourn and weep.

Luk 6:26 Woe unto you, when all men shall speak well of you! for so did their fathers to the false prophets.

Luk 6:27 But I say unto you which hear, Love your enemies, do good to them which hate you,

Luk 6:28 **Bless them that curse you, and pray for them which despitefully use you.**

Luk 6:29 And unto him that smiteth thee on the *one* cheek offer also the other; and him that taketh away thy cloke forbid not *to take thy* coat also.

Luk 6:30 **Give to every man that asketh of thee; and of him that taketh away thy goods ask *them* not again.**

Luk 6:31 And as ye would that men should do to you, do ye also to them likewise.

Luk 6:32 For if ye love them which love you, what thank have ye? for sinners also love those that love them.

Luk 6:33 And if ye do good to them which do good to you, what thank have ye? for sinners also do even the same.

Luk 6:34 And if ye lend *to them* of whom ye hope to receive, what thank have ye? for sinners also lend to sinners, to receive as much again.

Luk 6:35 But love ye your enemies, and do good, and **lend, hoping for nothing again**; and your reward shall be great, and ye shall be the children of the Highest: for he is kind unto the unthankful and *to* the evil.

Luk 6:36 Be ye therefore merciful, as your Father also is merciful.

Luk 6:37 Judge not, and ye shall not be judged: condemn not, and ye shall not be condemned: forgive, and ye shall be forgiven:

Luk 6:38 **Give, and it shall be given unto you; good measure, pressed down, and shaken together, and running over, shall men give into your bosom. For with the same measure that ye mete withal it shall be measured to you again.**

Ref Luke 06: 38

For you will be rewarded for what you give

Luk 6:38 **Give, and it shall be given unto you; good measure, pressed down, and shaken together, and running over, shall men give into your bosom. For with the same**

measure that ye mete withal it shall be measured to you again.

Ref Luke 09:1-6 & 10:1-4

Jesus appointed 12 Disciples & 70 Apostles to go out and spread the word.

Jesus sent them out with the power to use His Name to the various cities to spread the Gospel.

Luk 9:1 Then he called his twelve disciples together, and gave them power and authority over all devils, and to cure diseases.

Luk 9:2 And he sent them to preach the kingdom of God, and to heal the sick.

Luk 9:3 And he said unto them, Take nothing for *your* journey, neither staves, nor scrip, neither bread, neither money; neither have two coats apiece.

Luk 9:4 And whatsoever house ye enter into, there abide, and thence depart.

Luk 9:5 And whosoever will not receive you, when ye go out of that city, shake off the very dust from your feet for a testimony against them.

Luk 9:6 And they departed, and went through the towns, preaching the gospel, and healing every where.

Luk 10:1 After these things the Lord appointed other seventy also, and sent them two and two before his face into every city and place, whither he himself would come.

Luk 10:2 Therefore said he unto them, The harvest truly *is* great, but the labourers *are* few: pray ye therefore the Lord of the harvest, that he would send forth labourers into his harvest.

Luk 10:3 Go your ways: behold, I send you forth as lambs among wolves.

Luk 10:4 Carry neither purse, nor scrip, nor shoes: and salute no man by the way.

Ref Luke 10:38 - 42

Spend time with Him just enjoying His presence, and loving to be with Him. For this is His Will.

Luk 10:38 Now it came to pass, as they went, that he entered into a certain village: and a certain woman named Martha received him into her house.

Luk 10:39 And she had a sister called Mary, which also sat at Jesus' feet, and heard his word.

Luk 10:40 But Martha was cumbered about much serving, and came to him, and said, Lord, dost thou not care that my sister hath left me to serve alone? bid her therefore that she help me.

Luk 10:41 And Jesus answered and said unto her, Martha, Martha, thou art careful and troubled about many things:

Luk 10:42 But one thing is needful: and Mary hath chosen that good part, which shall not be taken away from her.

Ref Luke 11:13

ask The Holy Spirit to enter into you

Luk 11:13 If ye then, being evil, know how to give good gifts unto your children: how much more shall *your* heavenly Father give the Holy Spirit to them that ask him?

Ref Luke 12:22 – 34

Jesus Himself repeated God's law

Luk 12:22 And he said unto his disciples, Therefore I say unto you, Take no thought for your life, what ye shall eat; neither for the body, what ye shall put on.

Luk 12:23 The life is more than meat, and the body *is more* than raiment.

Luk 12:24 Consider the ravens: for they neither sow nor reap; which neither have storehouse nor barn; and God feedeth them: how much more are ye better than the fowls?

Luk 12:25 And which of you with taking thought can add to his stature one cubit?

Luk 12:26 If ye then be not able to do that thing which is least, why take ye thought for the rest?

Luk 12:27 Consider the lilies how they grow: they toil not, they spin not; and yet I say unto you, that Solomon in all his glory was not arrayed like one of these.

Luk 12:28 **If then God so clothe the grass, which is to day in the field, and to morrow is cast into the oven; how much more *will he clothe* you, O ye of little faith?**

Luk 12:29 And seek not ye what ye shall eat, or what ye shall drink, neither be ye of doubtful mind.

Luk 12:30 For all these things do the nations of the world seek after: and your Father knoweth that ye have need of these things.

Luk 12:31 **But rather seek ye the kingdom of God; and all these things shall be added unto you.**

Luk 12:32 Fear not, little flock; for it is your Father's good pleasure to give you the kingdom.

Luk 12:33 Sell that ye have, and give alms; provide yourselves bags which wax not old, a treasure in the heavens that faileth not, where no thief approacheth, neither moth corrupteth.

Luk 12:34 For where your treasure is, there will your heart be also.

Ref Luke 13:22-31

They fell into the trap and will be the Last for all eternity because they made themselves the first on earth.

Luk 13:22 And he went through the cities and villages, teaching, and journeying toward Jerusalem.

Luk 13:23 Then said one unto him, Lord, are there few that be saved? And he said unto them,

Luk 13:24 Strive to enter in at the strait gate: for many, I say unto you, will seek to enter in, and shall not be able.

Luk 13:25 When once the master of the house is risen up, and hath shut to the door, and ye begin to stand without, and to knock at the door, saying, Lord, Lord, open unto us; and he shall answer and say unto you, I know you not whence ye are:

Luk 13:26 Then shall ye begin to say, We have eaten and drunk in thy presence, and thou hast taught in our streets.

Luk 13:27 But he shall say, I tell you, I know you not whence ye are; depart from me, all *ye* workers of iniquity.

Luk 13:28 There shall be weeping and gnashing of teeth, when ye shall see Abraham, and Isaac, and Jacob, and all the prophets, in the kingdom of God, and you *yourselves* thrust out.

Luk 13:29 And they shall come from the east, and *from* the west, and from the north, and *from* the south, and shall sit down in the kingdom of God.

Luk 13:30 And, behold, there are last which shall be first, and there are first which shall be last.

Luk 13:31 The same day there came certain of the Pharisees, saying unto him, Get thee out, and depart hence: for Herod will kill thee.

Ref Luke 15:07

when just one person accepts the escape route and is <u>saved then there is great joy in Heaven</u>

Luk 15:7 I say unto you, that likewise joy shall be in heaven over one sinner that repenteth, more than over ninety and nine just persons, which need no repentance.

Ref Luke 22:25-27
tries to enforce authority over you they are misled
Luk 22:25 And he said unto them, The kings of the Gentiles exercise lordship over them; and they that exercise authority upon them are called benefactors.
Luk 22:26 But ye *shall* not *be* so: but he that is greatest among you, let him be as the younger; and he that is chief, as he that doth serve.
Luk 22:27 For whether *is* greater, he that sitteth at meat, or he that serveth? *is* not he that sitteth at meat? but I am among you as he that serveth.

Ref Malachi 03:03
God sits as a silver smith refining His people
He will continue to place you in the fire
Mal 3:3 And he shall sit *as* a refiner and purifier of silver: and he shall purify the sons of Levi, and purge them as gold and silver, that they may offer unto the LORD an offering in righteousness.

Ref Malachi 03:06
He is the same, yesterday, today and forever
Mal 3:6 For I *am* the LORD, I change not; therefore ye sons of Jacob are not consumed.

Ref Mark 03:28-29
Jesus specifically warns that anyone who says anything against The Holy Spirit

Mar 3:28 Verily I say unto you, All sins shall be forgiven unto the sons of men, and blasphemies wherewith soever they shall blaspheme:

Mar 3:29 But he that shall blaspheme against the Holy Ghost hath never forgiveness, but is in danger of eternal damnation:

Ref Mark 04:22-24

Do not be so quick to judge others, or God will judge you in the same light.

Mar 4:22 For there is nothing hid, which shall not be manifested; neither was any thing kept secret, but that it should come abroad.

Mar 4:23 If any man have ears to hear, let him hear.

Mar 4:24 And he said unto them, Take heed what ye hear: with what measure ye mete, it shall be measured to you: and unto you that hear shall more be given.

Ref Mark 09:41

help their congregation brothers and sisters first

Mar 9:41 For whosoever shall give you a cup of water to drink in my name, because ye belong to Christ, verily I say unto you, he shall not lose his reward.

Ref Matthew 03:7

John the Baptist called the Pharisees snakes

Mat 3:7 But when he saw many of the Pharisees and Sadducees come to his baptism, he said unto them, O generation of vipers, who hath warned you to flee from the wrath to come?

Ref Matthew 05:31-32

Does your Church Condone or treat as normal, accept or tolerate, Same Sex Marriages, or Sex before Marriage, or Divorce?

Mat 5:31 It hath been said, Whosoever shall put away his wife, let him give her a writing of divorcement:

Mat 5:32 But I say unto you, That whosoever shall put away his wife, saving for the cause of fornication, causeth her to commit adultery: and whosoever shall marry her that is divorced committeth adultery.

Ref Matthew 06:9-13

The most powerful prayer is to pray the Prayer Jesus Taught us while reverently understanding each word

Mat 6:9 After this manner therefore pray ye: Our Father which art in heaven, Hallowed be thy name.

Mat 6:10 Thy kingdom come. Thy will be done in earth, as *it is* in heaven.

Mat 6:11 Give us this day our daily bread.

Mat 6:12 And forgive us our debts, as we forgive our debtors.

Mat 6:13 And lead us not into temptation, but deliver us from evil: For thine is the kingdom, and the power, and the glory, for ever. Amen.

Ref Matthew 06:12

Anyone who prays The Lord's Prayer is actually making it very clear that God should ONLY forgive them if they have already forgiven everyone else

Mat 6:12 And forgive us our debts, as we forgive our debtors.

Ref Matthew 06: 14 & 15

<u>You will be tormented until you forgive others</u>

Mat 18:34 And his lord was wroth, and delivered him to the tormentors, till he should pay all that was due unto him.

Mat 18:35 So likewise shall my heavenly Father do also unto you, if ye from your hearts forgive not every one his brother their trespasses.

Ref Matthew 07:01-05

<u>Take the plank out of your own eye</u>

<u>Do not be so quick to judge others, or God will judge you in the same light.</u>

Mat 7:1 Judge not, that ye be not judged.

Mat 7:2 For with what judgment ye judge, ye shall be judged: and with what measure ye mete, it shall be measured to you again.

Mat 7:3 And why beholdest thou the mote that is in thy brother's eye, but considerest not the beam that is in thine own eye?

Mat 7:4 Or how wilt thou say to thy brother, Let me pull out the mote out of thine eye; and, behold, a beam *is* in thine own eye?

Mat 7:5 Thou hypocrite, first cast out the beam out of thine own eye; and then shalt thou see clearly to cast out the mote out of thy brother's eye.

Ref Matthew 07:21-23

<u>They fell into the trap and will be the Last for all eternity because they made themselves the first on earth.</u>

<u>If you do not, then Jesus says to you "Away from me you evil doers"</u>

Mat 7:21 Not every one that saith unto me, Lord, Lord, shall enter into the kingdom of heaven; but he that doeth the will of my Father which is in heaven.

Mat 7:22 Many will say to me in that day, Lord, Lord, have we not prophesied in thy name? and in thy name have cast out devils? and in thy name done many wonderful works?

Mat 7:23 And then will I profess unto them, I never knew you: depart from me, ye that work iniquity.

Ref Matthew 12:31-32

Jesus specifically warns that anyone who says anything against The Holy Spirit

Mat 12:31 Wherefore I say unto you, All manner of sin and blasphemy shall be forgiven unto men: but the blasphemy *against* the *Holy* Ghost shall not be forgiven unto men.

Mat 12:32 And whosoever speaketh a word against the Son of man, it shall be forgiven him: but whosoever speaketh against the Holy Ghost, it shall not be forgiven him, neither in this world, neither in the *world* to come.

Ref Matthew 16:1-11

You did not take personal responsibility for ensuring that the people you are following are following what the Bible teaches.

Mat 16:1 The Pharisees also with the Sadducees came, and tempting desired him that he would shew them a sign from heaven.

Mat 16:2 He answered and said unto them, When it is evening, ye say, *It will be* fair weather: for the sky is red.

Mat 16:3 And in the morning, *It will be* foul weather to day: for the sky is red and lowring. O *ye* hypocrites, ye can discern the face of the sky; but can ye not *discern* the signs of the times?

Mat 16:4 A wicked and adulterous generation seeketh after a sign; and there shall no sign be given unto it, but the sign of the prophet Jonas. And he left them, and departed.

Mat 16:5 And when his disciples were come to the other side, they had forgotten to take bread.

Mat 16:6 Then Jesus said unto them, Take heed and beware of the leaven of the Pharisees and of the Sadducees.

Mat 16:7 And they reasoned among themselves, saying, *It is* because we have taken no bread.

Mat 16:8 *Which* when Jesus perceived, he said unto them, O ye of little faith, why reason ye among yourselves, because ye have brought no bread?

Mat 16:9 Do ye not yet understand, neither remember the five loaves of the five thousand, and how many baskets ye took up?

Mat 16:10 Neither the seven loaves of the four thousand, and how many baskets ye took up?

Mat 16:11 How is it that ye do not understand that I spake *it* not to you concerning bread, that ye should beware of the leaven of the Pharisees and of the Sadducees?

Ref Matthew 16:15-19

But whom say ye that I am?

Mat 16:15 He saith unto them, But whom say ye that I am?

Mat 16:16 And Simon Peter answered and said, Thou art the Christ, the Son of the living God.

Mat 16:17 And Jesus answered and said unto him, Blessed art thou, Simon Barjona: for flesh and blood hath not revealed *it* unto thee, but my Father which is in heaven.

Mat 16:18 And I say also unto thee, That thou art Peter, and upon this rock I will build my church; and the gates of hell shall not prevail against it.

Mat 16:19 And I will give unto thee the keys of the kingdom of heaven: and whatsoever thou shalt bind on earth shall be bound in heaven: and whatsoever thou shalt loose on earth shall be loosed in heaven.

Ref Matthew 18:15-17

Should the offender not listen to this rebuke and continue to sin, then It should be brought before all the members of the church.

ALL THE MEMBERS OF THE CHURCH had to treat him/her as one who does not know Christ.

Mat 18:15 Moreover if thy brother shall trespass against thee, go and tell him his fault between thee and him alone: if he shall hear thee, thou hast gained thy brother.

Mat 18:16 But if he will not hear *thee, then* take with thee one or two more, that in the mouth of two or three witnesses every word may be established.

Mat 18:17 And if he shall neglect to hear them, tell *it* unto the church: but if he neglect to hear the church, let him be unto thee as an heathen man and a publican.

Ref Matthew 18: 18-20

"Wherever two or more of you agree on anything in My Name, it will be done for you by My Father in Heaven."

Mat 18:18 Verily I say unto you, Whatsoever ye shall bind on earth shall be bound in heaven: and whatsoever ye shall loose on earth shall be loosed in heaven.

Mat 18:19 Again I say unto you, That if two of you shall agree on earth as touching any thing that they shall ask, it shall be done for them of my Father which is in heaven.

Mat 18:20 For where two or three are gathered together in my name, there am I in the midst of them.

Ref Matthew 18: 34&35

You will be tormented until you forgive others

Mat 18:34 And his lord was wroth, and delivered him to the tormentors, till he should pay all that was due unto him.

Mat 18:35 So likewise shall my heavenly Father do also unto you, if ye from your hearts forgive not every one his brother their trespasses.

Ref Matthew 18: 21-35

Is it made clear to members that those who do not forgive others ARE going to go to Hell?

You will be tormented until you forgive others

Mat 18:21 Then came Peter to him, and said, Lord, how oft shall my brother sin against me, and I forgive him? till seven times?

Mat 18:22 Jesus saith unto him, I say not unto thee, Until seven times: but, Until seventy times seven.

Mat 18:23 Therefore is the kingdom of heaven likened unto a certain king, which would take account of his servants.

Mat 18:24 And when he had begun to reckon, one was brought unto him, which owed him ten thousand talents.

Mat 18:25 But forasmuch as he had not to pay, his lord commanded him to be sold, and his wife, and children, and all that he had, and payment to be made.

Mat 18:26 The servant therefore fell down, and worshipped him, saying, Lord, have patience with me, and I will pay thee all.

Mat 18:27 Then the lord of that servant was moved with compassion, and loosed him, and forgave him the debt.

Mat 18:28 But the same servant went out, and found one of his fellowservants, which owed him an hundred pence: and he laid hands on him, and took *him* by the throat, saying, Pay me that thou owest.

Mat 18:29 And his fellowservant fell down at his feet, and besought him, saying, Have patience with me, and I will pay thee all.

Mat 18:30 And he would not: but went and cast him into prison, till he should pay the debt.

Mat 18:31 So when his fellowservants saw what was done, they were very sorry, and came and told unto their lord all that was done.

Mat 18:32 Then his lord, after that he had called him, said unto him, O thou wicked servant, I forgave thee all that debt, because thou desiredst me:

Mat 18:33 Shouldest not thou also have had compassion on thy fellowservant, even as I had pity on thee?

Mat 18:34 And his lord was wroth, and delivered him to the tormentors, till he should pay all that was due unto him.

Mat 18:35 So likewise shall my heavenly Father do also unto you, if ye from your hearts forgive not every one his brother their trespasses.

Ref Matthew 19:1-9

Does your Church Condone or treat as normal, accept or tolerate, Same Sex Marriages, or Sex before Marriage, or Divorce?

Mat 19:1 And it came to pass, *that* when Jesus had finished these sayings, he departed from Galilee, and came into the coasts of Judaea beyond Jordan;

Mat 19:2 And great multitudes followed him; and he healed them there.

Mat 19:3 The Pharisees also came unto him, tempting him, and saying unto him, Is it lawful for a man to put away his wife for every cause?

Mat 19:4 And he answered and said unto them, Have ye not read, that he which made *them* at the beginning made them male and female,

Mat 19:5 And said, For this cause shall a man leave father and mother, and shall cleave to his wife: and they twain shall be one flesh?

Mat 19:6 Wherefore they are no more twain, but one flesh. What therefore God hath joined together, let not man put asunder.

Mat 19:7 They say unto him, Why did Moses then command to give a writing of divorcement, and to put her away?

Mat 19:8 He saith unto them, Moses because of the hardness of your hearts suffered you to put away your wives: but from the beginning it was not so.

Mat 19:9 And I say unto you, Whosoever shall put away his wife, except *it be* for fornication, and shall marry another, committeth adultery: and whoso marrieth her which is put away doth commit adultery.

Ref Matthew 19:3-6

God's design for a family is a Man and a Woman joined in Holy Matrimony that God joins together in some unknown and supernatural way.

Mat 19:3 The Pharisees also came unto him, tempting him, and saying unto him, Is it lawful for a man to put away his wife for every cause?

Mat 19:4 And he answered and said unto them, Have ye not read, that he which made *them* at the beginning made them male and female,

Mat 19:5 And said, For this cause shall a man leave father and mother, and shall cleave to his wife: and they twain shall be one flesh?

Mat 19:6 Wherefore they are no more twain, but one flesh. What therefore God hath joined together, let not man put asunder.

Ref Matthew 21: 21 - 22

Now I am in agreement with God's will.

Mat 21:21 Jesus answered and said unto them, Verily I say unto you, If ye have faith, and doubt not, ye shall not only do this *which is done* to the fig tree, but also if ye shall say unto this mountain, Be thou removed, and be thou cast into the sea; it shall be done.

Mat 21:22 And all things, whatsoever ye shall ask in prayer, believing, ye shall receive.

Ref Matthew 22: 23 - 30

There is no marriage after death

Mat 22:23 The same day came to him the Sadducees, which say that there is no resurrection, and asked him,

Mat 22:24 Saying, Master, Moses said, If a man die, having no children, his brother shall marry his wife, and raise up seed unto his brother.

Mat 22:25 Now there were with us seven brethren: and the first, when he had married a wife, deceased, and, having no issue, left his wife unto his brother:

Mat 22:26 Likewise the second also, and the third, unto the seventh.

Mat 22:27 And last of all the woman died also.

Mat 22:28 Therefore in the resurrection whose wife shall she be of the seven? for they all had her.

Mat 22:29 Jesus answered and said unto them, Ye do err, not knowing the scriptures, nor the power of God.

Mat 22:30 For in the resurrection they neither marry, nor are given in marriage, but are as the angels of God in heaven.

Ref Matthew 22:36-40

"Master, which *is* the great commandment in the law?

Mat 22:36 Master, which *is* the great commandment in the law?

Mat 22:37 Jesus said unto him, Thou shalt love the Lord thy God with all thy heart, and with all thy soul, and with all thy mind.

Mat 22:38 This is the first and great commandment.

Mat 22:39 And the second *is* like unto it, Thou shalt love thy neighbour as thyself.

Mat 22:40 On these two commandments hang all the law and the prophets.

Ref Matthew 23:8-10

This of course is how God has designed Heaven
In the Church, there is no place for such a hierarchy

Mat 23:8 But be not ye called Rabbi: for one is your Master, *even* Christ; and all ye are brethren.

Mat 23:9 And call no *man* your father upon the earth: for one is your Father, which is in heaven.

Mat 23:10 Neither be ye called masters: for one is your Master, *even* Christ.

Ref Matthew 23:8-12

Jesus made it very dear that there was not to be a hierarchy within the Church.
Servant hood to God and to others

<u>All believers are equal in authority and none are subject to another</u>

Mat 23:8 But be not ye called Rabbi: for one is your Master, *even* Christ; and all ye are brethren.

Mat 23:9 And call no *man* your father upon the earth: for one is your Father, which is in heaven.

Mat 23:10 Neither be ye called masters: for one is your Master, *even* Christ.

Mat 23:11 But he that is greatest among you shall be your servant.

Mat 23:12 And whosoever shall exalt himself shall be abased; and he that shall humble himself shall be exalted.

Ref Matthew 25:31-46

<u>Help your congregation brothers and sisters first</u>
<u>If you do not, then Jesus says to you "Away from me you evil doers"</u>

Mat 25:31 When the Son of man shall come in his glory, and all the holy angels with him, then shall he sit upon the throne of his glory:

Mat 25:32 And before him shall be gathered all nations: and he shall separate them one from another, as a shepherd divideth *his* sheep from the goats:

Mat 25:33 And he shall set the sheep on his right hand, but the goats on the left.

Mat 25:34 Then shall the King say unto them on his right hand, Come, ye blessed of my Father, inherit the kingdom prepared for you from the foundation of the world:

Mat 25:35 For I was an hungred, and ye gave me meat: I was thirsty, and ye gave me drink: I was a stranger, and ye took me in:

Mat 25:36 Naked, and ye clothed me: I was sick, and ye visited me: I was in prison, and ye came unto me.

Mat 25:37 Then shall the righteous answer him, saying, Lord, when saw we thee an hungred, and fed *thee?* or thirsty, and gave *thee* drink?

Mat 25:38 When saw we thee a stranger, and took *thee* in? or naked, and clothed *thee?*

Mat 25:39 Or when saw we thee sick, or in prison, and came unto thee?

Mat 25:40 And the King shall answer and say unto them, Verily I say unto you, Inasmuch as ye have done *it* unto one of the least of **these my brethren** [Referring to those who first gave themselves to God and were reborn as a spirit and who also prove they are His by doing these things], ye have done *it* unto me.

Mat 25:41 Then shall he say also unto them on the left hand, Depart from me, ye cursed, into everlasting fire, prepared for the devil and his angels:

Mat 25:42 For I was an hungred, and ye gave me no meat: I was thirsty, and ye gave me no drink:

Mat 25:43 I was a stranger, and ye took me not in: naked, and ye clothed me not: sick, and in prison, and ye visited me not.

Mat 25:44 Then shall they also answer him, saying, Lord, when saw we thee an hungred, or athirst, or a stranger, or naked, or sick, or in prison, and did not minister unto thee?

Mat 25:45 Then shall he answer them, saying, Verily I say unto you, Inasmuch as ye did *it* not to one of the least of these [Referring as per above to His brethren], ye did *it* not to me.

Mat 25:46 And these shall go away into everlasting punishment: but the righteous into life eternal.

Ref Matthew 28:18-20
This is also true. Jesus has also appointed
Jesus gave a final commandment at his ascension

Mat 28:18 And Jesus came and spake unto them, saying, All power is given unto me in heaven and in earth.

Mat 28:19 Go ye therefore, and teach all nations, baptizing them in the name of the Father, and of the Son, and of the Holy Ghost:

Mat 28:20 Teaching them to observe all things whatsoever I have commanded you: and, lo, I am with you alway, *even* unto the end of the world. Amen.

Ref Numbers 22: 28

God Is not confined to simply saving souls.

Num 22:28 And the LORD opened the mouth of the ass, and she said unto Balaam, What have I done unto thee, that thou hast smitten me these three times?

Ref Philippians 04:08-09

whatever is of a good report, think on these things

Php 4:8 Finally, brethren, whatsoever things are true, whatsoever things *are* honest, whatsoever things *are* just, whatsoever things *are* pure, whatsoever things *are* lovely, whatsoever things *are* of good report; if *there be* any virtue, and if *there be* any praise, think on these things.

Php 4:9 Those things, which ye have both learned, and received, and heard, and seen in me, do: and the God of peace shall be with you.

Ref Philippians 04:11-13

could do all things through Christ who strengthens him

I have learnt to be content in all things

Php 4:11 Not that I speak in respect of want: for I have learned, in whatsoever state I am, *therewith* to be content.

Php 4:12 I know both how to be abased, and I know how to abound: every where and in all things I am instructed both to be full and to be hungry, both to abound and to suffer need.

Php 4:13 I can do all things through Christ which strengtheneth me.

Ref Proverbs 06:16–19

There are 7 things mentioned in the Old Testament that God HATES AND CANNOT TOLERATE.

Pro 6:16 These six *things* doth the LORD hate: yea, seven *are* an abomination unto him:

Pro 6:17 A proud look, a lying tongue, and hands that shed innocent blood,

Pro 6:18 An heart that deviseth wicked imaginations, feet that be swift in running to mischief,

Pro 6:19 A false witness *that* speaketh lies, and he that soweth discord among brethren.

Ref Psalm 37:4

He gives you the desire to be in the place He wants you to be

He gives us the desires of our heart if we seek our happiness in Him.

Psa 37:4 Delight thyself also in the LORD; and he shall give thee the desires of thine heart.

Ref Revelation 3:15-19

He will spit you out of His mouth

Rev 3:15 I know thy works, that thou art neither cold nor hot: I would thou wert cold or hot.

Rev 3:16 So then because thou art lukewarm, and neither cold nor hot, I will spue thee out of my mouth.

Rev 3:17 Because thou sayest, I am rich, and increased with goods, and have need of nothing; and knowest not that thou art wretched, and miserable, and poor, and blind, and naked:

Rev 3:18 I counsel thee to buy of me gold tried in the fire, that thou mayest be rich; and white raiment, that thou mayest be clothed, and *that* the shame of thy nakedness do not appear; and anoint thine eyes with eyesalve, that thou mayest see.

Rev 3:19 As many as I love, I rebuke and chasten: be zealous therefore, and repent.

Ref Romans 03:23-26

all have sinned and fallen short of reaching God

Rom 3:23 For all have sinned, and come short of the glory of God;

Rom 3:24 Being justified freely by his grace through the redemption that is in Christ Jesus:

Rom 3:25 Whom God hath set forth *to be* a propitiation through faith in his blood, to declare his righteousness for the remission of sins that are past, through the forbearance of God;

Rom 3:26 To declare, *I say,* at this time his righteousness: that he might be just, and the justifier of him which believeth in Jesus.

Ref Romans 06:23

any Sin is punishable by Death

Rom 6:23 For the wages of sin *is* death; but the gift of God *is* eternal life through Jesus Christ our Lord.

Ref Romans 07:2-3

Does your Church Condone or treat as normal, accept or tolerate, Same Sex Marriages, or Sex before Marriage, or Divorce?

Rom 7:2 For the woman which hath an husband is bound by the law to *her* husband so long as he liveth; but if the husband be dead, she is loosed from the law of *her* husband.

Rom 7:3 So then if, while *her* husband liveth, she be married to another man, she shall be called an adulteress: but if her husband be dead, she is free from that law; so that she is no adulteress, though she be married to another man.

Ref Romans 08:01-17

why would He suffer the pain of watching <u>His only Son murdered to pay the price of sin, which is death</u>

Rom 8:1 *There is* therefore now no condemnation to them which are in Christ Jesus, who walk not after the flesh, but after the Spirit.

Rom 8:2 For the law of the Spirit of life in Christ Jesus hath made me free from the law of sin and death.

Rom 8:3 For what the law could not do, in that it was weak through the flesh, God sending his own Son in the likeness of sinful flesh, and for sin, condemned sin in the flesh:

Rom 8:4 That the righteousness of the law might be fulfilled in us, who walk not after the flesh, but after the Spirit.

Rom 8:5 For they that are after the flesh do mind the things of the flesh; but they that are after the Spirit the things of the Spirit.

Rom 8:6 For to be carnally minded *is* death; but to be spiritually minded *is* life and peace.

Rom 8:7 Because the carnal mind *is* enmity against God: for it is not subject to the law of God, neither indeed can be.

Rom 8:8 So then they that are in the flesh cannot please God.

Rom 8:9 But ye are not in the flesh, but in the Spirit, if so be that the Spirit of God dwell in you. Now if any man have not the Spirit of Christ, he is none of his.

Rom 8:10 And if Christ *be* in you, the body *is* dead because of sin; but the Spirit *is* life because of righteousness.

Rom 8:11 But if the Spirit of him that raised up Jesus from the dead dwell in you, he that raised up Christ from the dead shall also quicken your mortal bodies by his Spirit that dwelleth in you.

Rom 8:12 Therefore, brethren, we are debtors, not to the flesh, to live after the flesh.

Rom 8:13 For if ye live after the flesh, ye shall die: but if ye through the Spirit do mortify the deeds of the body, ye shall live.

Rom 8:14 For as many as are led by the Spirit of God, they are the sons of God.

Rom 8:15 For ye have not received the spirit of bondage again to fear; but ye have received the Spirit of adoption, whereby we cry, Abba, Father.

Rom 8:16 The Spirit itself beareth witness with our spirit, that we are the children of God:

Rom 8:17 And if children, then heirs; heirs of God, and joint-heirs with Christ; if so be that we suffer with *him,* that we may be also glorified together.

Ref Romans 12:2

Why did he disrespect social standing so much

Rom 12:2 And be not conformed to this world: but be ye transformed by the renewing of your mind, that ye may prove what *is* that good, and acceptable, and perfect, will of God.

Ref Romans 12:5

<u>According to the word of God</u>

Rom 12:5 So we, *being* many, are one body in Christ, and every one members one of another.

Ref Romans 12:1-21

<u>Why did he disrespect social standing so much</u>

Rom 12:1 I beseech you therefore, brethren, by the mercies of God, that ye present your bodies a living sacrifice, holy, acceptable unto God, *which is* your reasonable service.

Rom 12:2 And be not conformed to this world: but be ye transformed by the renewing of your mind, that ye may prove what *is* that good, and acceptable, and perfect, will of God.

Rom 12:3 For I say, through the grace given unto me, to every man that is among you, not to think *of himself* more highly than he ought to think; but to think soberly, according as God hath dealt to every man the measure of faith.

Rom 12:4 For as we have many members in one body, and all members have not the same office:

Rom 12:5 So we, *being* many, are one body in Christ, and every one members one of another.

Rom 12:6 Having then gifts differing according to the grace that is given to us, whether prophecy, *let us prophesy* according to the proportion of faith;

Rom 12:7 Or ministry, *let us wait* on *our* ministering: or he that teacheth, on teaching;

Rom 12:8 Or he that exhorteth, on exhortation: he that giveth, *let him do it* with simplicity; he that ruleth, with diligence; he that sheweth mercy, with cheerfulness.

Rom 12:9 *Let* love be without dissimulation. Abhor that which is evil; cleave to that which is good.

Rom 12:10 *Be* kindly affectioned one to another with brotherly love; in honour preferring one another;

Rom 12:11 Not slothful in business; fervent in spirit; serving the Lord;

Rom 12:12 Rejoicing in hope; patient in tribulation; continuing instant in prayer;

Rom 12:13 Distributing to the necessity of saints; given to hospitality.

Rom 12:14 Bless them which persecute you: bless, and curse not.

Rom 12:15 Rejoice with them that do rejoice, and weep with them that weep.

Rom 12:16 *Be* of the same mind one toward another. Mind not high things, but condescend to men of low estate. Be not wise in your own conceits.

Rom 12:17 Recompense to no man evil for evil. Provide things honest in the sight of all men.

Rom 12:18 If it be possible, as much as lieth in you, live peaceably with all men.

Rom 12:19 Dearly beloved, avenge not yourselves, but *rather* give place unto wrath: for it is written, Vengeance *is* mine; I will repay, saith the Lord.

Rom 12:20 Therefore if thine enemy hunger, feed him; if he thirst, give him drink: for in so doing thou shalt heap coals of fire on his head.

Rom 12:21 Be not overcome of evil, but overcome evil with good.

Proof Bibles translated since 1881 are corrupt.

A manuscript is a hand-copied document. This was the method used for writing and duplicating existing literature prior to the invention of printing. There are over 5,300 (5,309 to be exact) existing manuscripts of the Scriptures. Some of these manuscripts contain a large portion of scripture, while others are fragments.

Let us first consider certain Greek texts from which all New Testament translations are derived:

1. the **Majority Texts** (_Textus Receptus_), and
2. the **Minority Texts** (primarily the <u>Westcott and Hort</u> Greek Text, based primarily on the _Codex Sinaiticus_ and the _Codex Vaticanus_).

For obvious reasons, the <u>Textus Receptus</u> is also referred to as the _"Majority Text"_ since the **majority** (95% or more) of existing manuscripts support this reading. These extant manuscripts were brought together by various editors such as Lucian (AD 250-312), Erasmus, Stephanus, Beza, and the Elzevir brothers. The most notable editor of all was Desiderius Erasmus (1466-1536) one of the greatest scholars the world has ever known. When the early Protestant Reformers of the 16th and 17th centuries decided to translate the scriptures directly from Greek into the languages of Europe, <u>they selected Textus Receptus as their foundation Greek document.</u>

The NASB, the NIV, the Jehovah's Witness bible ("New World Translation"), and most modern translations and paraphrases use the <u>Westcott and Hort</u> Greek Text, which is supported by only a **small portion** (5% or less) of existing manuscripts, including <u>Codex Vaticanus</u>, <u>Codex Sinaiticus</u>, Alexandrian Codex, Parisian Codex, and Codex Bezae.

For obvious reasons, this text is referred to as the *"Minority Texts."* <u>Westcott and Hort</u> relied heavily on the <u>Vaticanus</u> and <u>Sinaiticus</u> for their Greek Text, which is particularly odd, considering the fact that **these two** codices **contradict each other** over **3,000 times** in the gospels alone.

As stated above, there are more than 5,300 manuscripts in existence. These manuscripts are divided into several different formats:

1. *Papyrus fragments* -- papyrus was relatively inexpensive compared to vellum (animal skins), and therefore was widely used. However, it was not very durable and copies would wear out rather rapidly through usage. The size of these papyrus fragments range from a few verses to large portions of an entire book.
2. *Unical* -- these are copies that were written in capital letters.
3. *Cursive* -- those written in small hand.

Of these 5,300+ existing manuscripts, over 95% are in agreement with, and form the basis for the

Textus Receptus, which is the text which the King James translators used. Strange as it may seem, Westcott and Hort threw out the preponderance of manuscript evidence and opted rather to go with the Minority Texts! **Hence we have inherited an ongoing struggle among New Testament critics, accompanied by havoc and confusion in churches caused by the introduction of these conflicting New Testament Greek texts.** Since 1881, most subsequent versions have followed the Minority Texts.

Study the information in the following table. Although this data was compiled in 1967, recent archeological discoveries will not significantly effect the results. This data illustrates why the Textus Receptus is referred to as the "Majority Text."

Type of Manuscript	Total # of this type manuscript	Number that support WH*	Number that support TR**
Papyrus	88	13 (15%)	75 (85%)
Unical	267	9 (3%)	258 (97%)
Cursive	2764	23 (1%)	2741 (99%)
Lectionary***	2143	0	2143 (100%)

* WH indicates *Westcott-Hort Greek Text (Minority Text)*
** TR indicates *Textus Receptus (Majority Text)*
*** A lectionary is a book that contains a collection of scripture readings

The table gives the approximate number and percent of each type of Greek manuscript that supports the Westcott and Hort Greek Text, as well as the number and percent of each class that supports the Textus Receptus Greek text. These approximations are taken from the careful research of Dr. Jack Moorman in his book <u>Forever Settled</u>. [From: <u>THE FOUR-FOLD SUPERIORITY OF THE KING JAMES VERSION</u> By Dr. D.A. Waite]

There are a few other old manuscripts, even including fragmentary Greek papyri, whose textual character seems to conform more to the <u>Codex Sinaiticus</u> and <u>Codex Vaticanus</u> than to the <u>Textus Receptus</u>. However, these all have been traced (by liberal and conservative scholars alike) to a probable source in Alexandria, Egypt, in the 2nd or 3rd century. The most influential man among the "intellectual" community of Alexandria was the learned <u>Origen</u>, and it is believed by many that he was largely instrumental in developing the so-called "Alexandrian" text of the New Testament (of which the Vatican and Sinai manuscripts are representative), in contrast to the "Byzantine" text, from which the <u>Textus Receptus</u> has largely come.

With all his immense learning and zeal, however, **Origen was a heretic.** Like modern theistic evolutionists, he felt constrained to harmonize Christianity with **pagan** philosophy, especially that of Plato and the Stoics. This led him into excessive allegorization of Scripture, especially Genesis, and into denigrating the actual historical records of the Bible, **even that of the bodily resurrection of Christ**, as well as the literal creation of the world.

<u>Alexandrea was the centre of disbelief in Jesus.</u>

Whether or not Origen and his associates were first responsible for the differences in the Alexandrian text from the Byzantine, the fact remains that significant differences **do exist**, and that practically all modern English translations have been heavily influenced (via Westcott and Hort, etc.) in favor of the former, whereas the King James translation has its basis primarily in the latter.

The only place where these error laden, unreliable manuscripts excel is in the quality of the materials used on them. They have good bindings and fine animal skin pages. Their physical appearance, contrary to their worthless texts, are really rather attractive. But then we have all heard the saying, "*You can't judge a book by its cover.*" The covers are beautiful but their texts are reprehensible.

And yet in spite of these well-known corruptions, they are the basis for many new versions such as the NIV and the NASB, rendering these versions **critically flawed and unreliable**. I will give many, many examples of these errors and omissions when I deal with the altered verses. Many of the differences between the manuscripts involve significant watering down of even such basic doctrines as Biblical inerrancy and the perfect divine/human nature of Christ.

IMPORTANT NOTE: Please remember that, while the modern versions of the Bible do water down the truth and are not the BEST translations, they certainly do not completely eliminate these key doctrines, so it is still possible to discern these doctrines and to find the true gospel and way of salvation in many of the new texts or translations. My wife, for instance, was saved while reading the Good News Bible, which is a paraphrase based on the Minority Texts, which were corrupted. So you see, God uses even the flawed translations to accomplish His purposes and decrees.

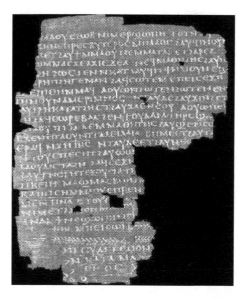

[The Lord wants to reach every generation with His Word.]

Think about it . . . can you really imagine the Lord of Lords, the Holy One of Israel hiding <u>Codex Vaticanus</u> away for over 1,000 years in the Vatican Library till 1481? Or better yet, can you imagine Him prompting the monks of St Catherine's Monastery to dump <u>Codex Sinaiticus</u> into a waste basket?

Remember, the early Christians **REJECTED** these manuscripts. So, they went into secret libaries...and there they lay...until they were later dug up as "ancient manuscripts."

So here's what likely happened: the corrupt Alexandrian text (also called the "Egyptian" or "Hesychian" type text) found its way into Constantine's bible (via <u>Origen</u> and Eusebius), one of which was the <u>Vatican</u> manuscript and another of which was the <u>Sinai</u> manuscript, but they were **rejected** and "thrown in the closet" by Christians of that day. However, after hundreds of years, they eventually were revived via the **Westcott and Hort [agnostics – did not believe Jesus is God]** Greek Text, and finally crept into the new "Bible" versions in your local "Christian" bookstore.

The Devil is out to destroy you and all you love. He will be happy if you stand by and watch him torture your loved ones, and then strip them, and suck the life out of them, and kill them while you watch.

You choose if you will allow this same devil to give you or your loved ones a lying bible (a map leading down the broad road to destruction).

As for me and my house, we will serve The Lord, and we will start with getting His Word right, and keeping our minds pure of satan's corruption. Personally, my family and I have burnt all of the bibles that lead to false worship, and now we only read from the Real Truth.

Therefore, when you hear or read of someone "correcting" the King James Bible with "older" or "more authoritative" manuscripts, you are simply hearing someone trying to use a **corrupted, pagan, gnostic, ecumenical, Roman Catholic** text to overthrow the God-honored text of the Protestant Reformation and the great revivals.

Reference: http://www.1611kingjamesbible.com/manuscripts.html/

Printed in the United States
By Bookmasters